DEATH INSIDE OUT

A Harper Forum Book ⏛

DEATH
Inside
Out

The Hastings Center Report

Edited by

Peter Steinfels AND Robert M. Veatch

HARPER & ROW, PUBLISHERS
New York, Evanston, San Francisco, London

DEATH INSIDE OUT. Copyright © 1974, 1975 by the Institute of Society, Ethics and the Life Sciences. All rights reserved. Printed in the United States of America. No part of this book may be used or reproduced in any manner whatsoever without written permission except in the case of brief quotations embodied in critical articles and reviews. For information address Harper & Row, Publishers, Inc., 10 East 53rd Street, New York, N.Y. 10022. Published simultaneously in Canada by Fitzhenry & Whiteside Limited, Toronto.

FIRST EDITION

Library of Congress Cataloging in Publication Data

Main entry under title:

Death inside out.

  (A Harper forum book)
  1. Terminal care. 2. Death. I. Steinfels, Peter.
II. Veatch, Robert M. III. Hastings Center.
R726.8.D4   616.07   74-25706
ISBN 0-06-067576-4
ISBN 0-06-067575-6 pbk.

75 76 77 78 79 10 9 8 7 6 5 4 3 2 1

Contents

1020

List of Contributors

PHILIPPE ARIÈS, a French civil servant and historian, is the author of the seminal work in the history of childhood, *Centuries of Childhood*. His most recent book is *Western Attitudes Toward Death: From the Middle Ages to the Present*.

ERIC J. CASSELL, M.D., Clinical Professor in Public Health at Cornell University Medical College, New York City, is the author of articles on subjects ranging from air pollution to medical education and care for the aging, in journals ranging from the *American Journal of Public Health* to *Commentary*. He also contributed the study "Being and Becoming Dead" to *Death in American Experience*.

H. TRISTRAM ENGLEHARDT, JR., M.D., is Assistant Professor of the Philosophy of Medicine at the Institute for the Medical Humanities and in the Department of Preventive Medicine and Community Health, University of Texas Medical Branch, Galveston, Texas. He is the author of *Mind-Body: A Categorical Relation* and *Medical Ethics* and translator of *The Structures of the Life World*, by Alfred Shutz and Thomas Luckmann.

IVAN ILLICH established the Center for Intercultural Documentation (CIDOC) in Cuernavaca, Mexico, where he is now Director of Research. Among other works, he is author of *De-schooling Society*, *Tools for Conviviality*, and most recently, *Medical Nemesis*.

LEON R. KASS, M.D., is Joseph P. Kennedy, Sr., Research Professor in Bioethics at the Kennedy Institute, Center for Bioethics, Washington, D. C. His articles on the ethical and social implications of biomedical advance have appeared in *Science*, *Theology Today*, *New England Journal of Medicine*, *Journal of the American Medical Association*, and other periodicals as well as in the volumes *The New Genetics and the Future of Man* and *Ethical Issues in Human Genetics*.

WILLIAM F. MAY is Chairman of the Department of Religious

Studies at Indiana University. He is author of *A Catalogue of Sins* and his essay, "The Sacral Power of Death in Contemporary Experience," appeared in *Death in American Experience.*

ROBERT S. MORISON, M.D., was Director of Medical and Natural Sciences at the Rockefeller Foundation in New York City and later Richard J. Schwartz Professor of Science and Society at Cornell University. He is now visiting professor at the Massachusetts Institute of Technology. He has written and lectured extensively on science, medicine, and social policy, and contributed the essay "Dying" to *Life, Death and Medicine.*

PAUL RAMSEY is Harrington Spear Paine Professor of Religion at Princeton University. Among other books he is the author of *The Ethics of Fetal Research, Fabricated Man: The Ethics of Genetic Control*, and *The Patient as Person.*

DAVID H. SMITH is Associate Professor of Religious Studies at Indiana University. Research for his chapter was done at the Kennedy Institute, Center for Bioethics, Washington, D. C. He is at work on a book on moral theology and euthanasia, suicide, and abortion.

DANIEL CALLAHAN is Director of the Institute of Society, Ethics and the Life Sciences, Hastings-on-Hudson, N.Y. He is author of *The Tyranny of Survival* and *Abortion: Law, Choice and Morality*, editor of *The American Population Debate*, and has written and edited other books.

PETER STEINFELS, Associate for the Humanities at the Institute of Society, Ethics and the Life Sciences, is editor of the *Hastings Center Report*. A former editor of *Commonweal*, he has contributed to numerous journals and several books.

ROBERT M. VEATCH is Associate for Medical Ethics at the Institute of Society, Ethics and the Life Sciences and is staff director of its Death and Dying Group. He has written widely on medical ethics and death and dying, is coeditor of *The Teaching of Medical Ethics* and editor of *Case Studies in Medical Ethics.*

Preface

DANIEL CALLAHAN

WHEN the Institute of Society, Ethics and the Life Sciences was founded in 1969, it was immediately evident that the question of human death would occupy a special place in our research and discussion. The Institute consisted of several dozen leading scholars from biology, medicine, philosophy, law, the social sciences, and other disciplines who worked together on ethical, social, and legal questions posed by what was then loosely called the "biological revolution." With the help of a small full-time staff in Hastings-on-Hudson, New York, these scholars formed permanent research groups in areas such as population policy, genetic counseling and engineering, behavior control, and death and dying.

In the late sixties several developments had linked death, the most ancient of humanity's riddles, with other "futuristic" issues raised by advanced technology. The first was the growing use of medical technology to support life to a point where life's only purpose sometimes seemed to be to support the further use of medical technology. A particularly dramatic extension of this development occurred in the cases in which medical technology was capable of maintaining the traditional indications of life—heartbeat and respiration—far beyond the point where, by other criteria, the patient could still be said to be "living." On top of these developments came the advent of heart and other organ transplantation, which posed difficult ethical, legal, and social questions about the definition of death, or, to be precise, about the conditions under which it becomes appropriate to pronounce a person dead. The need to find better ways of caring for the dying patient and the need to salvage organs in as good a state as possible for transplantation pressed on society and the medical profession extremely important but complicated policy questions.

These new difficulties in defining death and caring for dying patients, however, were only some dramatic instances of the accumulating evidence that a radical shift had taken place in the relationship between medicine and death. As a genuine "lifesaver," the history of modern medicine can be dated in decades not centuries; we often forget how recently it began to wield the prodigious powers now associated with its name. In the developing countries of the world, that power has been most obvious. The lowering of death rates, due to medicine's newly won victories over infectious disease, has become the source of rapid population growth. But this same medicine has not learned how to control birth rates equally well. In the developed countries, the impact of medicine's power over death has been less dramatic, spread out over several more decades, but no less real. The proportion of the aged in the population has climbed steadily. Roughly four percent at the turn of the century, the proportion of those over 65 in the American population is now nearly nine percent, and is expected to reach eleven percent by the year 2000.

Death remains as much a human reality as ever, but medicine has developed some skills in delaying its appearance. Not only has this delay created the specific problems referred to earlier, but when death does come, it now may seem even more unexpected and arbitrary. Medicine's triumphs have allowed us to be tantalized by the possibility that death is not all that inevitable. An absurd hope, perhaps, but one fueled by even modest success in staying death's hand. Save in those religious traditions where a belief in immortality is firmly fixed, death has always been the final boundary of human hope for the individual; life is set within a finite time-frame, one which has been elastic to some degree, but never enough so that one can expect to transcend the inexorable decay of the body. Thus death has been a source of terror, of fatalism, and, for many, of despair. It is hardly any wonder that even the faintest signs of success in changing the human relationship to death would be greeted with acclaim, especially that pragmatic acclaim which is expressed in large sums of public money invested in medical research.

This development has now given rise to more than a few ironies. Far from leading to a lowering of anxiety about death, the successes of medicine may well have increased it. That at least is one plausible interpretation of the attention paid to the problem of death in recent years. In any case, the ability of medicine to give more people more years of life has not been matched by an ability to deal with the infirmities and chronic illnesses which mark the lives of many of the old. And medicine has surely not been able to deal with the social, cultural, and psychological questions posed by the changing age structure of the population, with its increasing numbers of the elderly. Indeed, this is perhaps not even medicine's proper task.

To take another irony, the advent of organ transplantation has in great part required that some die in order that others may live. Successful transplantations seem to depend not only on remarkable medical skills, but also on a supply of young and healthy victims of homicides and motorcycle accidents. Or to turn to another irony, modern surgical techniques, which now allow many infants to be saved who in earlier years might have died—as in the case of a spina bifida—seem to have produced a curious result, namely a far more open public discussion about whether these babies should be saved at all. The final outcome has been that fewer rather than more babies may be kept alive by the new techniques.

The Hastings Center's research group on death and dying has, over the years, been attempting to analyze not only the specific issues of defining death and caring for the dying but also the larger changes in the relationship of medicine, and indeed of a host of social forces, to death. The Institute group, like all our research groups, has worked on the assumption that death is not the province of any one discipline; instead it must be looked at from a variety of angles, as a problem for philosophy, law, theology, the social sciences, literature, and history. Death at one and the same time poses the deepest and oldest of philosophical problems and the most immediate kind of public policy dilemmas. We have, then, tried to look simultaneously at both theory and practice, and the way they relate to each other. Often enough we have been pushed out of our depth. The question of death, if pursued hard enough, will invariably do that to those who seek its secrets. Often enough, too, we have not been able to reach any agreement on the issues, a fact which probably points less to differences in reasoning ability, or definitions of terms, than it points to the way in which the problem of death elicits very different perspectives on life itself—and thus often irreconcilable assumptions and visions about the nature of human existence.

In one very important respect, death is perhaps different from every other topic with which the Institute has dealt. Most such topics, from genetic counseling to the use of surgery or drugs for behavior control, touch upon all of us generally as *citizens*, and only a few of us particularly either as *subjects* or *professionals*. Death, however, confronts each of us as an individual, and our discussions inevitably gain in intensity—one hopes also in profundity—from these personal stakes.

The collection of essays published here does not, strictly speaking, represent either the work of our research group in its totality, or an attempt to put together a collection which reflects a single underlying theme or a developed sequence of topics. Instead, this collection represents what we believe to be a number of the most interesting and provocative articles which, in various ways, have been an outcome of the Institute's inquiries and most of which were published in the journal of the Hastings Center. The chapters by Ivan Illich and Eric J. Cassell, for in-

stance, were originally papers given in Mexico City at an Institute symposium, which in turn was part of an international congress cosponsored by the Mexican Council on Science and Technology and the American Association for the Advancement of Science. Although David H. Smith had previously written on euthanasia for an Institute workshop, the chapter published here was not done directly under the auspices of the research group either, but represents a significant contribution to an increasingly important problem which the group has addressed. A desire for greater historical perspective led the editors of the Hastings journal to translate and publish the essay by Philippe Ariès.

As Director of the Institute I would like to express our thanks to the authors of the articles collected here, to the other members of the research group on death and dying whose general participation and specific criticisms in the discussions of these issues has been of critical importance, and to the New York Foundation whose grants enabled us to put the research group on a firm footing.

Introduction
PETER STEINFELS

DYING, we have been told by Elisabeth Kubler-Ross, involves passing through several distinct stages: denial, anger, bargaining, depression, and acceptance. As with death, so with the contemporary discussion of it: we are passing through distinct phases. Two decades ago, denial was almost total. Geoffrey Gorer could well maintain in his essay "The Pornography of Death" that the acknowledgment of death was for us the equivalent of the acknowledgment of sex for the Victorians; it was taboo.[1] That statement cannot be made today without betraying a distressing insensitivity to the climate of our society.

True, it is still not easy to confront death honestly. It is still not easy to confront sexuality honestly either, despite (or perhaps because of) the absolute insistence upon candor and the cornucopia of assistance offered us in school courses, newspapers, magazines, books, TV talk shows, and therapies of every sort. For reasons I need not elaborate, death may never become as popular as sex, but as a topic of public discussion it is certainly not doing badly.

Before the sixties, books on death tended to be psychiatric explorations of the death instinct or the fear of death, pastoral or theological considerations of death for religious audiences, anthropological studies of rituals surrounding death in primitive societies, or philosophical monographs on the treatment of death by some philosopher (usually Heidegger). Few of these works reached out to a wide audience; death in popular periodicals was typically represented by accounts of brave individuals, often children, whose dying was sad—never bitter—but finally peaceful.

Sometime after the middle of the sixties this situation changed. The number of books on death multiplied; and what is more significant, they were being written for, or read by, the general reader. After 1970, these books began appearing at the rate of about one per month. The *New York Times Book Review* found itself reviewing eight such books at a time, and the reviewer could refer to ten other works in this "avalanche," this "death renaissance." Sales for Kubler-Ross's path-breaking *On Death and Dying* approached a half-million. The *Cumulated Index Medicus* for 1973 listed over a hundred titles on dealing with death.[2] What began with books soon made its way into monthly magazines, newsweeklies, daily papers, and the classroom. Each of the major television networks has ventured into

---

[1]Geoffrey Gorer, *Death, Grief and Mourning* (New York Doubleday, 1965), pp. 192-99.

[2]According to Franz J. Ingelfinger, M.D., in *The New England Journal of Medicine* 291 (October 17, 1974), p. 46.

this area with at least one major production concerning the "right to die." Courses on death and dying were initiated in medical schools and seminaries; they are now found in colleges, adult education programs, and even in grammar schools.

How and why this change has come about no one has yet seriously tried to explain. Those scores of books included some that were moving, persuasive, and widely read. But the reception of a book may be as much effect as cause. Jessica Mitford's *American Way of Death* was a best-seller in the early sixties, but both the author's tone and the audience's mood limited the controversy stirred by the book largely to a "consumers' protest" against the funeral industry. The willingness, even eagerness, of the public to go beyond this response probably rests on the impact of other shifts in our society.

But which ones? And in what proportions? To begin with, the way people die has continued to change: more in hospitals, more under intensive, high-technology medical care.[3] And it is true that our society has become more "open," or at least more talkative: How long could death remain the exception? Some would add that the sequence of assassinations of such public leaders as the Kennedys and Martin Luther King forced the issue into our consciousness. In a thoughtful report on television's handling of death, Michael J. Arlen has pointed out that "in public America—though the surface appears impervious to death—it was, ironically, television that, some time ago, on the occasions of the deaths of the two Kennedy brothers and Dr. Martin Luther King, helped the American people break through their apparent fear of death and death's

imagery."[4] Certainly the prolonged and well-publicized agony of Vietnam increased our awareness of death's presence. Others have looked further for the cause. "Ultimately, it is the knowledge of our own potential destructiveness that forces us today to confront ourselves with the meaning of life and death," writes Kubler-Ross, referring to the concentration camps, to Hiroshima and Nagasaki, to Vietnam, Biafra, Bangladesh, and the Middle East.[5] Perhaps that is too "ultimate." Perhaps it is an error to read in this new awareness a major transformation of the zeitgeist. And yet this willingness, this eagerness, to discuss death openly has gone far beyond the ranks of those touched in any immediate way by the specific problems of medical technology.

Death has always been the final objection, the last arrow in the quiver of critics of the scientific, technological "project" on which the Western world has been embarked for several hundred years. As a polemical, even a political device, perhaps the memento mori should therefore be distrusted; and yet it is undeniable that within our Faustian effort has lurked the drive to conquer death and failing that, as we are doomed to do, to evade our real destiny through endless activity, self-deceptive and often self-destructive. Faust, after all, was a physician whose quest for knowledge began with frustration at his inability to cure and whose greatest achievements not only failed to banish death but brought death with them.

It is reported—though exactly by whom I cannot recall—that at one of the big Communist-sponsored conferences of intellectuals in the thirties, André Malraux interrupted an enthusiastic discussion of the utopian society supposedly just around the corner. But what about the young girl accidentally killed by a streetcar, asked Malraux. Consternation. The conference officials met and drafted a conclusive reply to Malraux: in the

[3]Torturing the dying with "scientific" kindliness is not new, however: the description of the final hours of George Washington, written by one of the attending physicians—an account of a relentless series of bleedings, purgings, and blisterings—suggests that the distance between the treatment meted out to Washington and that received by Harry Truman or Eleanor Roosevelt is not so great as our concentration on the "dehumanizing" technical equipment may sometimes lead us to believe.

[4]Michael J. Arlen, "The Air: The Cold, Bright Charms of Immortality," *The New Yorker*, January 27, 1975, pp. 73-78.
[5]Elisabeth Kubler-Ross, "Foreword," *Jewish Reflections on Death*, ed. Jack Riemer (New York: Schocken, 1974), pp. 1-3.

utopian society of the future streetcars will *not* run down young girls!

The promise to build a society in which there are no streetcar accidents is only an exaggerated version of what the entire West came to expect generally from science and technology. These expectations are by no means dead; but the circle of those in whom expectation is accompanied by foreboding, or at least by a disenchanted doubt, has grown much wider. It is in this climate of disenchantment that the discussion of death has flourished.

No one should suppose that this flourishing is unambiguously "healthy." In *The Waning of the Middle Ages* the great Dutch historian Johan Huizinga portrayed a society in which death had suddenly seized the center of attention. Mendicant preachers and morose poets vividly reminded their audiences of fleshly decomposition; the newly popular *Ars moriendi* instructed the dying in proper behavior. The grotesque dance of death appeared on churchyard walls; later Hans Holbein's woodcut rendition of the same subject would become a best-seller. The important thing to remember, however, is that Huizinga was describing a society in decline; its obsession with death reflected the seeping away of its creative force, not the energy to construct a more livable and die-able world. Is it possible that the future historian of our time will decipher in our own sudden interest in death not an influx of wisdom but rather the cracking of our cultural nerves? It is *possible*; I repeat, *possible*. On balance, I do not believe this to be the case; but recognizing the possibility may help us temper our enthusiasm.

There is another possibility we should recognize. If the present "crisis of death" is a crisis of our drive, now several centuries old, to control all aspects of human existence, then that drive may only reassert itself in new efforts at controlling death. This moment of renewed attention to the question death poses, the *why* of our lives, may be quickly submerged by the more familiar, and easier, question of *how*. We can exhaust our energies (and our fears) protesting the laws and medical practices which make dying needlessly hard—and indeed there is much to protest. We can go further and construct how-to-do-it guides for the dying. Or further yet, and look for a technological "solution" to dying whether in medical rejuvenation, cryonics, or those combinations of classification, coercion, and benevolence which the imaginations of numerous novelists have glimpsed in our future.

Such a process, I believe, is already underway. It is revealed in the well-intentioned but naive proposals of popular books like Marya Mannes's *Last Rights*, where a humane indignation at the loss of dignity inflicted on the dying by medical, religious, and cultural orthodoxies sits side by side with an irritation at those dying individuals who refuse the new orthodoxy of the "good death." It is reflected in the titles of books like *Living Your Dying*, or *Death Is All Right*, or *To Die With Style*! Concluding an article comparing Ms. Mannes's book to Stewart Alsop's *Stay of Execution*, a moving but unsentimental account of confronting death from cancer, Paul Ramsey warns that "the same outlook and program" which gave us "calisthentic sexuality," when "addressed to 'the last taboo' can only lead eventually and logically to the same thing: to 'calisthentic dying.' "[6] How long before some *Joy of Dying* ("A Gourmet Guide to Passing Away") makes the best-seller lists?

Even work displaying such obvious sensitiveness as Elisabeth Kubler-Ross's *On Death and Dying* can be misused when seized upon by a technological mood that refuses to admit the unalterably tragic into its horizon. The five stages through which Dr. Kubler-Ross observed terminal patients passing have been perceived by some in a mechanical fashion as providing a surefire progression to a happy ending; the stages (which not all observers of the dying accept as general) shift from descriptive categories to normative ones,[7] and

---

[6]Paul Ramsey, "Death's Pedagogy," *Commonweal*, September 20, 1974, p. 502.

[7]Roy Branson argues that the source of ambiguity in Dr. Kubler-Ross's stages—are they descriptive or prescriptive?—is partially the noted physician's own views. At least the final stage in her scheme, acceptance, is normative for Kubler-Ross; if a person

dying persons who do not follow the script run the risk of being considered failures or even of forfeiting the compassion of those caring for them, just as terminal patients who showed signs of despair or withdrawal were considered ungrateful and uncooperative by hospital personnel in the fifties.

These reflections return us directly to our original point: the discussion of death has moved into a second phase, a phase where it is not enough simply to recognize death "as a fact of life" or to challenge with justified horror the unnecessary indignities heaped upon the dying. We are now obliged to probe further into the sources of our attitudes toward death and into the full implications of changes in those attitudes.

Not that the problems which the first phase of the discussion brought into view have disappeared: the denial of death which left the dying unprepared and isolated; the many instances of overtreatment and the substitution of science for sensitivity; the refusal to prepare, either as individuals or as a society, the means to maintain our humanness as much as possible in the face of illness, aging, and death. Indeed, Michael Arlen, in the article to which I referred earlier, concludes that "television—this great communicating force—has settled into a role of largely ignoring the reality of death." It does this, yes, by silence, but even more "by asserting that the whole reality of death is violence." On entertainment programs, nameless, faceless people are matter-of-factly killed. On the news, deaths are anonymous, sudden, distant, and "usually reported to us in the sterility of . . . 'body counts.' . . . We do not die, apparently, except in numbers, or in Rangoon, or with blank faces in a gunfight." The deaths which most of us have ex-

perienced, or will experience—"this great commonplace matter," which now leaves us "frozen at gravesides into our separate overcoats," which has in the past been integrated into the full cycle of our lives by tribal custom or religious rites—this death is still missing.[8]

The second phase of discussing death must therefore not reverse the previous discussion but consolidate it, refine it, prevent it from degenerating into slogans, insure that it does not issue in those unintended consequences that so often have marred the outcome of our best impulses. Finally, the second phase of the discussion must push beyond the immediate issue of how we should order our dying to the underlying and essential question: How should we order our living?

The essays in this book are representative of the second phase. Is death best thought about as "process" or as "event"? (Robert S. Morison and Leon R. Kass). Have historical changes in Western attitudes toward death deprived individuals of their deaths? (Philippe Ariès). Has the once revolutionary notion of fending off "unnatural" death become an instrument of social control in the West and of cultural disruption in the developing world? (Ivan Illich). Is death the "enemy" of humanity—and of medicine? Is man truest to himself in accepting his finitude or in struggling against it? (H. Tristram Engelhardt, Jr.). What has been the consequence of the shift of death from the "moral order" to the "technological order"? (Eric J. Cassell). Has secularization stripped the family of its capacity to cope with death? What should be our stance not only toward the dying but toward the newly dead body? (William May). And at the beginning of the life cycle, how should we be guided in intensifying or limiting efforts to preserve the lives of severely defective newborns? (David H. Smith). The essays in this book assume that their audience has been introduced to the topic of death, that this audience needs no convincing of its importance or "thinkableness," but now desires to pursue the mat-

---

passes from acceptance, say, to anger, then he "regresses" or has been improperly handled. See "Is Acceptance a Denial of Death? Another Look at Kubler-Ross," *The Christian Century*, May 7, 1975, pp. 464-68.

One report of the inability of other researchers to verify Kubler-Ross's five-stage model can be found in Richard Schulz and David Aderman, "Clinical Research and the Stages of Dying," *Omega* 5 (1974), pp. 137-43.

---

[8]Arlen, "The Air," pp. 76-78.

ter more deeply. This assumption is true even of the essays which originated almost five years ago, when questions of care for the dying had intersected with questions posed by the development of organ transplantation about the adequacy of traditional criteria for pronouncing death. "Most discussions of death and dying . . ." begins Robert S. Morison's analysis of death as an "event," setting his views from the start in the context of an ongoing intellectual effort.

One set of the essays, however, makes its place in a second phase of discussion explicit. The exchange of views between Paul Ramsey, Robert S. Morison, and Leon R. Kass on "the indignity of 'death with dignity'" begins with a deliberate stocktaking of the direction of our consideration of death. The exchange does not linger unduly on this point—the authors' intentions are prescriptive rather than descriptive—but it is not too much to claim that these three views on the senses in which we can honestly and humanely link the words "death" and "dignity" will become touchstones for future intelligent reflection on the subject.

The authors in this volume represent no single viewpoint, other than a common seriousness of purpose and a determination to be no more complacent about the new conventional attitudes toward death than they were about the old. I do not agree with them all, obviously, since they do not agree with one another. Yet I have come away from these essays with certain conclusions about the way the discussion of death must proceed.

1. *Death must be viewed as a mystery, not a problem.* Paul Ramsey uses this distinction in his *Commonweal* article when he writes of the danger of "turning mysteries to be contemplated and deepened altogether into problems to be solved."[9] Mystery in this sense is a reality which calls forth a certain attitude: openness to the unexpected, trepidation, awe, respect. For me the distinction between mystery and problem has been given the most substance by the philosopher Gabriel Marcel. In the words of one of his best expositors:

The distinction between problem and mystery is also a distinction between scientific and philosophical knowledge. The order of problems is that of things that can be inventoried, characterized, and manipulated. Problems are open to solution by the creation and application of special techniques. Progress in a unilinear direction is possible here, since results can be measured in terms of output and increased control. The mind passes from one problem to the next . . . without attempting philosophical penetration of an ever recurring mystery.

The problematic method is proper to the special sciences, since they study objective essences apart from the nature of the inquirer. But . . . it is incapable of handling cases where the attitude of the subject toward a question is of crucial importance for understanding the issues. Evil, suffering, and death are instances where the entire situation is altered when the inquirer ceases to cut his own personal destiny off from the matter under discussion. The full force of the evidence is not realized until it is also envisaged as bearing upon his own life and conduct. Hence Marcel defines a mystery as a problem that is constantly encroaching upon its own data and hence going beyond the condition of a problem. In the face of a problem, the investigator retains his superiority and distance: when these are threatened and invaded by the direction of the study, then the threshold of mystery is crossed.[10]

To say that death should be viewed as mystery does not mean that it should be viewed as unknowable or unthinkable. Mystery signifies not the unknowable but the inexhaustible, that which unfolds before us as we proceed. Death may be done with us but we will not be done with it.

2. *We will not be able to speak with any wisdom about the future of death unless we have examined the past of death.* Nothing could be more self-deceiving, or more ludicrous, than the impression occasionally communicated that death, shrouded in fear for so long, has now been "discovered." Removed at last from the dark corner where

---

[9]Ramsey, "Death's Pedagogy," p. 502.

[10]James Collins, *The Existentialists* (Chicago: Henry Regnery Gateway Edition, 1952), pp. 149-50.

it crouched for centuries, it is about to yield its terrors before the bright beacons of our reason and honesty. On the contrary, we may approach the record of how people have died before us in many ways, with a sense of loss or with a critical spirit, but approach this record we must. We may search for examples of how societies and individuals have coped with this final transformation in different places, in the rituals of "primitive" societies, in the traditions of world religions, or in the teachings and acts of great men and women, but search we must. What we cannot do is rely on our own thin slice of experience and reason in the face of such a question.

3. *Death cannot be discussed profitably without a strong awareness of the "underside" of human nature and behavior.* This conclusion, I suppose, is implied in the first two. By "underside" I simply mean all that does not fit easily into the categories of modern rationalism: the dark fears, inner contradictions, deep attachments, aesthetic responses, capacities both for unspeakable cruelty and astonishing, self-sacrificing service, all of which have been more successfully expressed in our myths, our images, our plays, our novels, our poetry than in the propositions of our natural and social sci- ences. Death is the shadow which has ab- sorbed all the substance of life: it is heavy with meaning and nonetheless elusive. With- out a sensitivity to shadow, we will be dis- cussing nothing more than a shadow of the shadow. Banish the darkness, and we will miss the reality.

4. *Discussions about death must be dis- cussions about life.* Death cannot be fenced off as a discrete "field" of concern, the way the dying are too often fenced off in our institutions. It cannot be handed over to specialists, nor entered into a shopping list of projects for social reformers. Death with dignity, as the writers in this volume make clear, is not an issue to be separated from life with dignity. Control over one's own death is not a matter distinct from control over one's life. The fact that dying takes place in institutional settings, or has shifted into the "technological order," or reflects the dilemma of the family in a post-tra- ditional world, reminds us that all this is true of living, too. To pose questions about the good death is to pose questions about the good life and the good society.

Ultimately this is what the contributors to this volume do.

I.
The Transformation
of Death

1

Death inside out

PHILIPPE ARIÈS

THE ATTITUDES commonly held about death by modern man—whether sociologists, psychologists or doctors—are so novel and bewildering that scholars have not yet been able to detach them from their modernity and situate them within a broader historical perspective. This is what I shall attempt to do in the following chapter, with respect to three themes: the dispossession of the dying person, the denial of mourning and the new funeral rites in America.

I. How the Dying Person is Deprived of His Death

For thousands of years man has been the sovereign master of his death and the circumstances attending it. Today he no longer is and these are the reasons why.

First of all, it was always taken for granted that man knew he was going to

This chapter was translated from the French by Bernard Murchland. Translation by permission from the European Journal of Sociology VIII *(1967), 169-95. An opening, brief bibliographic commentary intended for a European audience has been deleted from this translation.*

die—whether he came by this knowedge on his own or was told by somebody else. The story-tellers of former times assumed as a matter of course that man is aware of his forthcoming death. La Fontaine is an example. In those days, death was rarely sudden, even in cases of accident or war. Sudden death was very much feared not only because it did not allow time to repent but more importantly because it deprived man of his death. Most people were forewarned of their death, especially since most diseases were fatal. One would have had to be a fool not to perceive the signs of death; moralists and satirists took it upon themselves to ridicule those who refused to admit the obvious. Roland was aware that death was about to carry him off; Tristan felt his life ebbing away and knew that he was going to die; Tolstoi's peasant, responding to an inquiry about his health, says: "Death is at hand." For Tolstoi as for La Fontaine, men adopted a familiar and resigned attitude before death. This does not mean that thinking about death remained the same over this long period of history. Nonetheless, some basic similarities survived in certain classes from one age to another despite the emergence of other attitudes.

When the dying person failed to perceive his lot, it fell to others to tell him. A pontifical document of the Middle Ages made this a responsibility of physicians, and for centuries they executed it faithfully. We find one at Don Quixote's bedside: "A physician was sent for, who, after feeling his pulse, took a rather gloomy view of the case, and told him that he should provide for his soul's health, as that of his body was in a dangerous condition." The *Artes Moriendi* of the fifteenth century stipulated a "spiritual" friend for this task (as opposed to a "carnal" friend) who was called the *nuntius mortis,* a title and a role that is more than a little shocking to our modern sensibility.

As we advance through history ascending the social ladder in an urban environment, we find that man adverts less and less to his impending death. He must be prepared for it by others upon whom he consequently becomes more and more dependent. Probably sometime in the eighteenth century, the physician renounced a role that had long been his. By the nineteenth century, the doctor spoke only when questioned and then with certain reservations. Friends no longer intervened as they did in the time of Gerson or even as late as Cervantes. From the seventeenth century onward, the family assumed this responsibility, which may be taken as a sign of the evolution in family sentiment. For example: The year is 1848 and we are with a family called La Ferronnays. Madame La Ferronnays falls sick. A doctor diagnoses her case as serious and shortly afterwards calls it hopeless. The woman's daughter writes: "When she finished her bath and as I was about to tell her what the doctor had said, she suddenly said to me: 'I can no longer see anything and fear I am going to die.' She then recited a short prayer. How consoling those calm words were to me in that terrible moment!" The daughter was relieved because she was spared the painful task of telling her mother that she was going to die. Such relief is a modern trait but the obligation to inform another of imminent death is very ancient.

The dying were not to be deprived of their death. Indeed, they had to preside over it. As one was born in public so too one died in public. This was true not only of kings (as is well known from Saint-Simon's celebrated account of the death of Louis XIV) but of everyone. Countless tapestries and paintings have depicted the scene for us! As soon as someone fell ill, the room filled with people—parents, children, friends, neighbors, fellow workers. All

windows and doors were closed. The candles were lit. When people in the street saw the priest carrying viaticum, custom as well as devotion dictated that they follow him to the dying person's bedside, even if the person were a stranger. As death approached, the sick-room became a public place. In this context we understand the force of Pascal's words: "We die alone." They have lost much of their meaning for modern man because we literally do die alone. What Pascal means was that, despite the crowd gathered about, the dying person was, in the end, alone. Progressive doctors in the late eighteenth century were firm believers in the curative powers of fresh air and complained bitterly about this public invasion of the rooms of the dying. To their minds, it would have been far healthier to open the windows, put out the candles, and send everyone home.

The public presence at the last moments was not a pious practice imposed by the Church, as we might think. The clergy, or at least the more enlightened of them, had tried long before the doctors to restrain this mob in order to better prepare the sick person for an edifying end. Beginning with the fifteenth century, the *Artes Moriendi* recommended that the dying person be left alone with God so as not to be distracted from the care of his soul. As late as the nineteenth century, very pious individuals, having submitted to all these customary practices, might request that the many onlookers leave the room so that nothing would disturb their final conversations with God. But these were cases of rare and exemplary devotion. Long-standing custom dictated that death be the occasion of a ritual ceremony in which the priest had his place, but so did numbers of other people. The primary role in this ritual was played by the dying person himself. He presided with controlled dignity; having been a participant himself in many such occasions, he knew how to conduct himself. He spoke in turn to his relatives, his friends, his servants, including "the least of them," as Saint-Simon put it in describing the death of Madame de Montespan. He bade them adieu, asked their forgiveness, and gave them his blessing. Invested with a sovereign authority by approaching death (this was especially true in the eighteenth and nineteenth centuries), he gave his orders and made his recommendations. This was the case even when the dying was a very young girl, virtually a child.

Today, nothing remains of this attitude toward death. We do not believe that the sick person has a right to know he is dying; nor do we believe in the public and solemn character accorded the moment of death. What ought to be known is ignored; what ought to be a sacred moment is conjured away.

A Reversal in Sentiment

We take it for granted that the first duty of the family and the physician is to keep the dying person uninformed about his condition. He must not (exceptional cases apart) know that his end is near; he dies ignorant of his death. This is not merely an accidental feature of our contemporary mores; on the contrary, it has taken on the force of a moral rule. Vladimir Jankélévitch made a clear statement in proof of this at a recent medical conference on the theme: Should We Lie to the Sick?[1] "In my mind," he declared, "the liar is the one who tells the truth. I am against the truth, passionately against the truth. For me there is one law that takes precedence over all others and that is the law of love and charity." Since traditional morality made it mandatory to inform the dying of their state, Jankélévitch's law presumably has been universally violated until recent times. Such an attitude is the measure of an extraordinary reversal in sentiment and thought. What has happened? How has this change come about? We might suppose that modern societies are so fixed upon the goals of affluence and material well-being, that there is no place in them for suffering, sorrow, or death. But this would be to mistake the effect for the cause.

This change in attitude toward the dying is linked to the changing role of the family in modern society and its quasi-monopoly over our emotional lives. We must seek the cause of modern attitudes toward death in the relationship between the sick person and his family. The latter does not consider it

[1]Vladimir Jankélévitch, *Médecine de France* [177] (1966) 3-16; reprinted in *La mort* (Paris: Flammarion, 1966).

dignified or a mark of self-esteem to speak frankly about the imminence of death. How often have we heard it said of a loved one: "I at least have the satisfaction of knowing that he died without being aware of it." The "without being aware of it" has replaced the "being aware of one's approaching death" of other times, when every effort was made to make the dying aware of what was happening.

In fact, it may be that the dying frequently know perfectly well what is happening, but remain silent to spare the feelings of those close to them. (Of course, the dead do not share these secrets.) In any case, the modern family has abdicated the role played by the *nuntius mortis,* who from the Middle Ages until the dawn of modern times was not a member of the immediate family. As a result, the dying have also abdicated their role. Why? Because they fear death? Hardly. Fear of death has always existed, and was always countered, often with humor. Despite a natural fear of death, society obligated the dying to play out the final scene of farewell and departure. The fear of death, it is said, is ancestral, but so are the ways of overcoming it. No, the fear of death does not account for the modern practice of denying one's own death. Again, we must turn to the history of the family for an explanation.

In the late Middle Ages (the age of Roland which lives on in the peasants of Tolstoi) and the Renaissance, a man insisted upon participating in his own death because he saw in it an exceptional moment —a moment which gave his individuality its definitive form. He was only the master of his life to the extent that he was the master of his death. His death belonged to him, and to him alone. From the seventeenth century onward, one began to abdicate sole sovereignty over life, as well as over death. These matters came to be shared with the family which had previously been excluded from the serious decisions; all decisions had been made by the dying person, alone and with full knowledge of his impending death.

Last wills and testaments provide evidence of this. From the fourteenth to the beginning of the eighteenth century, they were a spontaneous and individual means of expression, as well as, a sign of distrust— or, at least, the absence of trust—toward the family. Today the last will and testament has lost its character of moral necessity; nor, is it any longer a means of warm and personal expression. Since the eighteenth century, family affections have triumphed over the testator's traditional distrust of his heirs. This distrust has been replaced by a trust so absolute that written wills are no longer necessary. Oral wills have recently become binding for the survivors and are now scrupulously respected. For their part, the dying confidently rely on the family's word. This trusting attitude, which emerged in the seventeenth and eighteenth centuries, and developed in the nineteenth, has become, in the twentieth, a prime source of alientation. No sooner does a member of the family fall mortally ill than the rest conspire to conceal his condition from him, depriving him of information, as well as his freedom. The dying person becomes, in effect, a minor like a child or mental defective. His relatives take complete charge of him and shield him from the world. They supposedly know better than he what he must do, and how much he should know. He is deprived of his rights, particularly the formerly sacred right of knowing about his death, of preparing for it, and organizing it. Now he allows this to be done for him because he is convinced that it is for his own good. He gives himself over to the affection of his family. And if, despite all, he divines his condition, he pretends not to know. In former times, death was a tragedy —often lightened by a comical element—in which one played the role of the dying person. Today, death is a comedy—although not without its tragic elements—in which one plays the role of the "one who does not know" he is going to die.

Of itself, the pressure of family sentiment probably would not have changed the meaning of death so drastically, had it not been for the progress of medical science. It is not so much that medicine has conquered disease, however real its achievements in this realm, but that it has succeeded in substituting sickness for death in the consciousness of the afflicted man. This substitution began to take place in the second half of the nineteenth century. When a sick peasant in Tolstoi's *Three Deaths* (1859) is asked how he is, he answers, "death is at hand." On the contrary, in *The Death of Ivan Ilych*

(1886), after overhearing a conversation that leaves no doubt in Ivan's mind about his condition, he obstinately believes that his floating kidney and infected appendix will be cured by drugs or surgery. His illness becomes an occasion for self-delusion. His wife supports this illusion, blaming his illness on his refusal to obey the doctor's orders to take his medicine regularly.

Of course, it is true, with advances in medical science, serious illness terminates less frequently in death. And chances of recovery are greatly improved. Even when recovery is partial, one can still count on many years of life. Thus, in our society (where we so often act as though medicine had all the answers, or look upon death as something that happens to others, but never to oneself) incurable disease, and especially cancer, has taken on, in the popular imagination, all the frightening and hideous traits depicted in ancient representations of death. Even more than the skeletons or macabre mummies of the fourteenth and fifteenth centuries, cancer is today the very image of death. Disease must be incurable, and regarded as such, before we can admit the reality of death and give it its true name. But the anguish caused by this kind of honesty is so great that it constrains society to hastily multiply those many inducements to silence that reduce a moment of high drama to the banality of a Sunday afternoon picnic.

As a consequence we die in virtual secrecy, far more alone than Pascal could have imagined. This secretiveness comes from a refusal to openly admit the death of those we love and a proclivity to soften its reality by calling it a disease that may be cured. There is another aspect to this problem that American sociologists have noted. In what one might be tempted to regard as nothing more than illusory conduct, they have shown the de facto presence of a new style of death, in which discretion is the modern form of dignity. With less poetry, this is the kind of death approved of by Jankélévitch in which the hard reality is coated over with soothing words of deception.

A New Model of Death

In their *Awareness of Dying* Glaser and Strauss report on their study of six hospitals in the San Francisco Bay area.[2] They recorded the reactions to death of an interrelated group that included the patient, his family, and the medical personnel (doctors and nurses). What happens when it becomes clear that the patient is near death? Should the family be told? The patient? And when? How long should a life be artificially maintained? At what moment should the patient be allowed to die? How should doctors and nurses act in the presence of a patient who does not know, or at least appears not to know, that he is dying? Or one that does know? Every modern family is certainly confronted by such questions, but in a hospital context an important new factor is present: the power of modern medicine. Today, few people die at home. The hospital has become the place where modern man dies, and this fact lends added importance to the Glaser and Strauss study. But the interest of their book goes beyond its empirical analysis. The authors have in fact uncovered an ideal of death that has replaced its traditional public character, as manifested for example in the theatrical pomp of the Romantic era. We now have a new "style of dying" or rather "an acceptable style of living while dying," "an acceptable style of facing death." The emphasis is on *acceptable*. What is important is that one die in a manner that can be accepted and tolerated by the survivors.

Doctors and nurses (although the latter less so) wait as long as possible before telling the family, and scarcely ever tell the patient himself, because they fear becoming involved in a chain of emotional reactions that would make them lose self-control. To talk about death, and thus admit it as a normal dimension of social intercourse, is no longer socially acceptable; on the contrary, it is now something exceptional, excessive, and always dramatic. Death was once a familiar figure and the moralists had to make it hideous in order to inspire fear. Today, mere mention of the word provokes an emotional tension that jars the routine of daily life. An "acceptable style of dying" is, therefore, a style which avoids "status forcing scenes," scenes which tear one from one's social role and offend our sensibility. Such scenes are the

crises of despair the sick go through, their tears, their cries and, in general, any exceptional emotive or noisy outburst that would interfere with hospital routine and trouble others. This is an example of what Glaser and Strauss call, "embarrassingly graceless dying," the very opposite of an "acceptable style of dying." Such a death would embarrass the survivors. This is what must be avoided at all costs and this is the reason why the patient is kept uninformed. What basically matters is not whether the patient knows or does not know; rather, if he does know he must have the consideration and courage to be discreet. He must conduct himself in such a way that the hospital staff is not reminded that he knows and can communicate with him as though death were not in their midst. For communication is necessary. It is not enough for the dying to be discreet; they must also be open and receptive to messages. Their indifference in this matter should be as embarrassing to the medical personnel as an excessive display of emotion. Thus, there are two ways of dying badly: one can be either too emotional or too indifferent.

The authors cite the case of an old woman who was at first well behaved, in accord with acceptable conventions; she cooperated with the doctors and nurses and bore her illness courageously. One day she decided that she had struggled enough, that the time had come to give up. Whereupon she closed her eyes, never to open them again, signifying in this way that she had withdrawn from the world and wished to await her end alone. In former times, this withdrawal would have been respected and accepted as normal. But in a California hospital it disconcerted the medical staff so much that they flew in one of her sons from another city to persuade her to open her eyes on the grounds that she was "hurting everybody." Sometimes patients turn to the wall and refuse to move. We recognize in such acts one of the oldest gestures of man in the face of death. In this way did the Jews of the Old Testament die. So died Tristan who turned toward the wall and exclaimed that he could no longer keep a hold on life. But in such ancestral reactions the California doctors and nurses saw only an antisocial refusal to communicate, a culpable renunciation of the will to live.

[2]B. G. Glaser and A. L Strauss, *Awareness of Dying* (Chicago: Aldine, 1965).

Let us note that patients are not blamed in such cases merely because they have demoralized the medical staff, or because of failure to perform their duty but more seriously because they are considered to have lessened the capacity to resist the sickness itself—an eventuality that becomes as fearsome as a "status forcing scene." That is why American and English doctors are today less inclined to keep patients in the dark about their condition. But we must not exaggerate the significance of such signs. They may indicate no more than the pragmatic hope that the patient will respond better to treatment if he knows his condition and will, in the end, die as discreetly and with as much dignity as if he knew nothing. In *Reflections on America*, Jacques Maritain describes the good American's death: The medical staff induces in him a kind of dream-like state in which he thinks that to die amidst these smiling faces and these uniforms, white and immaculate like the wings of angels, is a genuine pleasure, or at least a moment of no consequence—"Relax, take it easy, it's nothing."[3] Take away the professional smile and add a little music, and you have the contemporary philosopher's ideal of the dignified, humanistic death: "To disappear *pianissimo* and, so to speak, on tip toe" (Jankélévitch).

II. The Denial of Mourning

We now see how modern society deprives man of his death. Whatever dignity remains must be purchased at the price of not troubling the living. Reciprocally, modern society forbids the living from showing too much emotion over the death of a loved one; they are permitted neither to weep for the departed nor to appear to mourn their passing.

In times past mourning was the ultimate expression of sorrow. It was both legitimate and necessary. Grief over the death of a close one was considered the strongest and most spontaneous expression of emotion. During the Middle Ages, the most hardened warriors and the most renowned kings broke into tears over the bodies of friends and relatives. They wept, as we would say today,

like hysterical women. King Arthur is a good example. He often fainted, struck his breast, and tore at his skin until the blood flowed. On the battlefield, he fell to the ground in a swoon before his nephew's body and then set out in tears to find the bodies of his friends. Upon discovering one of them, he clasped his hands and cried out that he had lived long enough. He removed the helmet from the dead man's body and, after gazing upon him for a long time, kissed his eyes and mouth. We find many instances, in those times, of the most extraordinary and uninhibited emotional outbursts. But, with the exception of those few whose sorrow was so great that they had to retire to a monastery, the survivors soon resumed normal life.

From the thirteenth century on, we notice that expressions of mourning begin to lose their spontaneity and become more and more ritualized. The grand gesticulations of the early Middle Ages are now simulated by professional mourners (who can be found in some parts of Europe even today). The Spanish hero, El Cid, requested in his will that there be no flowers or mourners at his funeral, as had been the custom. The iconography of fourteenth and fifteenth-century tombs depict mourners around the body of the deceased, clothed in black robes with their heads buried in penitent-like cowls. We learn from sixteenth and seventeenth-century documents that funeral processions were composed largely of substitute mourners: mendicant monks, the poor, and orphans, all clothed for the occasion in black robes furnished by the deceased. After the ceremony, each received a portion of bread and a little money.

Apparently close relatives did not attend the funeral services. Friends were offered a banquet—banquets so excessively festive that the Church tried to suppress the practice. Last wills refer to such festivities less and less, or mention them only in censorious language. We notice that the dying frequently requested and sometimes insisted upon the presence of a brother or a son in the funeral procession. Often this was a child, who was offered a special legacy for his much desired presence. Would this have been the case had the family attended funerals as a matter of course? Under the old regime we know that women did not

---

[3]Jacques Maritain, *Reflections on America* (New York: Scribner's, 1958).

attend funerals. It is probable that from the end of the Middle Ages with the increasing ritualization of mourning rites, society imposed a period of seclusion upon the immediate members of the family, a seclusion which would have excluded them from the obsequies. They were represented by priests and professional mourners, religious, members of pious organizations, or simply those who were attracted by the alms distributed on such occasions.

The period of seclusion had two purposes. First of all, it gave the bereaved some privacy in which to mourn their loved ones. Protected from the gaze of the world, they waited for their sorrow to pass as a sick person waits for his illness to abate. One, Henri de Campion, makes mention of this in his *Mémoires.* In June, 1659, his wife died in childbirth and the child, a daughter, died shortly afterwards. He wrote:

I was heartbroken and fell into a pitiful state. My brother and my sister took me to Conches where I remained seventeen days and then returned to Baxferei to put my affairs in order. Not being able to inhabit my house because it reminded me too much of my beloved wife, I bought a property in Conches and lived there until June, 1660 (which is to say until the first anniversary of my wife's death) at which time I perceived that my sorrow had followed me. So I returned to my former home in Baxferei with my children, where I am presently living in great sadness.

Second, the period of seclusion prevented the survivors from forgetting the deceased too soon. It was in fact a time of penance during which they were not permitted the activities and pleasures of normal life. This precaution was not unhelpful in preventing a hasty replacement of the dead person. Nicolas Versoris, a Parisian merchant, lost his wife to the plague on September 3, 1522, one hour after midnight. On December 30 of that same year, he was engaged to a doctor's widow, whom he married as soon as he could, which is to say on January 13, 1523, "the first festive day after Christmas."

This custom continued through the nineteenth century. When someone died the immediate family, servants, and often the domestic animals as well, were separated from the rest of society by drawn curtains

and black mourning crepe. By this time, however, the period of seclusion was more voluntary than obligatory: it no longer prohibited close relatives from participating in the funeral service, pilgrimages to the graveside, or the elaborate memorial cults that characterized the Romantic Age. Nor were women any longer excluded from the obsequies. In this regard, the bourgeoisie were the first to break with tradition, followed some time later by the nobility, among whom it had been considered good taste for a widow not to attend her husband's funeral. At first the nobility ceded to the new practices discreetly, usually hidden in some dark corner of the church with ecclesiastical approval. Little by little the traditional custom of seclusion gave way to the new practice of honoring the dead and venerating their tombs. Women's presence at funerals, however, did nothing to radically change the private character of mourning: entirely clothed in black, the *mater dolorosa,* she is hidden from the world's sight except as symbol of sorrow and desolation. Nonetheless, mourning was now more moral than physical in nature. It was less a protection of the dead from oblivion than an affirmation that the living must remember them, that they could not go on living as before. The dead no longer needed society to protect them from the indifference of their close relatives; nor did the dying any longer need written testaments to make their last will known to their heirs.

The new family sentiment of the late eighteenth and early nineteenth centuries thus combined with the ancient tradition of seclusion to transform the mourning period from an imposed quarantine into a right to express, with all due propriety, deeply felt sorrow. This marked a return to the spontaneity of the high Middle Ages while conserving the formal rituals that had been introduced around the twelfth century. If we were to trace the historical curve of mourning it would look like this: until the thirteenth century, a time of uninhibited and even violent spontaneity, followed through the seventeenth century by a long period of ritualization, which gave way in the nineteenth to an age when sorrow was given full and dramatic expression. It is likely that the paroxysm of mourning in the nineteenth century stands in some direct relationship to its attenuation in the twentieth century in somewhat the same way as the "dirty death" of Remarque, Sartre, and Genet in the postwar period emerged as the other side of the "noble death" celebrated by Romanticism. Thus, the significance of Sartre's gesture, more laughable than scandalous, of urinating on Chateaubriand's tomb. It took a Chateaubriand to produce such a Sartre. It is a relationship of the sort that links contemporary eroticism to Victorian sexual taboos.

Mourning Becomes Forbidden

Some form of mourning, whether spontaneous or obligatory, has always been mandatory in human society. Only in the twentieth century has it been forbidden. The situation was reversed in a single generation: what was always commanded by individual conscience, or the general will, is now rejected. And what was, in former times, rejected is now recommended. It is no longer fitting to manifest one's sorrow or even give evidence of experiencing any.

Credit for uncovering this unwritten law of our civilization goes to the British sociologist, Geoffrey Gorer. He was the first to understand that certain facts, neglected or poorly understood by the humanistic moralists, did, indeed, constitute a characteristic attitude toward death in industrial societies. In an autobiographical introduction to his *Death, Grief and Mourning,* Gorer recounts some personal experiences which led him to the discovery that death is the principal taboo of our time.[4] The sociological inquiry he undertook in 1963 on attitudes toward death and mourning in England merely confirmed, detailed, and enriched ideas he had already published in his "The Pornography of Death," a remarkable article based upon his personal experiences and reflection.[5]

Gorer was born in 1910. He recalls that the whole family mourned the death of Edward VII. He learned, as do French children, to take off his hat when a funeral procession passed in the street and to treat those in mourning with special respect— practices which seem strange to the British

today. In 1915, his father was lost in the sinking of the *Lusitania,* and Gorer was, in his turn, given special attention. "I was treated with great kindness, like an invalid; no demands were made on me, I was indulged, conversation was hushed in my presence." One day during a walk, he attempted to convey his desolation by telling his Nanny that he would never be able "to enjoy flowers again," whereupon she reprimanded him and told him not to be morbid.

Because of the war his mother was allowed to take a job where she found diversion from her sorrow. She would not have had such a recourse at any earlier date; but at a later date she would not have had the support of the mourning ritual. Thus Gorer experienced in his childhood the traditional manifestations of mourning and they must have made a strong impression on him for they remained vivid in his memory many years later. During his youth in the postwar period, he had no further experience of death. Once he saw a cadaver in a Russian hospital he visited in 1931; unaccustomed to the sight of death, this chance viewing seems to have captured his imagination. Gorer's case was not unusual. Unfamiliarity with death is common today—the long, unnoticed consequence of greater longevity. J. Fourcassié has shown how it is possible for today's children to grow to adulthood without ever seeing anyone die. Gorer was, however, surprised when his inquiry revealed that more people had witnessed death than he would have suspected. But he also observed that they quite spontaneously adopted the same behavior patterns as those who had never seen a death, and forgot it with all possible haste.

Gorer was later surprised when his brother, a well-known physician, fell into a state of depression after his wife's death. Intellectuals in England had already begun to abandon the traditional funeral rites and external manifestations of sorrow as so many primitive and superstitious practices. But Gorer did not at the time see any connection between his brother's pathological despair and the absence of mourning rituals. The situation was different in 1948 when he lost a close friend who left a wife and three children. Gorer wrote:

[4]Geoffrey Gorer, *Death, Grief and Mourning* (New York: Doubleday, 1965).

[5]*Ibid.,* pp. 192-99. See Gorer, for this article and subsequent quotes.

When I went to see her some two months after John's death, she told me, with tears of gratitude, that I was the first man to stay in the house since she had become a widow. She was being given some good professional help from lawyers and the like who were also friends; but socially she had been almost completely abandoned to loneliness, although the town was full of acquaintances who considered themselves friends.

Gorer then strongly suspected that the changes that had taken place in mourning customs were neither anecdotal or insignificant. He was discovering the importance and serious consequences of these changes, and a few years later, in 1955, he published his famous article.

Decisive proof came in 1961 when his brother, who had remarried, was diagnosed as suffering from incurable cancer. His brother's doctor, a friend since they were in medical school together, "asked me to decide whether his wife, Elizabeth, should be informed; he had already decided to hide the truth from Peter; and he and his colleagues engaged in the most elaborate and successful medical mystification to hide from Peter's expert knowledge the facts of their diagnosis." He consulted an old and respected friend about his dilemma and was advised that Elizabeth should be told. "One of the arguments he advanced was that, if she were ignorant, she might show impatience or lack of understanding with his probably increasing weakness, for which she would reproach herself later; she could use the final months of their marriage better if she knew them for what they were." The prognosis was for a lingering illness but much to everyone's surprise Peter died suddenly in his sleep. Everyone concerned congratulated themselves that he had died without knowing it, an eventuality widely regarded as a desirable one in our culture. In this family of intellectuals, there would be no funeral vigil and no exposure of the body. Since his death took place at home, the body would have to be prepared. Gorer evokes what took place in colorful language:

It was arranged for a pair of ex-nurses to come to lay out the body. They imparted a somewhat Dickensian tone; they were fat and jolly and asked in a respectful but cheerful tone, "Where is the patient?" Some half hour later their work was done, and they came out saying, "The patient looks lovely now. Come and have a look!" I did not wish to, at which they expressed surprise. I gave them a pound for their pains; the leader, pure Sarah Gamp, said, "That for us duck? Cheers!" and went through the motions of raising a bottle and emptying it into her mouth.

No mention was made through all of this of either death or the corpse. Peter was still regarded as a "patient" despite the biological transformation that had taken place. Preparing the body for burial is an ancient rite. But its meaning has changed. It formerly had as its object to make the body reflect the ideal image of death prevalent in society; the intention was to create a sense of dependency, to present the body in a helpless state, with crossed hands, awaiting the life to come. The Romantic Age discovered the original beauty that death imparts to the human face and these last ablutions were designed to rescue this beauty from the pain that had generated it. In both cases, the intention was to create an image of death: to present a beautiful corpse but a corpse nonetheless. Today we no longer have a corpse but something almost alive. "The patient looks lovely now." Our fairy's touch has given it the appearance of life. All signs of pain have been erased, not in order to capture the hieratic beauty of the dead or the majesty of those in repose, but to present a cadaver that retains the charms of something living, something "lovely" and not at all repulsive. The preparation of the body is today intended to mask the reality of death and give the pleasing illusion of life. We must remember that in Gorer's England this practice was just emerging, which is why the family could not share the old nurses' enthusiasm for their handiwork. In the United States, on the other hand, embalming is a fine art and corpses are exhibited in funeral homes with great pride.

The Meaning of Cremation

Gorer's family was deluded by neither the beliefs of another age nor the flashy talents of American morticians. Peter's body was to be cremated, and cremation in England (and no doubt in Northern Europe generally) has a special meaning which Gorer's study clearly brought out. Cremation is no longer chosen, as was long the case, in defiance of the Church and tradiditional Christian customs. Nor is it chosen solely for reasons of convenience or economy, reasons which the Church would be disposed to respect in memory of a time when ashes, like those of Antigone's brother, were as venerable as a body that was buried. The significance of cremation in modern England cuts deeper; it reflects the rational spirit of modern times and is nothing less than a denial of life after death, although this was not immediately apparent from the results of Gorer's inquiry. Of sixty-four persons interviewed, forty favored cremation over burial and they offered two basic reasons for this preference. It was first of all considered the most efficient means of disposing of the body. Thus one of the respondents in the study had her mother cremated because it was "healthier" but stated, "I think for my husband, who was buried, cremation would have been too final."

The second reason is connected to the first: cremation makes cemetery rituals and periodic visitation to the graveside unnecessary. But it should be noted that such practices are not necessarily eliminated by cremation. On the contrary the administrators of crematoriums do everything in their power to enable families to venerate their dead just as they do in the traditional cemeteries. In the memorial rooms of crematoriums one can have a plaque installed which performs a function analogous to that of the tombstone. But of the forty persons interviewed by Gorer, only one had opted for such a plaque and only fourteen wrote their names in the memorial book which is opened each day to commemorate the day of the death. This may be seen as a kind of intermediary solution between complete oblivion and the permanency of the engraved plaque. If families choose not to adopt commemorative practices available to them it is because they see in cremation a sure means of avoiding any form of cultic homage to the dead.

It would be a serious mistake to see in this refusal to commemorate the dead a sign of indifference or insensitivity. The results of Gorer's study and his autobiographical

testimony is evidence to the contrary that the survivors are and remain deeply affected by a death in the family. For further proof of this let us turn to Gorer's account of his brother's cremation. Elizabeth, the widow,

> decided not to come to the cremation herself—she could not bear the thought that she might lose control and other people observe her grief; and she wished to spare the children the distressing experience. As a consequence, their father's death was quite unmarked for them by ritual of any kind, and was nearly even treated as a secret, for it was several months before Elizabeth could bear to mention him or have him mentioned in her presence.

Notice that her absence was not due to any of the traditional reasons or to indifference but to a fear of "losing control." This has become a new form of modesty, a convention which requires us to hide what we were formerly obliged to manifest, even if it had to be simulated: one's sorrow.

Notice, too, that children are also affected by this modern mandate. Even in France, where traditional practices are more in evidence, middle-class children rarely attend the funerals of their grandparents. Old people who are several times grandparents are buried by adults who are more rushed and embarrassed than grieved, with no grandchildren present. I was especially struck by this when in the course of my research I came across a number of documents dating from the seventeenth century in which the testator insisted that at least one of his grandchildren be in his funeral procession, although he may have been indifferent to the presence of other relatives. At that time, we might recall, mourners were often recruited among orphans. In numerous representations of the dying, the painter or engraver always included a child among those gathered about the deathbed.

So Elizabeth and her children stayed in their country home on the day of her husband's cremation. Geoffrey joined them that evening, overcome with grief and fatigue. His sister-in-law welcomed him in her usual self-assured manner. She told him that she had passed a pleasant day with the children. "They had taken a picnic to the fields where the grass was being cut for silage." Elizabeth, who was born in New England, quite naturally adopted the conduct she had been taught in America and which the English expected of her: she acted as if nothing had happened and so made it easier for others to do the same and thus permit social life to continue without even momentary interruption by death. Had she risked a public demonstration of her sorrow, society would have censored her like a fallen woman. She was, moreover, avoided by her and Peter's friends. They treated her, she said, "like a leper." Only if she acted as though nothing of consequence had happened was she again socially acceptable. Gorer observes that "at the period when she most needed help and comfort from society she was left alone." It was in the months following Peter's death that he decided to undertake a study of the modern refusal to mourn and its traumatizing effects.

From the Cabbage Patch to the Flower Garden

Gorer argues that this state of affairs began with the decline of social support for funereal rituals and the special status of the mourning period. He perhaps accords too much importance to the two World Wars as catalysts in this evolution. New conventions made their appearance gradually, almost imperceptibly in such a way that their originality went unnoticed. Even today they are not formalized in the manner of traditional customs. Yet they are just as powerful an influence on behavior. Death has become a taboo, an unmentionable subject (as Jankélévitch says over and over again in his book on death), something excluded from polite conversation. Gorer mounts impressive evidence to show that in the twentieth century death has taken the place of sex as the principal taboo. He writes that in our time,

> there has been an unremarked shift in prudery; whereas copulation has become more and more "mentionable"... death has become more and more "unmentionable" as a natural process.... The natural processes of corruption and decay have become disgusting, as disgusting as the natural processes of birth and copulation were a century ago; preoccupation about such processes is (or was) morbid and unhealthy, to be discouraged in all and punished in the

young. Our great-grandparents were told that babies were found under gooseberry bushes or cabbages; our children are likely to be told that those who have passed on (fie! on the gross Anglo-Saxon monosyllable) are changed into flowers, or lie at rest in lovely gardens. The ugly facts are relentlessly hidden; the art of the embalmers is an art of complete denial.

Children used to be told that a stork brought them but they could be present at deathbeds and attend funerals! Sometime after the middle of the nineteenth century, their presence caused a kind of malaise and there was a tendency to at least limit their participation when in fact it was not prohibited altogether. Children were present at the deaths of Emma Bovary and Ivan Ilych but they were permitted only a brief visit and then escorted from the room on the pretext that the agonies of the dying would be too much for them to bear. Although their presence at the deathbed was gradually prohibited, they were allowed their traditional place at the obsequies, clothed from head to foot in black.

Today children are initiated at an early age into the physiology of love and birth, but when they express curiosity about why they no longer see their grandparents they are told (at least in France) that they have gone on a long trip or (in England) that they are resting among the flowers. It is no longer a case of babies being found under the cabbages but of grandparents who disappear among the flowers! Relatives of the deceased are thus forced to feign indifference. Society demands of them a form of self-control similar to that demanded of the dying themselves. For the one as for the other, what is important is to show no sign of emotion. Society as a whole behaves like a hospital staff. Just as the dying must control their feelings and cooperate with the doctors and nurses, so must the bereaved hide their sorrow, reject the traditional period of seclusion (because this would betray their feelings), and carry on their normal activities without so much as missing a step. Otherwise, they would be ostracized by society, a form of seclusion that would have consequences quite different from the traditional mourning period. The latter was accepted by all as a necessary transition period and carried with it forms of behavior that were equally ritualistic such as obligatory visits of condolence, letters of sympathy, and the succors of religion. Today the bereaved are treated like sexual deviants, those afflicted with contagious diseases, or other asocial types. Whoever wishes to spare himself this stigma must hide his true feelings in public and reveal them only to his closest friends. As Gorer puts it, one weeps in private just as we undress and go to sleep in private, "as if it were an analogue of masturbation."

Society today refuses to recognize that the bereaved are sick people who need help. It refuses to associate mourning with illness. The traditional custom was in this respect more comprehensive, perhaps more "modern," more sensitive to the pathological effects of repressed moral suffering. Gorer considers it a mark of cruelty to deprive anyone of the beneficence guaranteed by the ancient custom. In their mourning, Gorer notes, those stricken by the death of a loved one need society's help more than at any other time, but it is precisely then that society withdraws its assistance and refuses to help. The price of this failure is very great in misery, loneliness, despair, and morbidity. This prohibition of a decent period of mourning forces the bereaved to bury himself in work; or to push himself to the very limits of sanity by pretending that the deceased is still living, that he never went away; or, what is worse, to imagine that he himself is the dead person, imitating his gestures, his voice, his idiosyncrasies, and sometimes simulating the symptoms of the sickness that carried him off. This is clearly neurotic behavior. We see in such behavior instances of those strange manifestations of exaggerated grief which seem new and modern to Gorer but are nonetheless familiar to the historian of customs. They once found an outlet in rituals which were acknowledged, recommended, and, indeed, even simulated during the prescribed period of mourning in traditional societies. But it must be admitted that only the appearances are the same. In former times such rituals had the purpose of liberating. Even when, as often happened in the Romantic Age, they exceeded the limits of custom and became pathological, they were not repressed as something monstrous but were patiently tolerated. This tolerance appears in a strik-ing manner in a novel by Mark Twain in which a woman refuses to accept the death of her husband and each year lives out his impossible return. Her friends conspire to support this illusion. Today we can't imagine anyone participating in such a dark comedy. Twain's characters acted out of kindness and generosity but their action would be viewed by today's society as something embarrassing and shamefully morbid, indeed, a sign of mental illness. We thus ask ourselves, with Gorer, whether or not a large part of contemporary social pathology does not originate in our refusal to confront the reality of death—in society's denial of mourning and the right to weep for the dead.

III. New Funeral Rites in the United States

Based on the foregoing analysis, we might be tempted to conclude that our suppression of the reality of death is part of the very structure of contemporary civilization. The elimination of death from conversation and from the communications media goes hand-in-hand with the priority of material well-being as the principal trait of industrial societies. This is especially the case in Northern Europe and America, the main geographical areas of modernity, although there are exceptions where older thought-patterns still prevail. I am thinking of some sectors of Catholic France and Italy, of Presbyterian Scotland, and of the lower classes even in countries that are industrially advanced. Modernity depends on social conditions as much as geography and even in the most progressive countries is limited to the educated classes, whether believers or sceptics. Where modernity has not penetrated we find that eighteenth and nineteenth century Romantic attitudes toward death still prevail, such as the cult of the dead and veneration in cemeteries. We should not be misled by the survival of such attitudes, however; while they characterize large numbers of people, they are seriously threatened today. They are doomed to inevitable decline, along with the earlier, less developed mentalities with which they are linked. They are also jeopardized by a model of future society which would continue the process of emptying death of all existential meaning, a model that already dominates middle-class families, whether liberal or conservative. We need not be entirely pessimistic about this evolution because it is probable that the denial of death is so bound up with industrial civilization that the one will disappear with the other. Nor is the denial of death universally the case, as we pointed out, because it is not found in many sectors of society. I am not thinking now of backward parts of Old Europe but of that stronghold of modernity, the United States. America has been the first among modern societies to attenuate the tragic sense of death. There we can observe firsthand the new attitudes toward death. Some of these were satirized in *The Loved One,* Waugh's novel, written in 1948.[6] In 1951, Roger Caillois saw in them an example of hedonistic sleight of hand:

> Death can be faced without fear, not because of some moral ability to transcend the fear it provokes, but because it is inevitable and because in fact there is no reason to dread it. *What we must do is simply not think or talk about it.*[7]

Everything we have said about death in the preceding pages—the alienation of the dying person, the denial of mourning, etc.—holds true for America with the one exception of burial practices. The Americans have not simplified funeral rites as much as the English. To understand this singularity we must continue our earlier account of how modern man dies, with the emphasis now on the time between death and burial. The time before death and after burial, together with the peculiar mourning rites modern man affects, is no different in America than in any other modern society. The difference comes in the intermediary period. We recall how the two nurses charged with preparing the body of Gorer's brother admired their own work. But in England this kind of enthusiasm is not shared by society at large. What matters to the English is to get rid of the body as decently and as quickly as possible. That is why they favor cremation.

In America, on the other hand, the art of laying out the body forms part of a series of new rites that are both complicated and sumptuous. These include: the embalming of the body, its exhibition in a funeral parlor, visitation by friends and relatives, flowers and music, solemn obsequies, and, finally, interment in a cemetery that looks like a park. The latter is embellished with monuments and is intended for the moral edification of visitors who are more like tourists than pilgrims. There is no point in describing these rites further. They are well known to a wide public as a result of Waugh's book, which has been made into a film, and Jessica Mitford's *The American Way of Death*.[8] Such books are misleading, however, insofar as they suggest that these rituals are no more than a form of commercial exploitation or a perversion of the cult of happiness held dear by Americans. More deeply, they testify to a refusal to have death emptied of all meaning, a refusal to let death pass without solemnizing the occasion ritualistically. This is one reason why cremation is less widespread in the United States.

American society is very attached to these rituals, although they seem somewhat ridiculous to Europeans and American intellectuals (whose attitudes are reflected in Mitford's book). So much so that for a time death is something familiar, something one can talk about. Ads of this sort are common in America: "The dignity and integrity of So-and-So Funeral Home costs no more. Easy access. Private parking for over one-hundred cars." Of course, there is no doubt that death is a consumer product. But what is noteworthy is that it has become so, together with all the publicity attendant upon its commercial status, despite the banishment of death elsewhere in society. American attitudes toward the immediately deceased constitute an exception to modern attitudes toward death in general. In this case, they break the normal pattern of modernity and grant the deceased the social space traditional societies had always reserved for them, space that has been practically eliminated in industrial societies. In their way, Americans are carrying on the

[6]Evelyn Waugh, *The Loved One* (London: Chapman and Hall, 1950).

[7]Roger Caillois, *Quatre essais de sociologie contemporaine* (Paris: Perrin, 1951).

[8]Jessica Mitford, *The American Way of Death* (New York: Simon and Schuster, 1963).

tradition of bidding a solemn farewell to the dead, and this in spite of the iron-clad rule of expediency that governs conduct in technological and consumer societies. In France many of the hospitals date from the seventeenth century (when the sick were

T he idea of making a dead person appear alive as a way of paying one's last respects may well strike us as puerile and preposterous. As is often the case in America, this practice is part and parcel of a syndrome that includes commercial interests and the language of advertising. But it also testifies to a rapid and unerring adaptation to complex and contradictory conditions of sensibility. This is the first time in history that a whole society has honored the dead by pretending that they were alive.

subjected to humiliating and coarse treatment at the hands of vagabonds and delinquents) and the bodies of the dead are still kept in cold rooms like so much meat. The French are, consequently, in a good position to appreciate the need for a time of recollection and solemnity that strikes a balance between the anonymity of a collective morgue and the finality of burial.

In another age such a time could have been observed in the home. But modern attitudes are set against having the corpse too close to the living. In Europe the intelligentsia rarely keep the body in the house,

even if the death occurs there. This is partly for hygienic reasons, but more because of a nervous fear of losing control. The American solution is to deposit the body in a neutral place, halfway between the anonymity of the hospital and the privacy of the home. This place is called a funeral home, a special building that is in charge of a kind of innkeeper who specializes in welcoming the dead. The time spent here is a compromise between the decent but hasty and deritualized services of Northern Europe and the more archaic ceremonies of traditional mourning. The new funeral rites created by the Americans are also a compromise between their desire to observe a period of solemnity after death and their general acceptance of society's taboos. That is why these rituals are so different from those we are used to and why, consequently, they strike us as somewhat comical, even though they retain some traditional elements. The half-closed coffin exposing the upper half of the body is not an invention of American morticians. It is a practice dating from the Middle Ages and can still be found in Mediterranean areas like Marseilles and parts of Italy. A fifteenth century fresco in the church of St. Petronius in Bologna depicts the remains of Saint Mark reposing in a coffin of this type.

The Mortician's Art

Still, it must be borne in mind that these funeral home rituals have quite radically changed the meaning of death. In fact, it is not death that is celebrated in these rituals; it is rather death transformed into the appearance of life by the mortician's art. Formerly embalming was intended primarily to impart something of the incorruptibility of the saints to the dead, especially those who had been celebrated and venerated in life. One of the miracles required for sainthood is an uncorrupted body. By helping to make the body more incorruptible, embalming was looked upon as a way of cooperating in the work of sanctification.

In modern America chemical techniques for preserving the body make us forget death by creating an illusion of life. What friends and relatives pay respect to amidst the banks of flowers and the soothing music is the life-like appearance of the deceased.

The idea of death is banished from this ritual as is all deep sorrow. Roger Caillois grasped this point so well when he noted that those fully clothed corpses give the impression that they are merely taking a nap. While it is a fact that this illusion is dispensed with in those sectors of English society described by Gorer and in the American intelligentsia, it is also a fact that the general public goes along with it and this is no doubt evidence of a profound trait in the American character.

The idea of making a dead person appear alive as a way of paying one's last respects may well strike us as puerile and preposterous. As is often the case in America, this practice is part and parcel of a syndrome that includes commercial interests and the language of advertising. But it also testifies to a rapid and unerring adaptation to complex and contradictory conditions of sensibility. This is the first time in history that a whole society has honored the dead by pretending that they were alive.

Something like this happened once before in history, but involved one person only. I refer to Louis XIV, King of France. When he died he was embalmed, clothed in the purple robes of his consecration, laid out on a bed that looked something like a judge's bench—all as though he would wake up at any moment. Banquet tables were set up, no doubt reminiscent of the ancient funeral festivities but more a symbol of the rejection of mourning. The king did not die in the minds of his subjects. Dressed in festive garments, like a rich Californian in a funeral parlor, he received his court for a last time. The idea of the continuity of the Crown dictated a funeral rite that was, in effect, much like those of contemporary America despite a time difference of several centuries, and like them it may be regarded as a compromise between the desire to honor the dead and the desire to put them out of mind as something unmentionable.

The Americans, who believe in their way of death (including the practices of their funeral directors) as they do in their way of life, give these rituals a further justification that is very interesting because it bears out in an unexpected way Gorer's theory about the traumatizing effects of the denial of mourning. Jessica Mitford reports this case: "Recently a funeral director told me of a woman who needed psychiatric treatment because her husband's funeral was with a closed casket, no visitation, and burial in another state with her not present." (In effect, this represents the practice of the progressive Englishman.) "The psychiatrist called him (the funeral director) to learn about the funeral or lack of one. The patient was treated and has recovered and has vowed never to be part of another memorial-type service," that is to say a simplified commemoration of the dead.[9]

Funeral directors, whose interests are threatened by a trend toward simplicity, draw upon expert psychological opinion to defend their business. They argue that by replacing sorrow with sweet serenity they are providing an important public service. Because it tempers the anguish of the bereaved and designs cemeteries for the happiness of the living, the funeral industry sees itself as having a beneficient moral and social function. In America today cemeteries play a role that was intended for future necropolises by French urban-planners at the end of the eighteenth century when a royal edict prohibited burial within the city walls. As a result, provisions for new cemeteries had to be made, and a vast literature described what they should be like and what in particular Père Lachaise of Paris (which became the model of all modern cemeteries in both Europe and America) should be like. One is struck by the resemblance between these eighteenth century texts and the prose of modern American funeral directors and the moralists who support them. Mitford's book offers abundant evidence of this similarity. America is rediscovering the tone and style of the Age of Enlightenment. Rediscovering? Perhaps we should say that they have never lost them. Some historians of American society think that the Puritanism of the eighteenth century impeded the development of a hedonistic attitude toward death and that contemporary optimism does not predate the twentieth century. Whether the influence is direct, then, or a repetition, after a century's interlude, in either case the similarity is striking.

Had it not been for the influence of Romanticism, Père Lachaise would have

---

[9]*Ibid.*, p. 93.

become another Forest Lawn, the famous cemetery in Los Angeles caricatured by Waugh. Romanticism thwarted a development in this direction and its influence still persists in the popular representations of death and in graveside cults. On the other hand, we get the impression that in America the Romantic influence was short-lived and that the spirit of the Enlightenment, although diminished by Puritanism, was more influential. If this is the case, Puritanism would have had the same braking effect in America as Romanticism did in Europe, but would have died out earlier, thus fostering a mentality much like that of the Enlightenment, the seedbed of so many modern attitudes. We cannot help thinking that in this matter as in so many others (in Constitutional law, for example) America is closer to the eighteenth century than Europe is.

The Crisis of Death and the Crisis of Individuality

We conclude that in the last third of the twentieth century something of monumental significance is taking place of which we are just becoming aware: death, that familiar companion of yore, has disappeared from our language. His name is anathema. A kind of vague and anonymous anxiety has taken the place of the words and symbols elaborated by our ancestors. A few writers like Malraux and Ionesco make some attempt to restore death's ancient name which has been obliterated from our language and social conventions. But in normal existence it no longer has any positive meaning at all. It is merely the negative side of what we really see, what we really know, and what we really feel.

This represents a profound change in attitude. In truth, death did not occupy a large place in the minds of men during the high Middle Ages or for some time afterwards. It was not outlawed by edict as it is today; rather its power was weakened by reason of its extreme familiarity. But from the twelfth century onwards, people became more and more preoccupied with death, at least this was the case among the clergy and the educated classes. This concern emerged gradually in connection with two distinct themes: in the twelfth and thirteenth centuries in connection with the theme of the Last Judgment and in the fourteenth and fifteenth centuries in connection with the theme of the art of dying. The *Artes Moriendi* depicted the whole universe in the death-room: the living of the earth, the blessed of heaven, and the damned of hell, all in the presence of Christ and his heavenly court. The life of the dying person was thus summed up for all time and, whoever he might be, he was in this restricted space and for this brief moment the very center of the natural and supernatural worlds. Death was the occasion for individual self-awareness.

We know from several sources that the late Middle Ages was a time of emerging individuality, when men began to define themselves as entities distinct from the collective representations of the human race. It was a time of rampant individualism in religion, in economics (the beginnings of capitalism), and in culture at large. The most conclusive evidence of this individualism is, in my opinion, to be found in the wills and last testaments of the time. These became a literary form in their own right and a means of individual self-expression. When a will is reduced to a mere means of disposing of the deceased's wealth as it is today, it is a sign of a decline or at the very least of a change in our conception of individuality. The progress of science, the affirmation of the rights of man, and the rise of the middle class in the eighteenth century testify that that age was also a heyday of individualism. But it was an individualism already in eclipse, for in the unnoticed intimacy of daily life, individual freedom was already threatened, on the one hand, by family constraints and, on the other, by the demands of professional life. The clear correspondence between the triumph over death and the triumph of individuality during the late Middle Ages invites us to ask whether a similar but inverse relationship might not exist today between the "crisis of death" and the crisis of individuality.

1020

2

The political uses
of
natural death
IVAN ILLICH

I N ANY society the dominant image of death determines the prevalent concept of health. In modern societies two contradictory concepts of death are simultaneously held, and this contradiction is accentuated and perpetuated by Janus-faced medicine. As a productive industry medicine is organized like an agency for the defense of mankind against a host of evil deaths, while as a world-wide ritual it is structured to foster the belief that natural extinction from peaceful exhaustion is the birthright of all men.

The Crisis of Medicine

The ritual nature of modern health procedures hides from doctors and patients the contradiction between the ideal of a natural death of which they want to die and the reality of a clinical death in which most contemporary men actually end. The concept of health is defined idealistically in reference to the former and the idea of sickness is an ambivalent

relationship to the two. The crisis of modern medicine can be faced only if this hidden contradiction is brought to light.

Public confidence in medical practice is close to a breakdown while just at this moment public dependence on medical care has reached unprecedented heights. People learn to depend on medical guidance for their food, their feelings, and their sex life, and at the same time discover that they have been damaged with the approval, or on the prescription of, doctors. As a consequence, attention is focused on the crisis in medical services while the much deeper crisis of medicine as a ritual agency amalgamating world-wide beliefs is pushed into the blindspot of social vision.

I want to focus on medicine as a ritual supporting a destructive myth and I want to avoid getting side-tracked into remedies which can improve the performance of medicine as an industrial enterprise.

Superficial Explanations

Remedies for inefficiency are usually sought in three categories of institutional defects: self-interested production of services, unjust delivery of benefits, and a professional monopoly over health care. This monopoly takes two forms: the exclusion of para-professionals from independent practice, and the imposition of allopathic medicine over all other persuasions.[1]

1. The collusion of doctors, pharmaceutical firms and hospital administrations is the first shortcoming which has attracted attention. It is true that modern medical services are usually operated by self-seeking professionals;[2] that delivery of health services is operated on feudal patterns; that research is conducted to perform miracles rather than face widespread needs; that failures of bio-medical intervention are hidden by blaming the patient, his culture or his government for his unwillingness to learn, to respond, or to survive; that total iatrogenic damages grow faster than demonstrable benefits.[3] As each of these forms of malpractice becomes more common and more blatant, the demand grows for more correction by public control. And each correction in turn provides more prestige to the medical product and more trusting dependence on the part of the consumer.

2. It is equally true that delivery systems in most countries are very unjust. Even after twenty years of socialism, the Chinese had to admit to a gulf between hospital-based, industrially-produced medical care for the few, and high-handed malpractice for the masses. After the short euphoria about nonprofessional, barefoot but modern healers, the new concern with international competition over miracle cures again concentrates benefits on those whom the doctors select. Everywhere, those on whom doctors can practice their virtuosity get disproportionately more attention than others. But this is not the only reason why health services, which are financed largely from taxes, are then cornered by the few. In capitalist economies, the rich transform medicine into a system of regressive taxation by using slight personal funds to purchase an edge of large public resources.

In South America hospitals supposedly private are often 80 percent supported by public funds. Social Security in Mexico is unable to overcome the inequitable distribution of medical services. Three percent of the population have access to what is, probably, the world's record in combining personal care with technological excellence. They are government employees who have truly equal access to ISSTE, whether they are ambassadors or drivers. To these 3 percent of privileged consumers, one-third of the country's hospital budget is allotted.

Other minorities are age-specific. The old in the U.S. constitute 10 percent of the population and consume 20 percent of health services, overwhelmingly for the treatment of arthritis, loneliness, cancer and other afflictions for which modern therapy cannot be shown to have either healing or soothing effects.

As public dependence on professional services becomes stronger, each of these forms of maldistribution becomes more irritating and, therefore, amenable to some management under protest. And each improvement of delivery increases total costs, spurs demand, and tends either to lower quality or to increase damage. The crisis of health delivery is, of course, analogous to that which we know from other industrial enterprises, each organized as a public utility and each defining its output as a basic necessity. More people develop tastes for increasingly more costly products, then learn to define them as basic needs, and soon their demand outruns the limits in-

[1]Cf. Rick J. Carlson, *The End of Medicine* (New York: John Wiley, in press). This is the clearest, most complete, and most readable summary of the arguments which explain the current institutional crisis in medicine.

[2]Cf. Eliot Freidson, *The Profession Of Medicine* (New York: Dodd, Mead, 1971).

[3]Cf. J. P. Dupuy, *et al.,* "La Consommation de médicaments: Approche psycho-socio-économique" (Paris: CEREB, 1971, mimeographed.)

herent in the method of supply. More people use vehicles, and block traffic for more people. More people get college degrees, and many more suffer by being defined as dropouts. More people want places in ambulances, hospitals and clinics, and the few who get them ask for increasingly more costly services. As the consumer pressure rises, society is so reorganized that the nonconsumer can no longer satisfy his simplest needs in traditional forms. Folk healers disappear and home remedies disappear soon afterwards. You cannot get to work without first consuming transportation, not get a job without first consuming education, not get the simplest medicine without first consuming the doctor's time who prescribes it. Agitation for *more* deepens the conviction that you can not do it on your own.

3. Higher quality in production and greater equity in distribution translate into higher professional controls. The resulting professional monopoly constitutes the third explanatory paradigm for the present crisis in medicine. This third paradigm enables criticism to go further than the previous two. It exposes the damage which contemporary medicine causes by its restrictions[4] on the nurse, the midwife, the bone-setter and the tooth-puller, by its discouragement of self-care, and by disparagement of the heterodox healer.[5] But just like faulty production and unjust delivery, so pro-

[4]Cf. Elaine Adamson, "Critical Issues in the Use of Physician Associates and Assistants" (San Francisco: University of California, Division of Ambulatory and Community Medicine), mimeographed. This paper delineates a method to increase the production and delivery of health care by the use of paraprofessional levels in the medical hierarchy, and reviews the cultural obstacles to such a policy. See also Oscar Gish, *Health, Manpower and the Medical Auxiliary* (London: Intermediary Technology Development Group, 1971).

[5]Academy of Parapsychology and Medicine, "The Varieties of Healing Experience," (transcript of the Interdisciplinary Symposium, October 30, 1971).

I have argued on other occasions that the crisis of the school system cannot be solved by recourse to more and better education . . . that the crisis of traffic systems cannot be solved by a change-over to rapid transportation. . . . I will now argue that the crisis in medical institutions cannot be solved by their reorganization under public or professional control. . . . It is not the industrial but the ritual nature of these institutions which must be brought to the fore; it is their power to generate expectations which by definition they cannot meet which must be clarified. In the case of medicine this can best be done by focusing on the historical evolution in the course of which we have constructed that social reality of health which now constitutes medicine's defining purpose.

fessional monopoly indicts medicine as a productive industry and not medicine as a mythopoetic ritual. It explains scarcity of outputs, not absurdity of shared beliefs. More self-care, acupuncture, astrology, radiesthesia, and yoga can be incorporated into a culture which wants to transform the world into a cosmic hospital for lifelong patients, just as contemporary bio-medicine can be used for the cure of self-reliant people.

Health care now is scarce, unjustly distributed, and prejudicial to self-care, and these defects keep iatrogenic damage within bounds. Improved outputs of a health-care system could render it—to use the phrase literally—more sickening. As long as medical practice supports society's death-oriented image of health, medicine will remain destructive.

Health in the Shadow of Death

I have argued on other occasions that the crisis of the school system cannot be solved by recourse to more and better education inside or outside of schools. I have equally argued that the crisis of traffic systems cannot be solved by a change-over to rapid transportation tax-free or fare-supported. I will now argue that the crisis in medical institutions cannot be solved by their reorganization under public or under professional control. As long as these large service industries remain subservient to quasi-religious goals such as universal education, higher speed, or better health, the only effect which their reorganization can have is to provide more luster to these myths and more professional exploitation. It is not the industrial but the ritual nature of these institutions which must be brought to the fore; it is their power to generate expectations which by definition they cannot meet which must be clarified. In the case of medicine this can best be done by focusing on the historical evolution in the course of which we have constructed that social reality of health which now

constitutes medicine's defining purpose.[6]

Health has become a multifaceted concept. It means different things to the geneticist and the clinician, for public hygiene and individual treatment, for the patient who feels ill and the doctor who defines his sickness. But in all these and other contemporary contexts, health means life in its struggle against death, and sickness implies the menace of death. The idea that all sickness is potentially unto death, and that sickness unto death should be interfered with by the doctor are both of recent origin; they can be understood only if the parallel development of the death image becomes equally clear.

In every society the image of death is a culturally conditioned anticipation of uncertain date. This anticipation determines a series of behavioral norms during life and the structure of certain institutions.[7] Insofar as death is a lifelong anticipation, the anthropologist or the literary critic can describe the death image of a society, the sociologist can study the different forms under which it spreads to age-groups and classes, the psychologist can investigate the personal progress of each member through this pre-existing cultural reality.[8] All of them will be able to tell

[6]Cf. Placidus Berger, "Religioeses Brauchtum im Umkreis der Sterbeliturgie in Deutschland," Zeitschr. Fur Missions und Religionswissenschaft, 48 (1964), 108-19, and 248.

[7]Cf. Herman Feifel, "Attitudes Toward Death in Some Normal and Mentally Ill Populations," in The Meaning of Death, ed. by Herman Feifel (New York: McGraw-Hill, 1965), pp. 114-33. Cf. Robert Olson, "Death," Encyclopedia of Philosophy, II, 307-09.

[8]Cf. Renée C. Fox, Experiment Perilous (Glencoe, Ill.: Free Press, 1959) and "Illness," International Encyclopedia of the Social Sciences (1968), VII, 90-95. She elaborates on the ideas of Talcott Parsons on the sick role. Cf. Robert Fulton, Death and Identity (New York: John Wiley, 1966), who has collected a broad spectrum of studies on the impact of the death-image on personal identity in modern societies. Elizabeth Kubler-Ross, On Death and Dying (New York: Macmillan, 1969),

us something about how a society's image
of death relates to its image of health.
At least they will be able to tell us if ill
health, pain or abnormality are rarely,
never, or usually seen as having a causal
relationship to ensuing death.[9]

The Western cultural ideal of natural
death is of quite recent origin. In 500
years it has evolved through four stages
and is now ready for another mutation.
A study of this history is the necessary
groundwork for any authoritative analysis of the present crisis.

I will deal with the stages under the
headings of (1) the skeleton man; (2)
the timely death of the aging lecher; (3)
death under the clinical eye; (4) union
demands for natural death; and (5) death
under intensive care. I will show that in
each of the first four stages a new social
ideal about the end of life called forth a
new form of medical activity. In each
stage the demands on medical performance preceded the demonstrated ability of

describes four typical attitudinal stages through
which her Chicago patients pass before death
and provides guidance to hospital personnel to
enable them to lead the dying patient through
these standard stages by using appropriate
therapy. Orville Brim *et al.*, *The Dying Patient*
(New York: Russel Sage Foundation, 1970),
deals first with the large range of professional
analysis and decisions in which health professionals are believed to be involved in determining how and when an individual's death
should occur, and then with their recommendations about what might be done to make the
process somewhat less graceless and less dis-
tasteful to the patient and his family. Robert
Hertz, *Death and the Right Hand* (Glencoe,
Ill.: Free Press, 1960), presents a dated but
well-documented ethnological study on the universal belief in survival, principally among
Malaya-Polynesians and their different forms
of collective representation of death. This is
still an essential work.

[9]Cf. Stephen Polgar, "Health and Human
Behavior," *Current Anthropology*, 3 (April,
1962), 159-205. A review of the literature up
to 1960 with comments by each of thirty-five
other specialists in the field. Also cf. Marion
Pearsall, *Medical Behavioral Sciences* (Lexing-
ton: University of Kentucky Press, 1963). This
is a more comprehensive bibliography which
has a subject index, but is not annotated.

medical practitioners to produce the results expected of them.

The Evolution of the Dance of Death

During the high Middle Ages, it was
not Death but Hell which kept people in
fear.[10] In the morality plays of the declining Middle Ages, however, a new kind
of Death appears. He is no longer the
Apocalyptic rider of the Gothic and
Roman reliefs, or the bat-like Maegera
who picks up souls in the Cemetery of
Pisa. He is no longer a messenger or
angel sent by God, but a very personal
figure who calls each man and woman
and insists on his own rights.[11]

In 1404, the Duke de Berry had the
first Dance of Death painted on the
Wall of the Cemetary of the Innocents at
Paris. King, peasant, and pope is each
beckoned to dance with a corpse. The
corpse reflects his features and his dress.
Everyman carries his own death with him
in the shape of his body. Until this period, man had been accustomed to choosing between angel and devil who struggle
for his escaping soul. Now, he sees himself in the mirror as his own lifelong
memento mori. It is not Death, but rather
his own dead self with whom he dances
through the autumn of the Middle Ages.
Life in front of the Mirror of Death
(Chastellain) acquires hallucinating poi-
gnancy. During the age of Chaucer and
Villon, Death becomes as sensual and as
intimate as pleasure.[12]

[10]Cf. Alberto Teneti, *Il senso della morte e
l'amore della vita nel Rinascimento* (Turin:
Einaudi, 1957), and cf. Berger, "Religioses
Brauchtum."

[11]Cf. J. Huizinga, *The Waning of the Middle
Ages*, Doubleday Anchor Books (Garden City,
New York: Doubleday, n.d. [original publication, 1924]) on the evolution of the death
image from the late thirteenth century to the
early fifteenth century in poetry and art. See
especially Chapter 11, "The Vision of Death,"
pp. 138-51.

[12]Cf. L. P. Kurtz, *The Dance of Death and
the Macabre Spirit in European Literature*
(New York: 1934, reprint Golden Press), for

By 1538, Hans Holbein the Younger published the first best selling picture book, his woodcuts on the Dance Macabre.[13] The mystically intimate death flavored by the *Devotio Moderna* was here replaced by an egalitarian natural force: from an encounter with the mirror image, the Dance of Death turned into frenzied exhaustion in the grip of anonymous nature. The dance partner has shed its putrid flesh and turned into a naked skeleton. The representation of each man entwined with his own death has turned into a natural force dragging all into the whirl and then mowing them down. Death held the hourglass or struck the tower clock. The new machine which could make time of equal length, day and night, now struck the hour for all. Survival in any form had ceased to be a demand of nature, and—in the theology of the Reformation era—had become a frightful punishment or an unmerited gift from God.[14] During the fifteenth century, death

had become the true end, equally so for all.[15] It had become more certain than immortality, more just than King or Pope or God, and the end of life rather than life's aim.[16] During the early sixteenth century, by becoming a force of nature, it cleared the way for reform and revolution of a new kind.

Once death had become a natural force, man wanted to master it by learning the art of dying. The instruction manual under the name of *Ars Moriendi*

within the church about death's relation to nature since the fourth century. For Pelagius, death was not a punishment for sin, and Adam would have died even had he not sinned. In this, he differs from Augustine's doctrine that Adam had been given immortality as a special gift from God, and even more from those Greek Church Fathers according to whom Adam had a spiritual, or "resurrectional" body, before he transgressed.

[15]Jacques Choron, *Modern Man and Mortality* (New York: Macmillan, 1964), deals with the fear and the hope related to death in a number of select philosophers since Socrates. He relates the idea of final and necessary natural death to the emergence of individuality and a changed time concept. Note that Choron does not deal with popular attitudes towards death. Cf. Teneti, *Il senso della morte,* for Renaissance death. See Jacques Choron, *Suicide* (New York: Scribner's, 1972), for changes in the attitudes towards suicide from the Middle Ages to the Renaissance, especially pertaining to Erasmus and Sir Thomas More.

[16]Death becomes the point at which linear clock-time ends, and eternity meets man, an eternity which during the Middle Ages had been (with God's presence) immanent in history. Cf. H. Plessner, "Ueber die Beziehung der Zeit zum Tode," *Eranos Jahrbuch* 5 (1951), 20. With the predominance of serial time, with concern for exact time-measurement and recognition of simultaneity of events, a new framework for the recognition of personal identity is constructed. The person's identity is sought in reference to a sequence of events rather than in the completeness of his life-span. Death ceases to be the end of a whole and becomes an interruption in the sequence. Cf. Alois Hahn, *Einstellung zum Tod und ihre Soziale Bedingtheit* (Stuttgart, 1968), on the effects which a change in time-perception had on the perception of death.

all of Europe and cf. Walther Rehm, *Der Todesgedanke in der Deutschen von Mittelatte bis zur Romantik* (1928, reprint Wissenschaft Buchgesellschaft), for Germany: Kurtz and Rehm provide detailed evidence from literature for my thesis of a major mutation in the death image around 1400 and again in 1520. See Johannes Kleinstueck, "Zur Auffassung des Todes im Mittelater," *Deutsche Vierteljahresschrift fur Literaturwiss enschaft und Geistesgeschichte* 28 (1954), 41, who criticizes Rehm and claims more continuity. (The moralists had to make death hideous to insist on its importance and imminence; death was too much a part of life to attract any attention otherwise.) For iconography, cf. K. Kuenstle, *Die Legende der 3 Lebenden und der 3 Toten* (n.p., 1908), who is easier to consult than Male.

[13]Cf. Hans Holbein the Younger, *The Dance of Death: a Complete Facsimile of the Original 1538 French edition* (New York: Dover, 1971).

[14]Paul Landsberg, *Essai sur l'expérience de la mort* (Paris: 1951). This is an important essay showing that the sense of finality and imminence of natural death can be considered the presupposition for a Christian view of the resurrection. Cf. G. B. Ladner, *The Idea of Reform* (Cambridge: Harvard University Press, 1959), especially p. 163 for the two currents

stayed on the best seller list during the next 200 years.[17] Medicinal folkways designed to help people meet their death multiplied.[18] People tried to learn how to face death, how to ease it, how to detach themselves from all bonds which would make it difficult to observe its command. Remedies against a difficult death proliferated. Pilgrimage centers flourished where the sick could consult oracles to determine if they should seek remedies or if the time had come to be ready for death. The dying man played a new role which had to be played very consciously. His children could help him to die, but only if they did not hold him back by crying. He was placed on the ground, and prayers were said; but people were not to look at him, so as not to frighten death away. The medical writers of the sixteenth century recognized clearly the two opposed services they could provide: health or a speedy death. In both cases, the doctor was anxious to assist nature. Reformed health generated its own ritual in support of the myth, and this ritual kept the doctor away from the deathbed of the peasant until late into the nineteenth century.

This ambiguous attitude towards death comes out very clearly in the writings of Paracelsus.[19] One recognizes him as one of the new doctors. "Nature knows the boundaries of its course. According to her own appointed term, she confers upon each of its creatures its proper life span, so that its energies are consumed during

---

Survival in any form had ceased to be a demand of nature, and . . . death had become the true end. . . . Once death had become a natural force, man wanted to master it by learning the art of dying.

---

the time that elapses between the moment of its birth and its predestined end." Death is a natural phenomenon: "What dies naturally has reached its appointed term, therein lies God's will and order. Even if death occurs through accident or illness, no reawakening is possible. Therefore, there is no defense against the predestined end. Nature, too, is full of anxiety; she has recourse to everything that God has given her in order to repel death;" and this death is final:

She tries to drive out harsh, bitter death, who fights against her; dreadful death, whom our eyes cannot see, nor our hands clutch. But nature sees, touches and knows him. Therefore she summons all her powers of heaven and earth to resist the terrible one. A man's death is nothing but the end of his daily work, an expiration of air, the consummation of his own balsamic

---

[17]For bibliography on the *Ars Moriendi*, see Mary Catherine O'Connor, *The Art of Dying* (New York: Columbia University Press, 1942, reprint New York: Abraham Magazine Service, 1967).

[18]These customs live on. Cf. Arnold van Gennep, *Manuel de folklore francais contemporain*, Vol. I, part 2, for the preparation for death in France and on procedures which are believed to ease death. See especially p. 649: *La mort comme phenomene contagieux la mort personnifiée, les neuf présages de la mort, procèdes pour hater l'agonie, arrêt de l'horloge,* etc. . . . See Lenz Kriss Rettenbêck, *Bilder und Zeichen Religioesen Volksglaubens* (Munich: George Calloway, 1963), for the extraordinary riches of plastic fold-art related to death which combines the sense of finality, necessity and horror of the grave with deep Catholic belief in salvation. This is a masterly study of mostly Bavarian folk-art.

[19]*Paracelsus*, ed. by J. Jacobi (Bollingen Ser., 1958), is an excellent, easily readable introduction to his thought.

curative power, the extinction of the rational light of nature, and a great separation of the three—body, soul, and spirit—a return to the womb. Death for Paracelsus has become a natural phenomenon, without excluding belief in transcendence.

The new concern with the art of dying helped to reduce the human body to a kind of object, which could be used to advance the art of healing. Throughout the Middle Ages, the human body has been sacred and its dissection was considered by humanist Gerson "a sacrilegious profanation, a useless cruelty exercised by the living against the Dead." This attitude still survives when modern law speaks about the "profanation" of graves, or of the "secularization" of a nondenominational cemetery which preceeds its transformation into a park.[20]

When the corpse appears in the mystery plays, it also moves into the arena of the amphitheater of universities. The first publicly authorized dissection took place in Montpellier in 1375. It was afterwards declared obscene and the performance could not be repeated for several years. Later, one corpse per year was authorized for dissection within the borders of the German Empire. One also was dissected each year just before Christmas at the University of Bologna, and the ceremony took three days. The

University of Lerida in Spain was entitled to the corpse of one criminal once every three years, to be dissected in the presence of a Notary assigned by the Inquisition. In England, in 1540, the faculties were authorized to claim four corpses a year from the hangman. But attitudes changed fast during the sixteenth century. By 1561, the Venetian Senate told the hangman to follow the instruction of Dr. Fallopius in order to provide him with corpses well suited for "anatomizing." Another sixty years later, public dissection was a favored subject for Flemish painters, the best known work probably being "Dr. Tulp's Lesson" by Rembrandt. At the same time, public dissections appeared as part of carnival programs.

The decay of the body had acquired a new finality. The heightened anguish was exorcized by a host of rituals surrounding the act of dying, by a new curiosity about the dead body, and by the production of phantasmic horror stories about the afterlife of the dead. The seventeenth-century's grotesque concern with ghosts and souls underlines the growing anxiety of man facing the empty grave. What people did to preserve their health or to cure their ills had little to do with what they did when they felt threatened by death. Medicine was ancillary to Nature, helping it to heal, or helping man to die.

The Rise of the Aging Lecher

By the early eighteenth century, the image of death which cuts all people to equal size had spread wide and far. It had been exported from Europe by missionaries of otherwise opposed sects and could be seen in every parish. The Dance of Death might still be painted on a wall of the village cemetery, showing the Duke holding the shepherd's knuckles, but the baroque Last Judgment painted on the opposite wall would have separate compartments in heaven and hell for kings, for virgins, and for commoners. The

---

[20]The transformation of the corpse into a thing that can be used for the advancement of science happens at this time. For a while, the corpse still has to be protected as a quasi-person. Cf. Paul Fischer, *Strafen und Sichernede Massnahmen gegen Tote im Germanischen und Deutschen Recht* (Dusseldorf, 1936), for the history of punishments meted out to the dead. Remember that various religions still accord or refuse "rights" to the dead. See Paul Julien Doll, "Les Droits de la science après la mort," *Diogène* 75 (July, 1971), on the survival of medieval traditions about the human body in contemporary law. Cf. Hans Hentig, *Vom Ursprung der Henkersmahlzeit* (Tubingen, 1958) on the widespread psychological attraction of the dead body.

same prayers were still said and the same superstitions observed and the same remedies given at the bedside of the rich and the poor, even though the rich now played the ritual much more pompously and their funerals became an occasion for public parades. During the third quarter of the eighteenth century, this equality ceased. Bacon had already begun to speak about a new task of medicine, the task of keeping death away. He divided "medicine into three parts or offices; first the preservation of health, second the cure of disease, and third the prolongation of life." He extolled the "third part of medicine regarding the prolongation of life: this is a new part, and deficient, although the most noble of all." But while a few doctors might believe in this new vocation, for 150 years after Bacon, for rich and poor alike, "death is the grand leveller." It is a "deadly disease neither physician nor physic can cure," for "while old men go to death, death comes to young men."

But then, during the 1760's, men became unequal in death. The reason for this was the rise of a new type of old man who refused to die in retirement and demanded to meet his death from natural exhaustion while on the job. It was not simply death in old age, but death in an active old age which he demanded—the old preacher expecting to go to heaven and the old philosopher denying the soul —both could agree now that natural death was only that death which overtook them at their desk. Where in the Middle Ages the same call from God came to sinners and saints, and in the Renaissance Nature brought the same end for all, in the seventeenth century death starts to come differently to different classes, it comes "timely" only for an elite.

The idea that natural death had to come in old age appeared, however, much earlier. Montaigne, in 1580, had ridiculed it: to die of old age is a death rare, extraordinary, and singular, and therefore

so much less natural than the others:

> 'tis the last and extremest sort of dying . . . what an idle conceit is it to expect to die of a decay of strength which is the effect of extremest age, and to propose to ourselves no shorter lease on life . . . as if it were contrary to nature to see a man break his neck with a fall, be drowned in shipwreck, be snatched away with pleurisy or the plague . . . we ought to call natural death that which is general, common and universal.

But though the dream is old, the ability to transform it into a cultural pattern begins to emerge about 1730. Technological changes by this time have greatly changed life.[21] The pampered rich could survive longer because living conditions had changed. Even more decisive was the change in working conditions. Sedentary work, hitherto rare, had come into its own. Also by this time, roads had improved: a general affected by the gout could command a battle from his wagon, and decrepit diplomats could travel through Europe. Office work multiplied and created the demand for a bourgeoisie. Rising entrepreneurship and capitalism favored the boss who had the time to accumulate capital or experience. The new class of old men survived because their lives at home, on the street, and on the job had become less extenuating. They refused to retire because an expanding bureaucracy favored the ageless who had

---

[21]Philippe Ariès, *Histoire des populations françaises: et de leurs attitudes devant la vie depuis le XVIIIᵉ Siecle* (Paris: Seuil, 1971 [originally 1946]). His chapter, "Les Techniques de la mort," pp. 373-88 contains a rich summary of information about the changing attitudes of different levels of the French population towards death during the eighteenth and nineteenth centuries. For those who know the author's *Centuries of Childhood*, it is especially interesting to observe that precisely those social classes which can afford to eliminate "social death" by means of traditional retirement create "childhood" as an institution for their children.

been around for a long time. Aging became a way of capitalizing life.[22]

To keep them out of the way and
simultaneously prepare them for eco-
nomically valuable lives, the young were
put into schools while the old stayed on
the job. With their economic status, the
value of the old man's bodily functions
also increased. In the sixteenth century a
"young wyfe is death to an old man"; and
in the seventeenth century "old men
who play with young maids embrace
death." This changes in the course of the
eighteenth century: the old lecher, who
had been a laughing stock under Louis
XIV, was envied at the Congress of
Vienna. The patriarch appears as a literary ideal. Wisdom is attributed to him,
just because of his age. It first becomes
tolerable and then appropriate that the
elderly rich should attend with solicitude
to the rituals deemed necessary to maintain their ailing bodies. The physician
whom they needed did not exist, since
he was neither the traveling quack, Jew,
or herbalist. Nor was he the resident
barber or surgeon who knew how to let
blood and set bones.

Formerly, only kings and poets had
been under the obligation to remain in
command to the day of their death. They
alone had recourse to the great doctors
from the universities, the Arabs of the
Middle Ages from Salerno, the Renaissance men from Padua or Montpellier.
To do what barbers did for the com-
moner, kings kept court physicians. Now
the aging bourgeois believed himself burdened by the duty of aging on the job.
The aging bureaucrat wanted to be cured
from what his grandfather or his maid
still accepted as a call to get ready for
death. He was out to confuse what until
then had been separate: on the one hand,

he wanted to identify retirement with
death; on the other hand, all ailments
which struck him threatened to be sickness unto death. He wanted a doctor to
drive away death, who also could give
dignity to his new role of valetudinarian.
He was willing to pay his doctor as
nobody had payed before, because bourgeois death was conceived as the absolute
price for the absolute economic value.
The rationale for the economic power of
the contemporary physician was thereby
created.[23]

The ability to survive longer, the refusal to retire and the demand for medical assistance for incurable illness had
joined to create a new definition of sickness: the type of health to which old age
could aspire. Since this was the health of
the rich and the powerful, malady soon
became fashionable for the young and
pretentious. Protracted ailments in preparation for natural death became a sign
of distinction. The poor were condemned
to die of untreated ills, which all lead
to untimely and therefore unnatural
death. It fitted the image one had of the
proletarian; he was also uneducated and
unproductive. Earlier, death had carried
the hour glass. If the victim refused, both
the skeleton and the onlooker grinned.
Now society takes the watch and tells
death when he may decently strike.
Health has become the privilege of waiting for a natural death. In the next epoch,
it becomes the ability to die with the rituals of medical ministration.

The Opening of the Clinical Eye

Two generations later it became highly
respectable to live as the client of a
famous doctor. Four generations later,
industrial workers demanded the right to
medical and retirement insurance. The
valetudinarian's image of timely extinction at the end of a pampered life first
mutated towards the solicitude of all

---

[22]Cf. Simone de Beauvoir, *The Coming of
Age* (New York: G. P. Putnam's, 1972). See
"Old Age in Historical Societies" for much
illustration on new types of old age in different layers of society during the sixteenth
through eighteenth centuries.

---

[23]Theodor Adorno, *Minima, Moralia, Re-
flektionen aus dem deschaedigten Leben*
(Frankfort, 1962).

ages to oppose death from a clinically defined sickness, and then to the claim by the unions to medical and old-age insurance against unnatural death. In barely a hundred years, the concept of natural death thus went through two distinct evolutions and in the process changed the ideas both of health and of social justice.

At first, untimely death got clinical names. Attention shifted from the sick to his sickness, from his being sick to his having a sickness.[24] Sickness became an entity or problem, and therapy, a procedure or solution which was effective if applied by the doctor. Once sickness could be treated by the doctor rather than letting nature assist in the person of the ailing man's own body (Paracelsus), medicine had moved into the industrial age. The relationship of the healer to the suffering man was now superceded by that of the medical institution to the patient. Man who must heal or die is substituted by the image of man the consumer. He functions as long as he gets therapy and health. Untimely death turns into underconsumption of clinical care, which can be explained by backwardness of medical science, self-seeking doctors, or unjust social arrangements. The stage is set for the idea of unnatural death as a result of under-consumption.

The first important step towards clinical production was taken by making hospitals out of eighteenth-century pesthouses, homes for the incurable, bedlams, and orphanages. Hospitals become industrial institutions for the mass-production of health services, repairshops for people. This establishment resulted from the idea of the same generation which discovered that defectives of every sort

had to be locked up among their like if they were to be bettered: in schools to be given education, in prisons to be given correction, and in hospitals to be returned to health. Only such institutional mass-production of services fits two key illusions of the industrial revolution: "better" satisfaction of man's needs by rational production, and the satisfaction of more needs for more people.

While the city doctor became a clinician, the country doctor became sedentary. It is important to remember that at the time of the French Revolution, he still belonged among the traveling folk. The surplus of army surgeons from the Napoleonic wars, all of them trained on the job, had to earn a living. They settled in villages and became the first class of resident healers. The simple people did not trust their new techniques, and the sedentary burghers were shocked by their rough ways. Their sons, around 1830, created the role of the country doctor which remained unchanged until the Second World War. His stable income was derived from the demands placed on him by the few middle class valetudinarians. He still had to compete with the medical technicians of old: the midwife, the dentist, the veterinarian, the barber, and sometimes the nurse. But within a generation, he could establish himself as a member of the solid middle class. The demand for his health services was sufficient both to provide him income and to send the sick to his clinical colleagues in town.The attempt to provide a natural death by referral through a hierarchy had begun.

Timely death under treatment of clinical symptoms emerged as the ideal of the middle class and its doctors.[25] Natural

[24]Michel Foucault, *The Birth of the Clinic* (New York: Pantheon, 1973) points out that sickness conceived against the backdrop of death ceases to be a negative entity, a disturbance of life which can never be fully ceased or defined, and becomes clearly definable and distinctly visible to the clinical eye. Sickness ceases to be a lack of health and acquires a body within the ailing body of the individual.

[25]Richard A. Kalish, "Death and Dying, a briefly Annotated Bibliography," in *Death and Dying*, ed. by Brim *et al.*, for a selected bibliography of English language literature on Death and Dying in a modern setting. It includes social science, medical and hospital administration items. Cf. John W. Riley, "Death,"

death during the first half of the nineteenth century was class-specific.

Union Claims for Equal Death

Then death became a union demand. The valetudinarian's health concept was written into labor contracts. The privilege of natural extinction from active old life in business was replaced by the mass demand for such a death for the pensioner.[26] The bourgeois image of the dirty old man still at his desk was replaced by the proletarian image of a healthy sex life on social security. The ideal of ending life on the job turned into the right to start life after retirement from it. The condition for the right of this proletarian form of natural death was lifelong clinical care for every clinical condition.[27] This vindication for health care was soon incorporated into political rhetoric and legal definitions. Natural death and the health-care preparation for it was something which society owed its members.

The death concept entered into social justice.[28] The right was formulated as a claim to equal consumption of social products rather than as a freedom from torts or new liberty for self-care. Just as, at this time, all men were defined as pupils, born in original stupidity and standing in need of several years of schooling before they could enter life, so they were defined as born patients who needed many kinds of treatment before they could leave life. Man now cannot take his place in the world before he has proven educational consumption and he cannot exit from the world without having been forced through medical programs. Just as compulsory educational consumption became a device to rationalize discrimination on the job, so compulsory medical consumption became a device for the rationalization of unhealthy work, cities, transportation, play, etc.

The redefinition of workers as health consumers had a double effect. At first it showed a revolutionary potential but soon it became a means for social control.[29]

International Encyclopedia of the Social Sciences (1968) IV, 19-25, for survey of social science literature trends in the United States in the study of death and bereavement. Cf. Robert W. Haberstein, *ibid.*, p. 26-8, for a short survey of contemporary American studies on the social organization of death.

[26]Werner Fuchs, *Todesbilder in der Modernen Gesellschaft* (Suhrkamp, 1969). Fuchs uses the content-analysis of obituaries as a means of ascertaining contemporary images of death. But he also suggests the use of dictionaries for this purpose. One of the major German encyclopedias of 1909 defines abnormal death as that which "is opposed to natural death because it results from sickness, violence, or mechanical and chronical disturbances." A very generally accepted dictionary of philosophical concepts defines natural death as that "which comes without previous sickness, without definable specific cause."

[27]Unions now seem to have travelled in a full circle. Daniel Maguire, "Freedom to Die," *Commonweal* (August 11, 1972), 423-7, suggests that by working creatively and in ways yet unthought of, the lobby of the dying and of the gravely ill could become a healing force in society. It could reconquer the "Freedom to Die."

[28]Just as universal education by means of compulsory schooling cannot promote equality but must favor those who start earlier, are healthier, and have greater learning opportunities at home, so equal opportunities for a timely death by means of free medical services can only raise the relative advantage of those who do not need these. The human cost of artificial prolongation of decrepitude inevitably weighs heavier on the poor than on the rich. Medical assistance was more effective in providing for the poor access to death from kinds of sickness which so far had been the privilege of the rich (old age and civilization sickness) than it was in helping the masses to end their lives in that kind of active and creative old age which the rich had claimed for themselves in the nineteenth century.

[29]Fuchs, *Todesbilder in Gesellscaft,* is the source for many of the ideas and the guide to some of the literature in this essay. The author tries to unmask the thesis about the repression of death in modern societies which he finds unfounded and instrumental. According to the author it is usually promoted by people of profoundly anti-industrial persuasions for the purpose of demonstrating the ultimate powerlessness of the industrial enterprise in face of

At the turn of the century, the euphoria over medicine's ability to ban untimely death provided ammunition to social critics. Every death without medical assistance was labeled untimely, and denounced as a scandal for whch a culprit had to be found. Of course, natural death was to be explained by a natural cause. It would not do to accuse the evil eye of the enemy, the evil intention of the magician, or the arbitrariness of a god. The culprit had to be found within society: the class enemy, the exploiting doctor, or the colonial master. The witch hunt at the death of a tribal chief was modernized into the hunt for those responsible for social injustice. Without this revolutionary use of a death ideal, the progress of social legislation during the first half of the twentieth century could not have happened. Without it, social agitators could not have enlisted support for reforming laws nor mobilized the guilt feelings necessary to enforce their enactment.

Contemporary social organization cannot be fully understood unless it is also seen in the perspective of a multifaceted exorcism of all forms of evil death.[30] Our major institutions constitute a gigantic defense program waged on behalf of "humanity and against unnatural deaths.[31] Not only medical agencies, but also welfare, international relief, and development programs are enlisted in this struggle. Ideological bureaucracies of all colors join in the crusade. Even war has been justified to defeat those who are blamed for wanton tolerance of sickness and death.

The revolutionary potential of the unionized death image became exhausted as soon as it had been written into the charters of established institutions. The production of natural death for all men is at the point of becoming an ultimate justification for social control.[32]

---

death. It is usually insisted upon to construct apologetical arguments in favor of the need for belief in God or afterlife. The fact that people have to die is taken as proof that they will never autonomously control reality. He interprets all theories which deny the finality of death as relics of a primitive past and considers as scientific and now tenable only those corresponding to a modern social structure. The death image of a society is a dependent variable in relation to it. He analyzes the contemporary image of death, principally by studying the language used in German obituaries. He believes that what is usually called "repression" of death is due to a lack of effective acceptance of the increasingly more generally accepted reality of death as an unquestionable and final end.

[30]Guenther Anders, *Endzeit und Zeiten-dende: Gedanken uber die atomare Situation,* (n.p., 1972). Not only the image of personal death is new. The image of the end of the world has also changed. Death is the end of *my* world. But each society has to live with an attitude towards the end of *the* world. The atomic situation has deeply affected attitudes about the Apocalypse. Rather than a mythological expectation it is a real contingency. Rather than being due to man's guilt, it is a possible consequence of man's direct decision. There is an uncanny analogy between atomic bombs and cobalt bombs: both deemed necessary for the good of mankind, both effective to provide man with the power to decide when the end shall come, and thereby strengthening the illusion that, by the proper use of these tools, it will come in a more natural way. See also, Robert J. Lifton, *Death in Life: Survivors of Hiroshima* (New York: Random House, 1968). See K. Jaspers, *Die Atombombe und die Zukunft des Menschen* (DTV, 1961).

[31]Bronislaw Malinowski, *Magic, Science and Religion,* introd. by Robert Redfield, Doubleday Anchor Books (Garden City, N.Y.: Doubleday, n.d. [1948]), p. 53. Malinowski argues that death among primitive people threatened the cohesion and survival of the group by leading to an explosion of fear of death and irrational expression of defences. Group solidarity is saved by making out of the natural event, a social ritual. Death becomes then an occasion for exceptional celebration of tribal or group unity. It might be argued that in an impersonal and industrial ritual, modern medicine celebrates the unity of mankind in their relatedness to an identical ideal death, and thereby diminishes the guilt and anxiety about the evidently different kinds of death that people die, who find their place on different levels of the medical consumer pyramid.

[32]William Ophuls, "Leviathan or Oblivion"

Only the culture which has evolved in highly industrialized societies could possibly have called forth the commercialization of the death image I have just described. In its extreme form, natural death is that point at which the human organism refuses any further input of treatment—when man becomes useless both as producer and as consumer.[33] It is the point at which a consumer trained at great expense must be written off as a total loss.[34] It is the ultimate form of consumer resistance.

Within an industrial society, medical intervention into everyday life does not change the image of health and of death which prevails, but rather caters to it. It diffuses the death image of elites to the masses and reproduces it for future gen-

erations.[35] But applied outside of a cultural context in which consumers prepare themselves religiously for a natural death, bio-medical engineering and modern medical practice inevitably constitute a form of imperialist intervention. They impose a compulsory socio-political image of death. People are deprived of their traditional vision of what constitutes health and death. The self-image which gives cohesion to their culture is dissolved, and atomized individuals can be incorporated into an international mass of health consumers.

(Cuernavaca: CIDOC, 1972), Limites no. 1, pp. 1-25. A provisional manuscript for a chapter in a learned and well-documented thesis within the context of which this issue could be well-discussed.

[33]Cf. Edgar Morin, *L'Homme et la mort* (Seuil, 1970), for whom the contradictions of bourgeois individualism are corroborated by man's inadaptation to any possible form of realistic death where the current industrial ideology prevails.

[34]Cf. Thomas Szasz, "Malingering: 'Diagnosis' or Social Condemnation? Analysis of the Meaning of 'Diagnosis' in the Light of Some Interrelations of Social Structure, Value Judgment, and the Physician's Role," *Archives of Neurology and Psychiatry* (A.M.A.) 76 (1956), 432. Szasz insists that the ritual of medicine takes, like other rituals of contemporary society, the form of a game. Therefore, the physician's chief function is that of an umpire: "he is the agent or representative of the social body (the game) and it is his duty to make sure that everyone plays the game according to the rules." The rules, of course, forbid leaving the game and dying except in carefully specified settings. Richard M. Bailey, "Economic and Social Costs of Death," in *The Dying Patient,* pp. 275-302, from an economic, analytical point of view, tries to specify how economics should attempt to measure the economic costs of death and the value of life. He argues that we cannot avoid placing dollar value on life, so let us do it explicitly. A new rationalization of the entire health-care system will result from cost-benefit analysis of terminal treatment.

[35]Various ideological bureaucracies lend important support to the double image of natural death. It would be interesting to study at least one in depth. For this purpose I would recommend research on Christian support for the Janus-faced modern death. See André Godin, "Has Death Changed?" *Death and Presence: the Psychology of Death and the Afterlife,* ed. by André Godin, in *Studies in the Psychology of Religion,* translated from French (Brussels: Lumen Vitae, 1972). Godin could provide a good starting point. This anthology contains a number of sociological and psychological studies concerned with a Christian education on (for?) death. Several studies highlight the greater anxiety and conflict of religious studies in the face of death. Pierre Delooz, "Who Believes in the Hereafter?" in Godin, *Death and Presence,* 1972, suggests that contemporary French-speakers have effectively separated belief in God from belief in the thereafter. P. Danblon, "How Do People Speak About Death?" in Godin, *Death and Presence,* 1972, studies the structured interviews of 60 French-speaking public figures. It would appear that cross-denominational analogies in their mode of expression, feelings and attitudes towards death are stronger than differences due to varying beliefs. Godin reviews studies on the changing image of death in our generation, and their relevance to Christian education and chaplaincy. None of these studies explicitly deal with medicine as a mythopoetic ritual engendering the tolerance for a contradiction between the reality which sick persons experience and the ideal which society pursues. They do not, therefore, deal directly with the crisis which arises from the simultaneous acceptance by a person of a Christian death and resurrection-oriented belief and the person's participation in the ritual of medicine which promises to banish death and suffering.

I was taught what this means on the frontier of Upper Volta. I asked a man if people over the border, in Mali, spoke the same tongue. He said: "No, but we

I asked a man if people over the border, in Mali, spoke the same tongue. He said, "No, but we understand them, because they cut the prepuce of their boys as we do, and they die our kind of death." Once a culture is deprived of its death, it loses its health.

understand them, because they cut the prepuce of their boys as we do, and they die our kind of death." Once a culture is deprived of its death, it loses its health. In the process of transition, people still have their way of knowing why and how death comes; but the modern doctor who comes to educate, claims to know better. He teaches them about a Pantheon of evil, clinical deaths, each one of which he will ban for a price. By his ministrations he urges them on the unending search for the good death of international description, a search which will keep them his clients forever.[36]

We have seen that in western society so far, medicine has served to legitimize changes which have taken place in a cultural context. In the last five centuries,

the idea of death and the demand for a new kind of health have evolved one step ahead of the necessary techniques and rituals of health-care. We have seen that just the opposite happens when the latest type of health care is introduced into a traditional society. The introduction of new techniques, there, leads to the adoption of a new ritual; as a result, a new myth about death emerges which in turn redefines health in relation to death. Of course, this myth is usually hybrid, like the saints of Latin America. At Guadalupe, priests minister to the Mother of Jesus who has taken the shape of a Mediterranean Gea while the people worship her in the guise of Tonanzin, the earth mother of the stars, who gives birth to them each evening and swallows them in the morning, filling her belly with bones. But inevitably the hybrid myth about health which results from the implantation of Western medicine defines health as a struggle against death by escalating application of industrial power. The hybrid myth has its place in the industrial world.

Health care is now a monolithic world religion whose tenets are taught in compulsory schools and whose ethical rules are applied by a bureaucratic restructuring of the environment. The struggle against death which in another century dominated the thoughts and lives of the rich, has now become the rule by which the poor of the earth are forced to conduct themselves. In the strict sense used by religious sociologists, medicine has become the dogma around which the structuring ritual of our society is organized. Like any effective ritual, participation in medical practice hides from the producer and the consumer the contradiction between the myth which the ritual serves and the reality which this same ritual enforces and reproduces. Bio-medical intervention into the life of the individual, the group and the biosphere, comes to be seen as the condition for a natural death. Inquisitorial supervision of com-

---

[36]F. N. L. Poynter, ed., *Medicine and Culture,* (London: Wellcome Institute of the History of Medicine, 1969).

pulsory treatment and the planned reorganization of the environment according
to the dictates of medical prejudices are
advocated as a condition for a "natural"
evil.[37] Nature exorcised from a hygieni-
cally planned life claims everyone—but
only at his or her grave. The right to die
of a natural death is turned into a duty on
which teachers, doctors, politicians, and
priests insist.[38]

Traditionally, the man best protected
against death was he whom society had
condemned to death. Society felt threatened that he could die without permission. Now the same authority is claimed
over every citizen.[39] What was a factual

necessity in the late Middle Ages is now
turned into a normative one. Natural
death has become a distorted mirror-
image of the death represented in the
dance macabre. It has resumed its egalitarian character; but while it was then a
natural force which stopped man with
the hourglass, it is now a chronometer
out to stop death. Man, faced by death,
was then asked to be aware that he was
finally, frighteningly, totally alone; society now obligates him to seek medicine's

W hile the
"Art of Dying" taught those
of the Reformation era to
face bitter death, to make
ready and hope for a speedy
end, compulsory treatments
now eliminate all final agonies
which might be easy but
are labeled unnecessary in
order to preserve modern man
for chronic disability or for
cancer and decrepitude.

[37]David Sudnow, "Dying in a Public Hospital." in Brim *et al., The Dying Patient.*
Sudnow describes how death becomes a self-
fulfilling prophecy of the medical ritual and
lists three stages of social death which precede
the wrapping of the body by orderlies. A sober
and hallucinating well-illustrated summary of
observations in U.S. Public hospitals. See also
Avery Weisman, *On Dying and Denying: Psychiatric Study of Terminality* (New York: Behavioral Publications, 1972), on the discrep-
ancy between the wish of people to die in
dignity and the actual services that they purchase.

[38]Joseph Fletcher, "Anti-Dysthanasia: the
Problem of Prolonging Death," *Journal of
Pastoral Care* 18 (1964), 77-84. In an article
against irresponsible life-prolongation, written
from the point of view of a hospital chaplain,
he argues: "I would myself agree with Pope
Pius XII and with at least two Archbishops of
Canterbury, Land and Fisher, who have addressed themselves to this question, that the
doctor's technical knowledge, his 'educated
guesses,' and experience, should be the basis
for deciding the question as to whether there
is any 'reasonable hope.' That determination is
outside a layman's competence.... But having
determined that a condition is hopeless, I cannot agree that it is either prudent or fair to
physicians as a fraternity to saddle them with
the onus of alone deciding whether to let the
patient go." This thesis is common, and shows
how even churches support professional judgment.

[39]According to Hentig, *Ursprung der Henkersmahlzeit,* 1958, ritual murder is not limited
to judicial execution, but wherever it is performed, a meal for the condemned man (some-

times today reduced to a last cigarette) pre-
cedes the ceremony, and a meal (breakfast of
the witnesses) usually follows. The author as-
sembles information from all countries and
epochs. He points out that only the soldier of
modern times is trained to kill rather than for
fighting and might be the first professional executioner not providing his victim with ritual
notice by means of a meal. Note that the modern doctor is also the first professional healer
who does not act as *nuntius mortis* when the
appropriate time has come.

protection and let the doctor fight.[40] Death has reacquired its pervasive threat. But where the skeleton man announced his coming by sickness unto death and each man's dignity demanded that he recognize the signs, institutional medicine now impresses on each man and woman their duty to watch by constant checkups for any symptom that would require clinical defense. While the "Art of Dying" taught those of the Reformation era to face bitter death, to make ready and hope for a speedy end, compulsory treatments now eliminate all final agonies which might be easy but are labeled unnecessary in order to preserve modern man for chronic disability or for cancer and decrepitude.[41] While the dancing partner of the Middle Ages was symbolic of something which really waits for each man, natural extinction from old-age exhaustion is a lottery ticket for only a few.[42]

[40]"L'homme du second Moyen Age et de la Renaissance (par opposition a l'homme de premièr Moyen Age, de Roland, qui se survit chez les paysans de Tolstoi) tenait à participer à sa propre mort, parce qu'il voyait dans cette mort un moment exceptionnel où son individualité recevait sa forme definitive. Il n'était le maître de sa vie que dans la mesure ou il était le maître de sa mort. . . . à partir du XVII siècle il a cessé d'exercer seul sa souveraineté sur sa propre vie, et par conséquent, sur sa mort. Il l'apartagée avec sa familee. Auparavant, sa famille était ecartée des decisions graves qu'il devait prendre en vue de la mort, et qu'il prenait seul." Philippe Ariès, "La Mort Inversée: Le changement des attitudes devant la mort dans les sociétés occidentales," *Archives Européenes de Sociologie* 8 (1967), 175.

[41]The *Ars Moriendi* charges the spiritual, as opposed to the "carnal" friend with the task of acting as *nuntius mortis* and of reminding the friend of approaching death. The more we rise in the social ladder through the eighteenth century, the less people perceive that death approaches; in the middle of the eighteenth century, the physician ceases to act as *nuntius mortis*. During the nineteenth century, he speaks only when pressed. Telling a person that death is near in some regions is a task taken over by the family, but only in the nineteenth century. The dying man ceases to preside over the ceremonial of his own death, and the doctor transforms it into the last stage of therapeutic pretensions. The death-chamber loses its candles, closed drapes, family reunions, and veracity, and becomes a hygenic, lonely, and professional environment for deception about the imminent.

[42]Other works which were consulted in the preparation of this chapter and may be of interest to the reader include:

A. Alvarez, *The Savage God* (New York: Random House, 1970); Werner Bloch, *Der Arst und der Tod in Bildern aus sechs Jahr-hunderten* (Stuttgart: 1966); Ladislaus Boros, *The Mystery of Death* (New York: Herder and Herder, 1965); R. Broca, *Cinquante Ans de conquêtes médicales* (Paris: Hachette, 1955); Harley L. Browning, "Timing Our Lives," Transaction, October, 1969, 22-7. G. Buchheit, *Totentanz* (1938); Eric J. Cassell, "Treating the Dying: the Doctor vs. the Man within the Doctor," *Medical Dimension,* March, 1972, 6-11; E. Codman, "The Product of the Hospital," *Surgery, Gynocology and Obstetrics* 18 (1914), 491-6; P. Delauney, *La Vie médicale aux XVIe, XVIIe, XVIIIe siècles* (Paris: 1935); Thomas M. Dunaye, "Health Planning: A Bibliography of Basic Readings" (Council of Planning Librarians, 1968; mimeographed); E. Doering-Hirsch, *Jenseits im Spaetmittelalter* (Berlin, 1927); José Echeverria, *Réflexions métaphysiques sur la mort et le problème du sujet* (Vrin: 1957); R. Ehlund, "Life between Death and Resurrection according to Islam," (Uppsala, Sweden: 1941; dissertation); Gabriel Fallopius, *Observationes anatomicae* (Venice, 1561); H. Fehr, "Tod und Teufel in Alten Recht," *Zeitschr. der Savignystiftung fur Rechtsgeschichte* 67 (1950?), 50-75; Christian von Ferber, "Soziologische Aspekte des Todes: Ein Versuch uber einige Beziehungen der Soziologie zur Philosophischen Anthropologie," *Zeitschr. Fur Evangelische Ethik* 7 (1963) 338-60; Albert Freybe, *Das Momento Mori in Deutscher Sitte, Bildlicher Darstellung und im Volksglauben* (1911); and *Das alte Deutsche Leichenmahl in Seiner Art und Entartung* (1909); H. Friedel, "L'Experience humaine de la mort," *Foi et Vie* 63, 105-17; Stanley Brice Frost, "The Memorial of the Childless Man: A Study in Hebrew Thought on Immortality" (Winnipeg: paper read to Canadian Biblical Society, Winnipeg, 1970); V. E. Frh. von Gebsattel, *Prolegomena einer Medizinischen Anthropologie* (Berlin: 1954); Siegfried Giedion, *Mechanization Takes Command* (Oxford: Oxford University Press, 1948); Oscar Gish, *Health, Man-*

power and the Medical Auxiliary (London: Intermediary Technology Development Group, 1971); Romano Guardini, The Death of Socrates, Meridian (New York: World Publishing, 1970); A. Guehring, De Todes—Auffassung der Deutschen Volks-Sage (Tubingen, 1956; dissertation); Pastor E. Heider, "Ausdruecke fur Tod und Sterben in der Samoanischen Sprache," Zeitschr. Fur Eingeborenensprachen 9 (1919), 66-88; Edgar Herzog, Psyche and Death (New York: G. P. Putnam's, 1967); Hans Jonas, "Technology and Responsibility: Reflections on the New Task of Ethics," Social Research 40 (1973), 31-54; John Koty, Die Behandlung der Alten und Kranken bei den Naturvoelkern (Stuttgart, 1934); Claude Levi-Strauss, The Savage Mind, Phoenix Series (Chicago: University of Chicago Press, 1969); John T. Marcus, "Death-Consciousness and Civilization," Social Research 35 (1964), 265-79; Karl Rahner, On the Theology of Death (New York: Herder and Herder, 1963); Jonas Robitscher, "The Right to Die: Do We Have the Right not to Be Treated?" Hastings Center Report [4] (1972); R. Shyrock, The Development of Modern Medicine (New York: Knopf, 1947); Charles Wahl, "The Fear of Death," Death and Identity, ed. by Robert Fulton (New York: Wiley, 1966).

3

Dying in a technological society

ERIC J. CASSELL

THE CARE OF the terminally ill in the United States has changed as the business of dying has shifted from the moral to the technical order. The moral order has been used to describe those bonds between men based in sentiment, morality, or conscience, that describe what is right. The technical order rests on the usefulness of things, based in necessity or expediency, and not founded in conceptions of the right.[1] The change of death from a moral to a technical matter has come about for many reasons based in social evolution and technical advance, and the effects on the dying have been profound.

One reason for the change has been the success of modern medicine in combatting death. For most, in the United States, premature death is no longer imminent. The death of infants is unusual, the death of children rare, and the death of young adults so improbable that it must be removed from the realistic possibilities of young life. Further, the nature of death has also changed. The degenerative diseases and can-

cer have become predominant. Lingering sickness in the aged is a less common event because medicine is able to combat the complications of chronic disease that so often in the past kept the sick person from functioning. Accompanying these changes brought about by technical advances, there has been a change in the place where death occurs. Death has moved from the home into institutions—hospitals, medical centers, chronic care facilities and nursing homes.

From the Moral to the Technical

There are other reasons for the shift of death in the United States from the moral to the technical order. One is the widespread acceptance of technical success itself. Because life expectancy has increased, the dying are old now. But, life expectancy is not an individual term, it is a statistical term. For individuals, what has changed is their death expectancy; they do not expect to die. They may use fantasies of early death or fears of death for personal or psychological reasons, but the reality belief is that death need not occur in the foreseeable future, that death is a reversible event. That belief in the reversibility of death, rooted in the common American experience of modern medicine, begins to move death out of the moral order. Death is a technical matter, a failure of technology in rescuing the body from a threat to its functioning and integ-

---

[1] Robert Redfield, *The Primitive World and Its Transformations* (Ithaca: Cornell University Press, 1953), pp. 20ff.

rity. For the moment, it does not matter that the death of a person cannot be removed from the moral order by the very nature of personhood; what matters is the mythology of the society. The widespread mythology that things essentially moral can be made technical is reinforced by the effect of technology in altering other events besides death; for example, birth, birth defects or abortion.

The fact that technology can be seen so often as altering fate nurtures an illusion that is basic to the mythology of American society—that fate can be defeated.

From the Family to the Hospital

Another reason why death has moved away from the moral order lies in the changes in family structure that have occurred over the past decades in the United States. The family remains the basic unit of moral and personal life, but with the passing of functionally meaningful extended families have come changes directly related to the care of the dying. The old, both the repository of knowledge about what is right and the major recipients of moral obligation, have left the family group. For many reasons, not the least their desire for continued independence in the years when previously material dependency would have been their lot, the aged frequently live alone. In retirement they may live far from their roots or their children, associating largely with others of their own age. An age-graded way of life has emerged that depends again on technical success and public responsibility (such as old age benefits) to solve problems for the aged that previously would have been the primary concern of the family. There is the belief, reinforced by the advantages of the change in family structure and geographic mobility, that essentially moral problems—obligations to parents, for example—have become part of the technical order amenable to administrative or technical solutions.

On the other hand, in his search for continued independence and comfortable retirement, the old person has allowed his family to separate, allowed the young to achieve their independence. In previous times and in other cultures, the mantle passed to the next generation only with the death of the old. Here it is voluntary. But, a problem is created for the dying patient. The old person who is going to die is already out of the family. To die amidst his family he must return to them—reenter the structure in order to leave it. Reenter it in denial of all the reasons he gave himself and his children for separation, reasons equally important to them in their pursuit of privacy and individual striving and in their inherent denial of aging, death and fate.

Thus, by reason of technological success and changes in family structure that are rooted in the basic mythology of America, death has moved from the moral order to the technical and from the family to the hospital.

The Context of Dying

It is interesting to examine some of the consequences and corollaries of the shift. In individual terms, moving the place of death from the home to the hospital, from familiar to strange surroundings, means changing the context of dying. The picture of the old person, independent and swinging free—promulgated as much by the old as by others—while part fact, is also a partial fiction dictated by the old person's love for, and nurturance of, the independence of the young. Becoming a burden is the great fear not only for what it may mean personally, but for the threat it poses to the fragile economic and personal structure of today's nuclear family. But part fiction or

The family remains the basic unit of moral and personal life, but with the passing of functionally meaningful extended families have come changes directly related to the care of the dying.

no, the hallmark of "golden age" is independence. With independence and its mobility, the belief arises that each person is the sole representative of his own beliefs, values and desires. In health that may seem to be true, but the fact is as fragile as the body. In health a person can struggle for his rights, pronounce his values and attempt their fulfillment. But the sick, bound to their bodies by their illness, are different. The values and desires dearly held during life give way in terminal illness. Pain and suffering erode meaning and deny dignity. The fiction of independence and the denial of fate give way to reality. In terminal illness, the individual must give over to others and to the context of his dying, the defense of his dignity and the statement of his values. But the context of dying and the people at the bedside have changed. The aged no longer die surrounded by their loved ones. An essentially private matter takes place in the public sphere surrounded by symbols of individual sameness, not personal difference. The family and its needs are the intruders. The patient's values, spoken by others, compete with the values of the institution. There is a final, ironic, independence as the person dies alone.

Thus, there are personal or value problems created for the individual when death moves from the moral to the technical order. Characteristically our society seeks solutions to these problems not by reasserting the moral, but by attempting technical solutions for moral imperatives. We are seeing increasing attempts in the United States to find quasi-legal or legal means to reassert the rights of the dying—some technical means to give as much weight to the person who dies as the hospital gives to his body.

Mechanical Events in the Moral Sphere

In the process of the shift of death from the moral to the technical a basic confusion arises that confounds the usefulness of technical solutions in what are essentially moral problems. The mechanical events involved in a body becoming dead, which occur in the technical sphere, are confused with the process of dying, which occurs in the moral sphere. It is a natural error but one that we do not frequently make in health. That is to say that while we are aware that the mechanical event that is a beating heart is essential to life, we do not confuse ourselves with our heartbeat. As a matter of fact if someone becomes too conscious of his heartbeat, we consider it a symptom, or neurosis. But in the sick or the dying the confusion is rampant. There are two distinct things happening in the terminally ill, the death of the body and the passing of the person. The death of the body is a physical phenomenon, a series of measurable events that are the province of physicians. The passing of the individual is a nonphysical process, poorly defined, largely unmeasurable and closely connected to the nature of the dying person. It is the process by which he leaves the group and during which we take leave of him. Indeed, in the manner in which many act towards the newly dead body—as though it still contained some part of the person—the passing of the individual, at least for the onlooker, may not end with death. It is obvious that in sudden death, a person may pass away who was never dying; or conversely, in the depressed, the person may be dying with no evidence of impending death.

The passing of the individual is also part of the work of physicians, but of more importance, it is the province of family, friends, and clergymen—indeed the entire group. But in a technical era, the passing of the person, since it is unmeasurable and does not fit the technical schema, is not a legitimate subject for public discourse.

Those feelings within that relate to the dying person are difficult to organize, to deal with, or to speak about. The social rituals that previously enabled those confused meanings and feelings to spend themselves appropriately have diminished or disappeared along with the extended family. In the moral order, time slows down for those around the dying; but in the world of things, of necessity or expediency, time moves on relentlessly, making its case for those around the dying to return to that world. Furthermore, with decreasing practice in moral matters, even when social forms remain, the content becomes increasingly sterile. Men obscure the moral content of the passing of the person by using the facts and artifacts of the death of the body as the vehicle for their interchanges—much as talk about the weather or sports draws the sting on other occasions.

The confusion of the mechanical events of the death of the body with the personal and social nature of the passing of the person confounds attempts to solve the essentially moral problems of the dying—problems of sentiment, conscience, or the knowledge of what is right. Thus, in matters such as when the respirators should be turned off, and by whom, essentially moral questions, the mechanical events loom so large that attention is diverted away from the moral, back to the technical. And this is the corollary problem to that raised earlier: the context of death no longer gives weight to the values of the dying person and forces a resort to legal or administrative protection of his rights.

Depersonalization of Care

The confusion of mechanical events for moral processes creates the further problem of depersonalization of care. And it is seen in the greater attention paid to diseases than to people by doctors and their institutions —a common complaint about physicians and particularly about physicians in their care of the dying. Frequently we explain this depersonalization by saying that it is the physician's psychological defense against the emotional burden imposed by the care of the dying. Though that may be true, it is only part of the truth. We have seen how the whole society has shifted its public focus from moral to technical in many areas of life: doctors are no exception to the trend. The problem cannot solely lie among physicians, or the society would not let them get away with it. Social forces would drive doctors back towards a more holistic view of their patients. Indeed, such a change is beginning to occur in response to the increasingly vocal dissatisfaction with medical care.

Because depersonalization is so much a part of the technical order, not only in medicine, and so antithetical to the values of personhood, let us further examine how depersonalization takes place. Each dying patient is not only a person, but also the container of the process or events by which his body is dying. By definition, since he is dying, these processes or events cannot be

controlled by existing technology. Because of the inability of the technology to control such things—and cancer or heart failure are examples—they acquire independent meaning apart from the person containing them. From the viewpoint of caring for the terminally ill, such depersonalization may be justly deplored. But from the viewpoint of medical science the pursuit of the meaning of the resistant body process, apart from the person containing it, is a legitimate end in itself. That is to say, the heart as an abstraction, as a pump, an electrical system or what have you, is a proper object of technical concern and quite distinct from the fact that human hearts are only found in humans. Further, it is the nature of any system of abstract or formal thought not to be content with mystery, but to continue operating on any problem until understanding results. Mystery is a threat to the adequacy of the system of thought itself. Consequently, the disease process must be probed and probed, not only because of its relevance to the care of the sick and dying, but also because lack of a solution poses a threat to the entire logical construct of which the body process is thought to be a part. Thus, the depersonalization and abstraction of body mechanics is both necessary and legitimate within the framework of science, and understanding of the body-as-machine is impeded by consideration of human values.

The problem of depersonalization depends in part on the degree to which the dying person's disease process is understood. For example, in the care of the patient with bacterial pneumonia, easily treated with antibiotics, depersonalization poses little difficulty. The abstractions necessary for understanding microbes, antibiotics and so forth, are so much a part of the physician's thinking that he or she is able to integrate them back into a total concept of man, patients, etc. Withdrawal and depersonalization are not frequent, I think, when experienced doctors and nurses care for the dying, if the cause of death is something acceptably inevitable, such as pneumonia in the very old, or stroke. If it is correct that persons dying of a poorly understood process are more likely to be depersonalized by their physicians, we can better understand why the accusation of depersonalization is most often brought against young physicians. To the inexperienced doctor almost everything about the dying person is unfamiliar or poorly understood thus requiring the abstraction that leads to depersonalization. Effective integration of the learned technical material with human needs, values, and desires comes only at a later stage of learning.

Temples of the Technical Order

In the United States, the modern medical center is the very temple of the technical order, revered both by medicine and the public. As medical science, in its effort towards understanding, has taken the body apart system by system, it has departmentalized the intellectual structure of the hospital. By that I mean not only the well known division of medicine into specialties, but the further subdivisions that represent specific body functions. The corridors of any American medical center reveal rooms whose doors bear titles such as pulmonary function laboratory, cardiographics laboratory, nuclear medicine, sonography and so forth. Each of these specialized functions has contributed immeasurably to the diagnostic and therapeutic power of the modern physician, and no doctor who has grown accustomed to their use will feel wholly comfortable in their absence. They are unlike the traditional clinical or research laboratory which when examining a function of the patient's body takes the whole patient along; it is not his blood or urine that goes to the laboratory, it is the patient. But it is not the person who holds the interest for the specialized laboratory; instead the interest centers on the person's lungs, or heart, or whatever. A good coronary arteriogram is not necessarily a good patient or even good for the patient, it is merely a technically good example of coronary arteriograms. Patients are usually not aware or interested in those distinctions and all too frequently, but in an opposite sense, neither is the physician who performed the test. One can see the hospital, thus compartmentalized, as the concrete expression of the depersonalization resulting from the abstract analytic thought of medical science. Thus, the dying patient in the modern hospital is in an environment ideally suited for the pursuit of knowledge and cure, but representing in its technology and idealized representative—the young doctor—technical values virtually antithetical to the holistic concept of person. This does not imply that the most personal and humane care cannot be and is not given in such hospitals, but rather that those who do give such care must struggle against their technical depersonalized thinking about the body, and against the structure of the hospital that such thought has produced.

If the modern hospital represents the positive strivings of medical science and the technical order—the belief that nature, disease, and fate can be conquered—the nursing home represents the tattered edges of that philosophy.

No discussion of the care of the terminally ill in the United States can avoid the problem of the nursing home. Whereas the modern hospital represents the positive strivings of medical science and the technical order—the belief that nature, disease, and fate can be conquered—the nursing home represents the tattered edges of that philosophy. Medicine and medical care are seen primarily as the application of medical science to disease: if science fails the body, medicine fails the person. Nursing homes contain the failures and frustrations of medicine, as well as the homeless or unwanted sick. They are a place to linger and to die. Walking their halls is deeply depressing because hopelessness is overwhelming. It is the hopelessness one experiences whenever one sees the sick completely overtaken by their sickness, forever apart from the comfort of group. None of the many reasons for their proliferation and crowding explains why they are the hopeless places that they usually are. We know they can be better because of the success of the occasional institution given over to the care of the terminally ill in a positive sense. Such successful nursing homes are often run by religious orders or by others whose belief in their mission is deeply moral. Thus, what we see in the usual American nursing home is by no means inevitable in the way that death is inevitable, but rather a vacuum of care. The promise of science and technology has failed here. The old family solutions to the problems posed by the care of the terminally ill have been altered past utility by social change. No new solution has come forward to fill the void.

We have seen how the care of the terminally ill has changed in the United States. They are older now and die more frequently in institutions. But that bare frame of facts conceals increasing distress within the society over the quality of their dying. When death occurs in the modern hospital there seems to be more concern for the disease than for the dying person, more concern for life as a succession of heartbeats, than life as meaning. When death occurs in nursing homes it is as if life just dribbled out—custodial care seemingly inconvenienced by individual difference or tenacity for life.

A Balance of the Moral and Technical

We have seen that the problem is larger than widespread insensitivity which might be corrected by new educational programs. Rather, there has been a shift of death from within the moral order to the technical order. The technical, the expedient, the utilitarian that has worked so well in so many material ways seemed to promise easier solutions to the problems previously seen as matters of conscience, sentiment, or obligations between men. But the promise has not been fulfilled; not in the United States nor elsewhere where the technical order spreads its dominance.

Even if it were possible, the solution is not a return of American society to technical innocence. I do not believe that men were inherently more moral in the past when the moral order predominated over the technical. The path seems to lie in the direction of a more systematic understanding of the moral order to restore its balance with the technical. Understanding the body has not made it less wonderful, and the systematic exploration of the moral nature of man will not destroy that nature but rather increase its influence. In the care of the dying, it may give back to the living the meaning of death.

4

The metaphysical plight of the family

WILLIAM MAY

THIS ESSAY is a preamble to a study of the rites that precede and follow upon the event of death. In our society, these rites raise chiefly the question of the role of the family and, even more particularly, the so-called nuclear family. It was not always so. In traditional society, each differentiated group within a culture had its role in the rituals surrounding death—even when the deceased was not a major public figure. The shaman, the priest, workers, and tribal leaders all had their part in a departure from this life. Not that these functionaries have entirely disappeared from the modern scene, but their roles have changed. Their presence has been privatized. They appear at the invitation and request of the family. This is true even for the modern minister, rabbi, or priest. The changed position of the religious leader is symbolized by the fact that his honorarium for the occasion often comes to him under the signature of the funeral director who presents a summary bill for services rendered to the family. Death is not viewed as an event of public significance in which public institutions have their own self-legitimating role. Their roles, insofar as they have them, are legitimated by request for services from the family, a social unit which, in turn, is much less public an entity than formerly. Indeed, the family is construed today as a shelter for privacy and intimacy.

There are certain exceptions to the increasing privatization of death. The Jew still observes the mourner's *kaddish,* a ritual that lifts up into public religious occasion private family grief, as members of the family stand, in the presence of the congregation, to acknowledge and honor the dead. An Episcopalian in mourning occasionally wears a black armband. Some vestigial remains of public participation may be found in still other religious traditions. The nation at large, moreover, has its memorial day for soldiers fallen in battle. The birthdays of some national leaders are, or used to be, celebrated. The death dates of national martyrs are remembered for a year or two. But a short list of these exceptions proves the point. Whatever happened to the death date of Martin Luther King? It has hardly become the public occasion that many expected. Death has become increasingly privatized. It is even so for Coretta King and Ethel Kennedy.

Thus any discussion of rites of preparation and mourning has to center in the family. From there it may proceed outward to include others, a circle of friends and professionals—nurses, doctors, lawyers, funeral directors, social workers, ministers—but all of their services direct inward toward the primary social unit, the patient and his family. Just how and why and in what form these services are needed and the peculiar social vectors that develop in the performance of such tasks will receive some attention in this chapter. But not until we have spent some time on what I consider to be the heart of the problem; namely, the metaphysical plight of the family, or, what might be called, if you will, the great family secret: God is dead.

Death and Ritual

A move in this essay from social analysis to philosophy or religion may seem somewhat arbitrary and indefensible. Why should a discussion of the role of the family in rites of preparation and mourning suddenly force a discussion of the metaphysical plight of the family? I believe the move is required by the very term, "rite." A human ritual, when it is genuine, is not perceived as something that men experimentally contrive, enact, tentatively indulge in with castanets and folk guitars, and subsequently evaluate with questionnaires and "feedback," in a kind of religious equivalent of the T.V. show that waits nervously for its Nielsen ratings. All such current trivializations of religious liturgy to the contrary, a ritual is enacted because men feel that reality itself mandates that the action be performed. There is no other choice. The particular ritual in question—to appeal to the stoic category—alone seems *fitting*. Anything else in a given situation would stick out as boorish, inappropriate, absurd. The ritual action alone is congruent with reality.[1]

Such an interpretation of ritual does not permit a man to take much credit for what he does liturgically, even when his own creativity and judgment enter into the action performed. The literary critic, Robert Gorham Davis, was embarrassed when he re-

---

[1] Arthur McGill, in a paper on the ethics of avoidance delivered in 1973 at a seminar sponsored by the Society for Religion in Higher Education, developed this analysis of behavior in the context of ethical action. He interpreted ethical action as that which is mandated by the real. While it seems clear to me that this definition is acceptable for ritual action, I am less convinced that ethical action can be fully subsumed under it.

ceived congratulations for an eloquent speech he made at the time of the Russian invasion of Hungary. He brushed flattery aside with the quite genuine acknowledgment that, under the circumstances, the speech wrote itself. So it is with ritual—doing what is called for; complying with the mandates of the real.

The Grand Inquisitor: An Arch-Humanist

We return, then, to the main question: What is the metaphysical plight of the family that shapes its ritual response to death? My short answer would be that it is very close to the metaphysical perception of the Grand Inquisitor in the legend that Dostoievski told in *The Brothers Karamazov*. I first read the story about the encounter of the Inquisitor with the returned Christ under the tutelage of a liberal Protestant philosopher at Yale who interpreted it as an attack on the Roman Catholic Church and its authoritarianism. A second lecturer in the course, Father John Courtney Murray, understandably enough, argued that Dostoievski's real target was another of his foes —authoritarian socialism. Taken either way, the Inquisitor is a rather ordinary villain. He is a power-seeker who deprives human beings of their freedom by giving them instead, miracle, mystery, and authority. In his lengthy monologue to the Christ, the Inquisitor explains why he felt it was necessary for him to deprive men of their freedom, and warns the Christ that if he should linger, he, the Inquisitor, would have to crucify him again.

It is my own conviction that the story is about a figure much more universal than either a church inquisitor or an authoritarian socialist. First and foremost, the Inquisitor is an arch-humanist. He is motivated by his urgent love of mankind. (Young college students who are regularly assigned the legend are not in a good position to understand the Inquisitor—except as a stereotypical villain—because most of them have not yet loved another human being for whom they have accepted responsibility and care. Not until they are in a family way will they understand the grandeur and tragedy of the Inquisitor. For he really loves mankind; he wants, above all else, to protect human beings from suffering. He wants their happiness.) In fact, from the perspective of the Inquisitor, there are only two realities in the world: his passionate love for human beings and the grim suffering from which he desires to protect them. There is no other factor in the picture, no other power that could possibly act in and through suffering. That is the Grand Inquisitor's secret, the great burden he and those like him bear on behalf of the happiness of mankind. The Grand Inquisitor (through the mouth of Ivan Karamazov) speaks:

> And all will be happy, all the millions of creatures except the hundred thousand who rule over them. For only we, who guard the mystery, shall be unhappy. There will be thousands of millions of happy babes, and a hundred thousand sufferers who have taken upon themselves the curse of the knowledge of good and evil. Peacefully they will die ... and beyond the grave they will find nothing but death. But we shall keep the secret, and for their happiness we shall allure them with the reward of heaven and eternity.[2]

Ivan's brother Aloysha, who listens attentively, breaks in upon the story and exclaims with regard to the likes of the Inquisitor:

> They have no ... great cleverness, and no mysteries and secrets.... Perhaps nothing but atheism, that's all their secret. Your Inquisitor does not believe in God, that's his secret.[3]

The modern conscientious parent occupies the same religious position as the Grand Inquisitor. Parents assume that there are only two realities in the world: their love for their child and the suffering from which they want, with their money, their advice, their urgency, and their moral support, to protect their own. They are keenly aware of all those catastrophic possibilities that lie in wait for their children—a Mack truck bearing down the highway, a skidding motorcycle, bad grades, a mediocre college, a disastrous love affair, a rudderless career, a bad marriage, and middle-age ennui. As conscientious parents, they operate as though the powers that are decisive in the universe

could not possibly do anything in and through the suffering of their children. They alone bear the burden of succor, wisdom, and counsel. They take upon themselves the responsibilities of a savior-figure; and, of course, because they cannot do a very good job of being saviors, they are filled with apprehension as they cope with their children. What an anomaly it must be for a child to see his parents attend a church or a synagogue and yet betray, by the worry written across their faces, their great secret fear that God is dead!

Atheism and Three Basic Perceptions of Death

What are, then, the perceived powers that threaten human beings and that render the existence of a good and nurturant God incredible? These powers are chiefly experienced as destructive.[4] The city of Dublin does not survive a single day except on the basis of wholesale butchery, observes Joyce in *Ulysses.* He names this power early on in the novel, *Dio Boia,* the "hangman God." Or again, "the whole world is organized by death," testifies one of the heroes in Camus' *The Plague.* The central anxiety of man, argues Joseph Rheingold of Harvard Medical School, is anxiety before death; not the scientist's natural death, not the philosopher's diluted experience of death as nonbeing, but fear of catastrophic death, a fear that includes the dread of mutilation and the fear of abandonment. This is what the headlines of our newspapers are all about and that is what dominates our nightmares: the catastrophe of physical mutilation, mangling, and destruction and the catastrophe of abandonment at the hands of the community. The child is fully acquainted with this double fear of death. He does not reduce the event to a purely *natural* experience, as recorded in the proposition that all creatures perish—like pears, puppies, and men. Neither is the child given to the romantic daydream of the existentialists who muse on nothingness. Rather he feels keenly the danger of being mutilated, dismembered,

---

[2]Fyodor Dostoievsky, *The Brothers Karamazov,* Modern Library (New York: Random House, 1952), p. 269.

[3]*Ibid.,* p. 271.

[4]See Arthur McGill, *Suffering: A Test of Theological Method* (Philadelphia: Geneva Press, 1968), Chap. 2; and William F. May, "Death: Its Religious Reality and its Theological Interpretation," in *Perspectives On Death,* ed. by Liston O. Mills (Nashville: Abingdon Press, 1969).

killed, suffocated, immobilized, deprived of sight, and lastly abandoned. In demanding the reassurance of a voice, the touch of a hand at bedtime, the child betrays that he knows all the issues involved in a sleep— a burial under the covers—that is early

T he great humanist, then, the Grand Inquisitor, is a religious man. His atheism is religiously inspired.

practice in dying. Death threatens all men with final abandonment, exclusion, oblivion.

Part of the awesomeness of the adventures of the astronauts is that they exposed themselves to these two elements of catastrophic death: the possibility that their bodies would be ripped apart by forces at a velocity that defies the imagination, but even more awesome, the possibility that they might die a staggering distance from home, abandoned in the wastes of space.

Moreover, the heroics of the astronauts are child's play when it comes to courting cataclysmic power. As Robert Jay Lifton has pointed out, the atomic bomb confronts not only individuals but mankind at large with the prospect of mutilation and abandonment—a mutilation genetically transmitted from generation to generation and an abandonment by virtue of which the human race itself would be severed from its nurturant world.

The great humanist, then, the Grand Inquisitor, is a religious man. His atheism is religiously inspired. He is tragically acquainted with those powers that environ us. He knows that his charges will find nothing beyond the grave. They belong eventually to death—utterly without remainder. And that is why on this side of the grave, given his overwhelming love, he wants to protect them, he seeks to offer them what Melville calls in *Moby Dick,* the Isle of Safety. He is the archetypal mother/father; the one who creates and provides for the family, who

seeks to establish some kind of temporary sanctuary, who knows that this isle of safety is not the organizing principle of the universe, but who seeks within its confines to found a tolerable degree of warmth, intimacy, and vitality—until the earth shakes, the tide rolls in, and the winds blow. Within this sanctuary, the ruling principle is the *avoidance* of suffering and death and therefore he must send the silent but disturbing stranger on his way. He cannot suffer the presence of the Christ whose life bears some mysterious connection with that suffering which is religiously abhorrent to the Inquisitor.

I should pause for a moment and defend the use of religious categories with respect to the contemporary reflex before death. Among the welter of attitudes to sacred power, the western religious tradition has found it possible to identify three basic relations to God: first, the man of faith who lives in dread, awe, or openness toward God; second, the Titan, the man of pride, who revolts against the deity; and, third, the philistine, the man of sloth, who avoids God's presence. The man of faith lives in dread of sacred power, the Titan defies it, and the philistine flees from it. These three, then, faith, resistance, and avoidance.

Dread, Flight, and Revolt

A contemporary body of literature substitutes death for God as the decisive event with which the modern consciousness must cope. In writing my own dissertation fourteen years ago, I worked on the thought of Heidegger and Camus, because they posed the question of death in a way that corresponds roughly to the western religious tradition. They exhibited in their writings three basic relations to death, comparable to the three responses to God posited in Christian thought: dread, flight, and revolt. For Heidegger, man's authentic existence is an openness toward his death; his inauthentic existence, an evasion of his end. For Camus, man's authentic existence is defined by a revolt against death; his inauthentic existence, either by a piety toward, or an evasion of, his end.

Beginning first with the response of revolt: the attitude of the Titan toward sacred power is that of presumption. In response to the powerfulness of the sacred object, the Tital attempts, in his own right, a seizure of power. Such a man does not pretend that the sacred does not exist. "On the contrary: Power is here frankly recognized and then a hostile attitude is adopted amounting to contempt; and thus man turns away from the power that arouses dread toward himself and toward his own powerfulness . . ."[5] In the full manifold of Camus' plays, novels, and philosophical essays, there emerges a hero who is inwardly nurtured by his resistance to death; the political rebel, the artist, and the medical doctor are varying examples of heroic protest against a world that is beset by destructive power and death. Within this vision of things, death is not reduced to a natural event; quite the contrary, it is supremely antihuman, the absolute enemy, the enemy that cannot be defeated, but which, nonetheless, must be resisted if man would affirm his humanity.

In the fashion of his time, Camus found this resistance in what he calls the absurdist experience (the experience of which Dostoievski's Ivan is fully aware); that is, the awareness of an irreconcilable conflict between the human demand for life and rationality and a world that disappoints this demand with meaningless death. In his essay on *Suicide and the Soul,* James Hillman more recently associates this ethic of resistance with the medical profession. It will not countenance suicide inasmuch as it accepts as its sacred duty the fight against death. The sociologist Gutmann tends to locate this attitude in the society at large in those octogenarians whom he calls the survivors, those who outlast their peers and who do so in part by being fighters, by turning toward themselves and their own powerfulness.[6]

The response of avoidance has had most of the attention from analysts recently. It embraces all those rites by virtue of which men not only avoid the obvious ordeals of sickness, aging, and dying, but also seek to repress those more subtle intimations of mortality—when a marriage turns stale, when the relations between the generations are burdened with the guilt of replacement, or when sexual intercourse is followed by letdown and melancholy. From the perspective of Camus, the Christian faith and the western philosophical tradition, insofar as they have promulgated a doctrine of the resurrection of the body or the immortality of the soul, have engaged in nothing more than an evasion of death; they have sought to put theological screens before the eyes of the condemned.

Heidegger adds to this analysis of evasion by observing that the avoidance of death is finally a self-evasion. This move on the philosopher's part takes us then into the third response to death, according to which man is essentially himself only in his openness to death. From this perspective, death and dying no longer appear as supreme enemy to the human. Quite the contrary, the authentic human being must experience the dreadfulness of death as essential to his very own existence. Only in anxiety before death does man come to himself as a man. The moral of the story is not: you travel this way but once, so grab for all the gusto you can; but, rather, you travel this way but once, so come to yourself, reckon with yourself, in your own induplicable freedom. A man's relationship to death is not merely one in a series of possible relations which are authentic or inauthentic, standing alongside relations to one's mother, one's job, or one's creativity. An authentic relationship to death is the touchstone of authenticity in all other relations. Man is this hyphenated reality, being-unto-death. Only in his progress toward death does he stand forth as a man and so gain possession of himself toward all else. Every strategy of escape, then, is a derivative, privative, and restricted mode of being for the being which is a being-unto-death. This is true whether man seeks refuge from death in the solaces of his collective life, in the solidities of the work-a-day world, or in the deliverances of objective thought. In all these ways, man but squanders himself.

Heidegger defines being-toward-death so idiosyncratically that it should not be confused with another more nihilistic form of openness to death. In this prospect, death appears as destructive power, without relief,

[5]G. Van der Leeuw, *Religion in Essence and Manifestation,* trans. by J. E. Turner (London: George Allen & Unwin, 1938), pp. 468-69.

[6]David Gutmann, "The Premature Gerontocracy: Themes of Aging and Death in the Youth Culture," in *Death in American Experience,* ed. by Arien Mack (New York: Schocken Books, 1973).

and yet men embrace it. Admittedly, Heidegger is interested in man's evaluation and ecstasy through a being-toward-death, but he does not mean thereby some sort of dark thralldom with the "negative," in the sense of the menacing and the destructive.[7]

Death as Destructive Power

Another literature explores more directly this preoccupation with death as destructive power. Malraux's novels, for example, are full of anarchists and terrorists who seek to surpass the relative tensions of political life, as they surrender themselves to the ecstasy of violence. Mishima, in his novel, *The Temple of the Golden Pavilion,* gives another example of the hero, who is fascinated with destruction. The Japanese novelist describes in Dostoievskian terms the career of a young Buddhist acolyte who seeks to overcome the contradiction between the beautiful realm of outer forms and the ugly introversion of his own life by a single pyromaniacal action in which he burns down his temple and thus releases the fires that wait impatiently beneath the surface of the universe. The quest for this sort of experience of destructive power may not be as eccentric as it appears, inasmuch as there is in the most ordinary of men a craving for the bad news of the day which follows a vicarious enjoyment of events more alluring than the incidents that fall within the daily routine.

Robert Jay Lifton has described the political dimension of all this in *Boundaries* with the term, "nuclearism." He reserves the terms for those who, once having caught a glimpse of destructive force, feel exalted and therefore safe only insofar as they themselves draw close to destructive power. Lifton, of course, has in mind the apologists of the military-industrial establishment who shield themselves from the powerfulness of the bomb in the hands of others by drawing near to it themselves—even though this power in their own hands purchases safety neither for friend or foe. Once again, the strategy has its domestic versions—in the alcoholic who goes for the bottle not only be-

cause it offers him comfort, but the comfort of poison, or the young who move into hard drugs because they find there an ecstasy that makes the everyday world and its safeties pale into the trivial.

Where does the Inquisitor fit in this analysis of several metaphysically plausible responses to death? Camus places Ivan, the narrator of the legend, in the camp of those atheists who are given to metaphysical rebellion. His atheism results from his perception of suffering and death. His humanism is a religious reflex before destructive power. His vision of the suffering of the innocent has made him lose his innocence. Henceforth he accepts the heavy burden. He acknowledges the fact that there are two kinds of men—those who are given to lucidity about the human condition and those who are like children in the diminished sense of that term, unaware, naive. The Inquisitor, painfully sensitive to the human condition, defies it by trying to provide his fellows with an isle of safety in which avoidance is possible. In so doing, he accepts the full burden of isolation from the human race. His knowledge deprives him of happiness, and his love deprives him of solidarity with his fellows. Lucid about his own condition, he practices deception on those who, by his deception, are reduced to the status of children.

While the Inquisitor presents in extreme the archetypal pattern of resistance, the ordinary parent, in coping with his children about death, represents some kind of combination of resistance and avoidance. Because he knows about the human condition, he does not want his children to know—too soon—and, because he half-knows, does not himself want to know too much.

He is like the Inquisitor in that he deceives, but, unlike the Inquisitor, in that he also seeks to self-deceive. He not only creates the isle of safety for his children, he tries to live in it himself. He is given to an unstable mixture of awareness and avoidance. Given this ambivalence, the parent, when he must face death in his own right, is tempted to look for someone who will serve him in turn as a kind of Grand Inquisitor. But more of the doctor later.

Further distinctions are required about the relations of parents to children, husband to wife, and parents to grandparents, in the

---

[7]All such nihilistic embrace of destruction is analyzed by Heidegger under the modalities of fear and desire and carefully distinguished from what he means by anxiety before death.

light of the metaphysical plight of the family and the three basic responses to that plight.

Parents and Children

I have already referred in the discussion of Dostoievski's legend to the parents' attempt to protect their children from suffering and death. These deliberate efforts at protection are reinforced at involuntary levels by the distance of the nuclear family from grandparents. Children are far removed from the process of aging, sickness, and death within their own families. Grandfather's death is a long-distance telephone call; hurried arrangements for plane tickets; otherwise, an abstraction. But even when the larger family is located in one area, children find themselves removed from the event. The number of persons dying in hospitals and nursing facilities increases apace. An estimated forty percent died at home in 1958 but only twenty percent die there today. By hospital rule, young people under fourteen are not permitted to visit the sick even though they may be central figures in their lives. The net effect is to remove young people from initiation into the event. Superficially, at least, within the nuclear family, they are protected, as much as possible, from suffering and death.

But at another level, children are not quite so insulated. Parents may soothe them to sleep with rumors of angels at their bedposts, but they cannot control their dreams, nor can parents control the reaction of their children to their own overprotectiveness. One group sloughs off parental concern about the dangers of the mortorcycle, drugs, or the cigarette, with the familiar assumption of immortality by saying, "What you describe may happen to others but not to me." A second group internalizes the fears of adults. They become anxious and unadventuresome souls in their own right. A third reacts to the dull, overanxious lives of their parents and responds with a nuclearism of their own. They deliberately court danger, finding in it, if not security, an expanded life against which the arguments of parents are unavailing.

After all, who are parents to talk? Concerned for the success of their children in a harsh world, they pressure them to become efficient, little overachievers, shrewd little connivers, clever in cadging the best grades that will open the doors to the best schools, that will lead to the best jobs, that will turn the keys in the best houses, that will open the gates to the best cemeteries. So complained R. D. Laing, in *The Politics of Experience,* of the brutalities of an educational system which he compared to the frantic realism of a London beggar who used to maim and mutilate his children in order to equip them to be overachievers in the family trade.

The very parent who acts to protect his child from conflict, suffering, failure, and death and who fears the child's incomprehensible nuclearism—the reckless love affair, the high-speed wreck, the vocational doldrums, the drifting and dozen false starts —indulges in an unwitting nuclearism of his own. He is committed to an educational system and a work ethic that in its own way courts mutilation, destruction, and death. That is the message behind the gothic exaggeration of R. D. Laing, in comparing a high-powered educational system to the low cunning of a Fagin. Most parents over forty are too much acquainted with the psychic mutilations of an educational system and a life-style that has meant too much insomnia and hypochondria, too many tranquilizers and too much alcohol, too many broken homes, and burnt-out cases, and too much cholesterol, altogether to deny the charge against their generation.

At this point, the responses of anxious

T he anxious man actually worries those powers he fears. He hunts them down in his dreams, even though his dreams are filled with flight; he imposes them upon his children, relentlessly reminding them of those disasters which he wants them at all costs to avoid.

avoidance of death and nuclear embrace reveal themselves to be closer together than first appear to be the case. Etymologists, if not psychoanalysts, have long ago recognized this fact. The worried man thinks of himself as harrassed by those evils that press in upon him. But the word "worry" itself is much more active/aggressive in origin. However bent on wholesome avoidance of evil he may think himself to be, the anxious man actually worries those powers he fears. He hunts them down in his dreams, even though his dreams are filled with flight; and he imposes them upon his children, relentlessly reminding them of those disasters which he wants them at all costs to avoid.

Husband and Wife

It was stated at the outset of this essay that the nuclear family seems to provide a sanctuary for intimacy in an otherwise large, impersonal, functionalized world. The *sanctum sanctorum* of this intimacy is the relationship betwen husband and wife. The first question we need to face is how the crisis of death and dying tests and strains that intimacy.

A sophisticated professional woman in her middle years, but newly married, argued at a recent conference that the inability of a husband and wife to talk to one another during the crisis of terminal illness betrays a lack of intimacy in their prior life together. The woman in question, an expert in modern literature, has a formidable literary example to back her point. Tolstoi's *The Death of Ivan Ilych* is a powerful account of the way in which the crisis of death can expose the inauthenticity of human relationships.

Tolstoi's point need be recalled but briefly. The story opens from the perspective of Ivan's colleagues at the government legal bureau where news has just been received of Ivan's death. Here the perspective is cold, careerist, and calculating. Who will get Ivan's job? Who will have to adjust certain plans for the evening and pay respects to the family? The office chatter shows up the work-a-day world for what it is: indifferent, impersonal, shallow, oriented to gossip and pleasures that grow restive with detour and delay.

But then the camera shifts, as it were, to the home of the bereaved. Here one would expect a level of intimacy and rapport, a genuineness of grief, so lacking in the public domain. Clearly, not so. While accepting condolences, the wife worries about the inadequacy of her insurance policies. While shedding a tear, she tends to emptying ashtrays for her guests.

In third perspective, the story moves back into Ivan's life and marriage and we are treated to an account that conforms to the professional woman's generalization about death as a test of intimacy. Ivan and his wife are unable to talk about his illness, unable to console one another in the face of his imminent death. Moreover, the impatience, the lies, the anger, the resentment, the cruelty, the abortive sentiments that pass between them in his final months only bring to the surface a fundamental fault already present in a shallow marriage. Intimacy fails between them at the end because it was never there in the first place.

Ivan and his wife lead parallel, calculating lives. Death reveals an outsidedness between them that has already overtaken them both. In this respect, Tolstoi's story is similar to D. H. Lawrence's little tale about a miner whose body is brought home to his wife. As she washes the corpse for the funeral, its strangeness overwhelms her, disclosing to her the foreigner that he had always been to her in the flesh.

> Elizabeth looked up. The man's mouth was fallen back, slightly open under the cover of the moustache. Life with its smoky burning gone from him, had left him apart and utterly alien to her. And she knew what a stranger he was to her. In her womb was ice of fear, because of this separate stranger with whom she had been living as one flesh. Was this what it all meant—utter, intact separateness, obscured by heat of living? In dread, she turned away. The fact was too deadly.... they had been two isolated beings, far apart as now.[8]

Martin Heidegger has tried to articulate this philosophically. Dying is always one's own, indeed one's innermost, unsubstitut-

_____

[8]D. H. Lawrence, "Odour of Chrysanthemums," *The Prussian Officer and Other Stories* (New York: B. W. Heubsch, 1916), p. 307.

able possibility. Even when another lays down his life for me, he cannot die for me. Each must do his own dying. Thus dying distances one from another, Elizabeth Kubler-Ross and her quest for intimacy to the contrary.

> We have no access to the loss of being as such which the dying man 'suffers.' The dying of others is not something which we experience in a genuine sense; at most we are just 'there alongside.'[9]

(Eventually, Ivan experiences community, but not with his wife; rather with his servant, Gerasim, who offers him the little relief from pain that he knows by hoisting Ivan's legs up on his shoulders—a simple work of mercy—and finally with his son in a gesture of understanding that passes between them just before his tortured end. Not much, to be sure, but enough to permit one to rename the story, "The Salvation of Ivan Ilych." His dying effects his harrowing transition from an empty life to the only authentic life he has ever known.)

Despite impressive literary backing from Tolstoi and Lawrence's stories, I would dispute the professional woman's assertion that the breakdown in communication between a husband and wife before the crisis of death exposes the lack of intimacy in the prior marriage. Certainly not inevitably. When serious illness comes and communication seems difficult or impossible, this does not necessarily mean that the couple enjoyed only a pseudo-intimacy before; rather, illness itself may have disrupted the very basis for the intimacy which had been theirs.

Intimacy, after all, depends upon a certain rhythm and balance in human relationships. The rhythm is easily broken; the balance, shattered by too much pressure or strain on one or the other of a couple. Without ever realizing what is happening, a distancing between husband and wife can occur. The crisis of sickness, dying, and death makes them strangers to one another.

One example. A certain women is extremely dependent on her husband. At first glance, he is the domineering member of the marriage. Final decisions are his. He has the line of command down to the children to which her own relationship is adjunctive. His intelligence and force of personality

make him the center of attention in the family from whom others take their bearings. Yet she is not without her resources for controlling her husband. Like most dependent people, she has learned long ago how to manage him in varying ways through her dependencies. Chiefly she wants his company as much as possible. To that end, she fills up his free time with household projects that will keep him occupied. Whatever time is left over, she steers into activities which she can share. He golfs, she takes up golf. As much as possible, she wants to be at his side; he is her familiar, near at hand.

But his terminal illness changes all that. After the onset of cancer, metastasized into the liver, and after the use of antidepressant drugs that had a toxic effect on his system and caused him for a time to hallucinate, the husband loses command. He is no longer captain of the ship. Even after he is withdrawn from the drugs and recovers lucidity, he is unable to recover sufficiently to reassert his old role in relationship to his family—his pain, his weakness, his sleeplessness, his weight loss, the imminence of death—all combine to dislocate utterly the prior bases for his life and his authority.

Meanwhile, the wife also seems to suffer a traumatic change in her relationship to her husband. Formerly unable to be with him enough, his current plight fills her with dread. Much to her daughter's chagrin, she seems withdrawn, immobilized, unable to care for him, as the daughter feels she ought. But her paralysis isn't a moral matter, it isn't even a question of her physical and emotional exhaustion at the age of seventy from the demands of sick care. The deeper problem is the drastic reversal that has occured in their relationship. The family captain is helpless, and, as such, he has become a *stranger* to her. As the saying goes with respect to illness, "He is not *himself.*" This is the feature of so many terminal illnesses that undercuts the usual basis for human relationships. The gregarious becomes reclusive; the manic, somewhat depressed; the witty, slurred and slow of speech; the dominant, detached; the dependent, demanding. The bases for intimacy have been jarred and disrupted, if not destroyed. For who is most likely to suffer from this alteration of personality than the person whose life, for better or for worse,

---

[9]*Sein und Zeit*, p. 239.

flourished in the medium of the self that he was? From this point on, it is not only the dying who become strangers to the living, but the living who seem like strangers to the dying.

It is not always possible to explain all this by imputing a prior lack of intimacy in the relationship between a couple. Imperfect? Yes. Lacking in intimacy? Not necessarily. What human relationship, even the most intimate, isn't burdened with its ironies, its tyrannies, its excesses, its imperfections, and its preposterous accommodations—all of which get welded together into the familiar world that each knows in and through the other, but a familiar world which the trauma of dying has a way of turning inside out.

There is some literary support, older than Tolstoi's work, for the point I am arguing; it is in one of the earliest of Western plays, *Everyman*. When the figure of death, the sheriff, comes to arrest him, Everyman seeks help from his possessions, from good company, from his five senses, and from his relatives. All abandon him; but the peculiar experience of desertion at the hands of relatives is finely expressed: they become as "strangers" to him. The same process of estrangement is apparent in the unpretentious, but sensitive film centering on the last weeks of Albro Piersall, a terminal cancer patient at the Calvary Hospital, located in the Bronx, N.Y. In the later stages of his illness, Albro Piersall views his own life in a detached, almost remote, perspective. His relatives visit, trying to keep up conversation within the terms of the intimate and the everyday, but Albro looks beyond them, like an Indian, with his eye on a horizon that no one else sees.

The film, of course, centers on the last days of detachment and cathexis; nevertheless, it points to the destination toward which the whole process of dying moves, a process which the family, on the basis of its own rituals of intimacy, has few resources to face. Death, in Lawrence's words, seals that unbridgeable outsidedness of one to another. No wonder, facing this crisis, the family so often requests outside agencies to take over. The chief outside agent, of course, is the doctor, because the doctor, it is hoped, will be able to restore the person to the former basis of life in the family. The doctor thus assumes the same role

toward the patient and his family as parents originally assumed toward their children, except, if anything, more intensively so, because the family now faces immediate crisis rather than diffuse vulnerability. The doctor assumes the role of the great humanitarian, equipped with the three resources of the Inquisitor: Miracle, Mystery, and Authority. The family looks to him for a medical miracle, wrapped up in a Latin mystery, and accompanied by authoritative instructions on how to behave, so that "everything may be done that has to be done."

Once again, the moral justification for the enterprise is the same as that invoked by the Inquisitor—the relief of suffering and the deferral of reckoning with death. In some such ways, he fights against those powers that have the last say in the universe for the sake of the happiness of his charges. Sometimes the twin aims come into conflict with one another; the relief of suffering can hasten the coming of death and the prevention of death can prolong human suffering. It would appear today that the aim of relief from suffering is assuming a certain priority, because suffering carries with it the terrible knowledge of those powers that rule the universe. Thus death-hastening drugs are justified if they relieve pain and compacts with doctors are encouraged that will instruct them concerning those conditions under which one would prefer to exit from this life. An increasingly attractive solution to the problem of suffering, so Arthur McGill put it, is to eliminate the sufferer.

Parents and Grandparents

Increasingly, the model for the relationship of parents to grandparents has become that of parents to children. The healthy have authority over the sick, the middle-aged over the elderly, the professional over the patient, as the parent exercises power over the child. Given the current prolongation of life and the increased incidence of feebleness and senility, there is a certain objective warrant for this asymmetrical behavior. But in one important way the elderly are granted even less dignity than children. The dependency of a child is directed toward an increase of life; the dependency of the aged is on the other side of a continental divide that slopes off toward the west and nightfall.

Thus the dependency of the aged is less tolerable. It reminds those in the fullness of their powers rather too vividly of their own imminent eclipse. The old injunction had it that children should be seen, but not heard. In encouraging the trek to Arizona and in depositing the elderly in old peoples' homes and centers for chronic care, we seem to be saying today that the elderly should be neither seen nor heard. In folklore, death appeared as the hider-goddess.[10] By excluding the aged from family life, we tell them, in effect, that as they approach the hider-goddess we prefer to have them hidden away.

Our current attitude toward the aged contrasts sharply with that of those cultures in which they commanded respect, if not veneration. In traditional culture, this veneration for the aged was partly a religious blind for a conservative politics and economics, but I think it goes deeper than that. It testifies that human beings have a value that transcends their utility. It argues that a distinction must be maintained between human being and human doing. The former cannot be reduced to the latter—modern pragmatic, utilitarian culture nothwithstanding.

The "secularization" of modern culture, in the most literal sense of that term, is not unrelated to our attitude toward the aged. The word "secular" has associations with the temporal. Most generally, it means "this-worldly," but more precisely it means an orientation to the present age, the current generation. What is valued is the work of the ruling generation, not the past generation or the generation to come. This generation is oriented to itself with a vengeance. Abortion protects it at one end and the discard pile for the aged protects it from inconvenience at the other.

I do not think that this charge of expedience that has intruded itself in the discussion is inconsistent with the preceding remarks about the protective instinct of the nuclear family. On the contrary, orientation to the nuclear family and the protection of its life against inconvenience and suffering

is spiritually consistent with the somewhat more calloused dismissal of what used to be called the extended family. The sociologist Slater summarized all this by referring to what he called the "toilet assumption" in American life. Instead of facing problems, we flush them; we seek to void them. Our nervous refusal to face those of diminishing social value betrays our own sense of resourcelessness, our own inner conviction that we ourselves are founded on and surrounded by a void. So we are not sure what to do except to evacuate.

And yet, we are not wholly successful in that. A family of grown and dispersed children gathers for the last days and funeral of a parent. The low-key middle class does its best to cope smoothly with the event. But then tempers flare, curses fly in the air, brothers come to blows. People on their best behavior suddenly find themselves offended and offending inexplicably. All the ancient resentments, with burial at hand, are disinterred. Who among the children will make the decisions? the oldest? the nearest? the most successful? the smartest? the most worldly-wise? And the most ridiculous of arguments break out over possessions—a piece of clothing, a cast-off chair, a piece of jewelry—while still others in the family withdraw from the scene to occupy the high ground of disdain and contempt.

The Church, the Family, and Dying

Given the way men quarrel with one another, suffer and die, no traditional religious solution to the problem of death is possible that conforms to the pattern of avoidance. Human conflict and suffering have a way of surfacing to mock the strategy of evasion. Yet the Christian Church has played its own role in avoidance. Many persons report that they have never heard their minister or priest take up frontally in a sermon the question of their own dying. Other clergymen preach the resurrection in such a way as to attempt a kind of verbal by-pass around the reality of death. Insofar as this avoidance takes place, the church betrays unconditionally the Christian message. The church offers only a momentary respite from secret apprehensions before each is called, tricked, or snatched from the sanctuary into the graveyard.

---

[10]The devouring goddess of the dead. See William May, "Attitudes Toward the Newly Dead."

To preach about death is absolutely essential if Christians are to preach with joy. Otherwise they speak with the profound melancholy of men who have separated the church from the graveyard. They make the practical assumption that there are two Lords. First, there is the Lord of the Sabbath, the God who presides over the affairs of cheerful philistines while they are still thriving and in good health. Then there is a second Lord, a Dark Power about which one never speaks, the Lord of highway wrecks, bedside squabbles, hospitals, and graveyards who handles everything in the end.

The Christian faith, however, does not proclaim two parallel Lords. The Lord of the church is not ruler of a surface kingdom. His dominion is nothing if it does not go at least six feet deep. This is the conviction that lies behind those terse statements about Jesus' career that found their way into the Apostle's Creed, "Suffered under Pontius Pilate, was crucified, died, and was buried." This peculiar confession insists that new life comes solely through an act in which the savior lays down his life for men. The mark of deity is not withdrawal—either from death or from the whole human arena of conflict, suffering, and dying. Quite the contrary, they are the medium in and through which new life is opened up.

This is the overwhelming message of the passion narrative that describes the last few days in Jesus' life. Nothing negative is suppressed, not even in the course of that potentially sentimental occasion on which Jesus eats a last meal with his disciples. The supper is absolutely riven with conflict. No sooner have the disciples taken bread than one of them is accused of treason. Then a dispute breaks out among them as to which is to be regarded the greatest; and, instead of flattering them all and smoothing over the squabble, Jesus says, "Let the greatest among you become as the youngest, and the leader as one who serves." He undercuts the pretenders by comparing himself to a servant. Still a third disciple tries to cover over the tension and recoup the occasion with an extravagant declaration of loyalty, but he in turn is exposed in imminent denial. As a social occasion, the dinner is a disaster—followed upon by yet further absurdities as the friends fall asleep during a last vigil, make futile efforts at defense, and, at the end, flee ignominiously—one of them so lacking in dignity as to run right out of his clothes in order to escape capture. And yet all of this is interpreted as the manifestation of a life and power that reveals itself in and through suffering and death rather than by dodging death and setting it aside. At the least, this narrative, when taken seriously, provides warrant for facing into all that men find negative, ugly, and ludicrous in human affairs without fearing their power to engulf.

Clearly this narrative is in the background of Dostoievski's novel with which this discussion of the family began. Ivan Karamazov's humanist cannot expose his charges to the knowledge of suffering and death. To save means to suppress. But the novel closes with a still further possibility for the family. Another Karamazov, the same brother who listened attentively to Ivan's legend, preaches a children's sermon at the funeral of a young boy. Aloysha Karamazov takes up his stand by Illusha's stone—not high ground removed from the human scene but on the very spot where the dead boy was persecuted by his friends hurling stones. Aloysha preaches, fully acknowledging the cruelty of the young boys and fully recognizing the pain, the illness, and the desperation of the father of the deceased; but, despite it all and in the midst of it all, Aloysha and the boys are bound together as one. Dostoievski therewith suggests another way than the way of avoidance and deception. On the killing ground itself, it is possible for men to remain human, to remember, to grieve, and even to rejoice.

II.
The Redefinition
of Death

5

Death: process or event?

ROBERT S. MORISON

MOST DISCUSSIONS of death and dying shift uneasily, and often more or less unconsciously, from one point of view to another. On the one hand, the common noun "death" is thought of as standing for a clearly defined event, a step function that puts a sharp end to life. On the other, dying is seen as a long-drawn-out process that begins when life itself begins and is not completed in any given organism until the last cell ceases to convert energy.

The first view is certainly the more traditional one. Indeed, it is so deeply embedded, not only in literature and art, but also in the law, that it is hard to free ourselves from it and from various associated attitudes that greatly influence our behavior. This chapter analyzes how the traditional or literary conception of death may have originated and how this conception is influencing the way in which we deal with the problem of dying under modern conditions. In part, I contend that some of our uses of the term "death" fall close to, if not actually within, the definition of what Whitehead called the "fallacy of misplaced concreteness."[1] As he warned, "This fallacy is the occasion of great confusion in philosophy," and it may also confuse our

handling of various important practical matters.

Nevertheless, there is evidence that the fallacy may be welcomed by some physicians because it frees them from the necessity of looking certain unsettling facts in the face.

In its simplest terms, the fallacy of misplaced concreteness consists in regarding or using an abstraction as if it were a thing, or, as Whitehead puts it, as a "simple instantaneous material configuration." Examples of a relatively simple kind can be found throughout science to illustrate the kinds of confusion to which the fallacy leads. Thus, our ancestors who observed the behavior of bodies at different temperatures found it convenient to explain some of their observations by inventing an abstraction they called heat. All too quickly the abstract concept turned into an actual fluid that flowed from one body to another. No doubt these conceptions helped to develop the early stages of thermodynamics. On the other hand, the satisfaction these conceptions gave their inventors may also have slowed down the development of the more sophisticated kinetic theory.

It should be quite clear that, just as we do not observe a fluid heat, but only differences in temperature, we do not observe "life" as such. Life is not a thing or a fluid anymore than heat is. What we observe are some unusual sets of objects separated from the rest of the world by certain peculiar properties such as growth, reproduction, and special ways of handling energy. These objects we

[1]A. N. Whitehead, *Science and the Modern World* (New York: Macmillan, 1967), pp. 51-55.

elect to call "living things." From here, it is but a short step to the invention of a hypothetical entity that is possessed by all living things and that is supposed to account for the difference between living and nonliving things. We might call this entity "livingness," following the usual rule for making abstract nouns out of participles and adjectives. This sounds rather awkward, so we use the word "life" instead. This apparently tiny change in the shape of the noun helps us on our way to philosophical error. The very cumbersomeness of the word "livingness" reminds us that we have abstracted the quality for which it stands from an array of living things. The word "life," however, seems much more substantial in its own right. Indeed, it is all too easy to believe that the word, like so many other nouns, stands for something that must have an existence of its own and must be definable in general terms, quite apart from the particular objects it characterizes. Men thus find themselves thinking more and more about life as a thing in itself, capable of entering inanimate aggregations of material and turning them into living things. It is then but a short step to believing that, once life is there, it can leave or be destroyed, thereby turning living things into dead things.

Now that we have brought ourselves to mention dead things, we can observe that we have invented the abstract idea of death by observing dead things, in just the same way that we have invented the idea of life by observing living things. Again, in the same way that we come to regard life as a thing, capable of entering and leaving bodies, we come to regard death as a thing, capable of moving about on its own in order to take away life. Thus, we have become accustomed to hearing that "death comes for the archbishop," or, alternatively, that one may meet death by "appointment in Samarra." Only a very few, very sophisticated old generals simply fade away.

In many cases then, Death is not only reified, it is personified, and graduates from a mere thing to a jostling woman in the marketplace of Baghdad or an old man, complete with beard, scythe, and hourglass, ready to mow down those whose time has come. In pointing to some of the dangers of personification, it is not my purpose to abolish poetry. Figures of speech certainly have their place in the enrichment of esthetic experience, perhaps even as means for justifying the ways of God to man. Nevertheless, reification and personification of abstractions do tend to make it more difficult to think clearly about important problems.

Abstractions Can Lead to Artificial Discontinuity

A particularly frequent hazard is the use of abstractions to introduce artificial discontinuities into what are essentially continuous processes. For example, although it is convenient to think of human development as a series of stages, such periods as childhood and adolescence are not discontinuous, sharply identifiable "instantaneous configurations" that impose totally different types of behavior on persons of different ages. The infant does not suddenly leave off "mewling and puking" to pick up a satchel and go to school. Nor at the other end of life does "the justice, . . . with eyes severe and beard of formal cut" instantly turn into "the lean and slipper'd pantaloon." The changes are gradual; finally, the pantaloon slips through second childishness into "mere oblivion, sans teeth, sans eyes, sans taste, sans everything."[2] Clearly we are dealing here with a continuous process of growth and decay. There is no magic moment at which "everything" disappears. Death is no more a single, clearly delimited, momentary phenomenon than is infancy, adolescence, or middle age. The gradualness of the process of dying is even clearer than it was in Shakespeare's time, for we now know that various parts of the body can go on living for months after its central organization has disintegrated. Some cell lines, in fact, can be continued indefinitely.

The difficulty of identifying a moment of death has always been recognized when dealing with primitive organisms, and the conventional concept has usually not been ap-

---

[2]Shakespeare, *As You Like It*, Act II, Scene vii, ll. 144-166.

plied to organisms that reproduce themselves by simple fission. Death as we know it, so to speak, is characteristic only of differentiated and integrated organisms, and is most typically observed in the land-living vertebrates in which everything that makes life worth living depends on continuous respiratory movements. These, in turn, depend on an intact brain, which itself is dependent on the continuing circulation of properly aerated blood. Under natural conditions, this tripartite, interdependent system fails essentially at one and the same time. Indeed, the moment of failure seems often to be dramatically marked by a singularly violent last gasping breath. Observers of such a climactic agony have found it easy to believe that a special event of some consequence has taken place, that indeed Death has come and Life has gone away. Possibly even some spirit or essence associated with Life has left the body and gone to a better world. In the circumstances surrounding the traditional deathbed, it is scarcely to be wondered at that many of the observers found comfort in personifying the dying process in this way, nor can it be said that the consequences were in any way unfortunate.

Now, however, the constant tinkering of man with his own machinery has made it obvious that death is not really a very easily identifiable event or "configuration." The integrated physiological system does not inevitably fail all at once. Substitutes can be devised for each of the major components and the necessary integration can be provided by a computer. All the traditional vital signs are still there—provided in large part by the machines. Death does not come by inevitable appointment, in Samarra or anywhere else. He must sit patiently in the waiting room until summoned by the doctor or nurse.

Perhaps we should pause before being completely carried away by the metaphor. Has death really been kept waiting by the machines? If so, the doctor must be actively causing death when he turns the machines off. Some doctors, at least, would prefer to avoid the responsibility, and they have therefore proposed a different view of the proc-

ess.[3] They would like to believe that Death has already come for the patient whose vital signs are maintained by machine and that the doctor merely reveals the results of his visit. But if Death has already come, he has certainly come without making his presence known in the usual way. None of the outward and visible signs have occurred—no last gasp, no stopping of the heart, no cooling and stiffening of the limbs. On the other hand, it seems fairly obvious to most people that life under the conditions described (if it really is life) falls seriously short of being worth living.

Is a "Redefinition" of Death Enough?

We must now ask ourselves how much sense it makes to try to deal with this complex set of physiological, social, and ethical variables simply by "redefining" death or by developing new criteria for pronouncing an organism dead. Aside from the esoteric philosophical concerns discussed so far, it must be recognized that practical matters of great moment are at stake. Fewer and fewer people die quietly in their beds while relatives and friends live on, unable to stay the inevitable course. More and more patients are subject to long, continued intervention; antibiotics, intravenous feeding, artificial respiration, and even artificially induced heartbeats sustain an increasingly fictional existence. All this costs money—so much money, in fact, that the retirement income of a surviving spouse may disappear in a few months. There are other costs, less tangible but perhaps more important—for example, the diversion of scarce medical resources from younger people temporarily threatened by acute but potentially curable illnesses. Worst of all is the strain on a family that may have to live for years in close association with a mute, but apparently living, corpse.

An even more disturbing parameter has recently been added to the equation. It appears that parts of the dying body may

[3]H. K. Beecher, *J. Am. Med. Assoc.* 205, 337 (1968).

acquire values greater than the whole. A heartbeat, a kidney, someday even a lung or a liver, can mean all of life for some much younger, more potentially vigorous and happy "donee."

Indeed, it appears that it is primarily this latter set of facts which has led to recent proposals for redefining death. The most prominent proposals place more emphasis on the information-processing capacity of the brain and rather less on the purely mechanical and metabolic activities of the body as a whole than do the present practices. The great practical merit of these proposals is that they place the moment of death somewhat earlier in the continuum of life than the earlier definition did. By so doing, they make it easier for the physician to discontinue therapy while some of what used to be considered "signs of life" are still present, thus sparing relatives, friends, and professional attendants the anguish and the effort of caring for a "person" who has lost most of the attributes of personality. Futhermore, parts of the body which survive death, as newly defined, may be put to other, presumably more important uses, since procedures such as autopsies or removal of organs can be undertaken without being regarded as assaults.

In considering the propriety of developing these new criteria, one may begin by admitting that there is nothing particularly unusual about redefining either a material fact or a nebulous abstraction. Physical scientists are almost continuously engaged in redefining facts by making more and more precise measurements. Taxonomists spend much of their time redefining abstract categories, such as "species," in order to take into account new data or new prejudices. At somewhat rarer intervals, even such great concepts as force, mass, honor, and justice may come up for review.

Nevertheless, in spite of the obvious practical advantages and certain theoretical justifications, redefinition of abstractions can raise some very serious doubts. In the present instance, for example, we are brought face to face with the paradox that the new definitions of death are proposed, at least in part,

because they provide that certain parts of the newly defined dead body will be *less dead* than they have been if the conventional definition were still used. Looked at in this light, the proposed procedure raises serious ethical questions.[4] The supporters of the new proposal are, however, confronted every day by the even more serious practical problems raised by trying to make old rules fit new situations. Faced with a dilemma, they find it easier to urge a redefinition of death than to recognize that life may reach a state such that there is no longer an ethical imperative to preserve it. While one may give his support to the first of these alternatives as a temporary path through a frightening and increasingly complicated wilderness, it might be wise not to congratulate ourselves prematurely.

As our skill in simulating the physiological processes underlying life continues to increase in disproportion to our capacity to maintain its psychological, emotional, or spiritual quality, the difficulty of regarding death as a single, more or less coherent event, resulting in the instantaneous dissolution of the organism as a whole, is likely to become more and more apparent. It may not be premature, therefore, to anticipate some of the questions that will then increasingly press upon us. Some of the consequences of adopting the attitude that death is part of a continuous process that is coextensive (almost) with living may be tentatively outlined as follows.

An unprejudiced look at the biological facts suggests, indeed, that the "life" of a complex vertebrate like man is not a clearly defined entity with sharp discontinuities at both ends. On the contrary, the living human being starts inconspicuously, unconsciously, and at an unknown time, with the conjugation of two haploid cells. In a matter of some hours, this new cell begins to divide. The net number of living cells in the organism continues to increase for perhaps 20 years, then

---

[4]P. Ramsey, in *Updating Life and Death*, D. R. Cutler, ed. (Boston: Beacon, 1969), p. 46; H. Jonas, in *Experimentation with Human Subjects*, P. A. Freund, ed. (New York: Braziller, 1970), pp. 10-11.

begins slowly to decrease. Looked at in this way, life is certainly not an all-or-none phenomenon. Clearly the amount of living matter follows a long trajectory of growth and decline with no very clear beginning and a notably indeterminate end. A similar trajectory can be traced for total energy turnover.

A human life is, of course, far more than a metabolizing mass of organic matter, slavishly obeying the laws of conservation of mass and energy. Particularly interesting are the complex interactions among the individual cells and between the totality and the environment. It is, in fact, this complexity of interaction that gives rise to the concept of human personality or soul.

Whatever metaphors are used to describe the situation, it is clear that it is the complex interactions that make the characteristic human being. The appropriate integration of these interactions is only loosely coupled to the physiological functions of circulation and respiration. The latter continue for a long time after the integrated "personality" has disappeared. Conversely, the natural rhythms of heart and respiration can fail, while the personality remains intact. The complex human organism does not often fail as a unit. The nervous system is, of course, more closely coupled to personality than are the heart and lungs (a fact that is utilized in developing the new definitions of death), but there is clearly something arbitrary in tying the sanctity of life to our ability to detect the electrical potential charges that managed to traverse the impedance of the skull.

If there is no infallible physiological index to what we value about human personality, are we not ultimately forced to make judgments about the intactness and value of the complex interactions themselves?

"Value" of a Life Changes with Value of Complex Interactions

As the complexity and richness of the interactions of an individual human being wax and wane, his "value" can be seen to change in relation to other values. For various reasons it is easier to recognize the process at the beginning than at the end of life. The growing fetus is said to become steadily more valuable with the passage of time:[5] its organization becomes increasingly complex and its potential for continued life increases. Furthermore, its mother invests more in it every day and becomes increasingly aware of and pleased by its presence. Simultaneous with these increases in "value" is the increased "cost" of terminating the existence of the fetus. As a corollary, the longer a pregnancy proceeds, the more reasons are required to justify its termination. Although it may be possible to admire the intellectual ingenuity of Saint Thomas and others who sought to break this continuous process with a series of discontinuous stages and to identify the moment at which the fetus becomes a human being, modern knowledge of the biological process involved renders all such efforts simply picturesque. The essential novelty resides in the formation of the chromosomal pattern—the rest of the development is best regarded as the working out of a complicated tautology.

At the other end of life the process is reversed: the life of the dying patient becomes steadily less complicated and rich, and, as a result, less worth living or preserving. The pain and suffering involved in maintaining what is left are inexorably mounting, while the benefits enjoyed by the patient himself, or that he can in any way confer on those around him, are just as inexorably declining. As the costs mount higher and higher and the benefits become smaller and smaller, one may well begin to wonder what the point of it all is. These are the unhappy facts of the matter, and we will have to face them sooner or later. Indeed, attempts to face the facts are already being made, but usually in a gingerly and incomplete fashion. As we have seen, one way to protect ourselves is to introduce imaginary discontinuities into what are, in fact, continuous processes.

A similar kind of self-deception may be involved in attempts to find some crucial

---

[5] D. Callahan, *Abortion: Law, Choice and Morality* (New York: Macmillan, 1970).

differences among the three following possibilities that are open to the physician attending the manifestly dying patient.

1) Use all possible means (including the "extraordinary measures" noted by the Pope) to keep the patient alive.

2) Discontinue the extraordinary measures but continue "ordinary therapy."

3) Take some "positive" step to hasten the termination of life or speed its downward trajectory.

Almost everyone now admits that there comes a time when it is proper to abandon procedure 1 and shift to procedure 2 although there is a good deal of disagreement about determining the moment itself. There is much less agreement about moving to procedure 3, although the weight of opinion seems to be against ever doing so.

The more one thinks of actual situations, however, the more one wonders if there is a valid distinction between allowing a person to die and hastening the downward course of life. Sometimes the words "positive" and "negative" are used, with the implication that it is all right to take away from the patient something that would help him to live but wrong to give him something that will help him to die.

The intent appears to be the same in the two cases, and it is the intent that would seem to be significant. Furthermore, one wonders if the dividing point between positive and negative in this domain is any more significant than the position of zero on the Fahrenheit scale. In practice, a physician may find it easier not to turn on a respirator or a cardiac pacemaker than to turn them off once they have been connected, but both the intents and the results are identical in the two cases. To use an analogy with mathematics, subtracting one from one would seem to be the same as not adding one to zero.

Squirm as we may to avoid the inevitable, it seems time to admit to ourselves that there is simply no hiding place and that we must shoulder the responsibility of deciding to act in such a way as to hasten the declining trajectories of some lives, while doing our best to slow down the decline of others. And we have to do this on the basis of some judgment on the quality of the lives in question.

Clearly the calculations cannot be made exclusively or even primarily on crude monetary or economic criteria. Substantial value must be put on intangibles of various kinds—the love, affection, and respect of those who once knew the fully living individual will bulk large in the equation. Another significant parameter will be the sanctity accorded to any human life, however attenuated and degraded it may have become. Respect for human life as such is fundamental to our society, and this respect must be preserved. But this respect need not be based on some concept of absolute value. Just as we recognize that an individual human life is not infinite in duration, we should now face the fact that its value varies with time and circumstance. It is a heavy responsibility that our advancing command over life has placed on us.

It has already been noted that in many nations, and increasingly in the United States, men and women have shouldered much the same kind of responsibility—but apparently with considerably less horror and dismay—at the beginning of the life-span. In spite of some theological misgivings and medical scruples, most societies now condone the destruction of a living fetus in order to protect the life of the mother. Recent developments have greatly broadened the "indications" to include what is essentially the convenience of the mother and the protection of society against the dangers of overpopulation.

A relatively new, but very interesting, development is basing the decision of whether or not to abort purely on an assessment of the quality of the life likely to be lived by the human organism in question. This development has been greatly enhanced by advances in the technique of amniocentesis, with its associated methods for determining the chromosomal pattern and biochemical competence of the unborn baby. Decisions made on such grounds are difficult, if not impossible, to differentiate, in principle, from decisions made by the Spartans and other earlier societies to expose to nature those infants born with manifest anatomical defects. We are being driven toward the ethics of an earlier period by the inexorable logic of the situation, and it may only increase our discomfort without changing our views to reflect that historians[6] and moralists[7] both agree that the abolition of infanticide was perhaps the greatest ethical achievement of early Christianity.

Issues Cannot Be Settled by Absolute Standards

Callahan, in *Abortion: Law, Choice and Morality*, has reviewed all the biological, social, legal, and moral issues that bear on decisions to terminate life in its early stages and argues convincingly that the issue cannot be settled by appeals to absolute rights or standards. Of particular importance for our purposes, perhaps, is his discussion of the principle of the "sanctity of life," since opposition to liberalizing the abortion laws is so largely based on the fear of weakening respect for the dignity of life in general. It is particularly reassuring, therefore, that Callahan finds no objective evidence to support this contention. Indeed, in several countries agitation for the liberalization of abortion laws has proceeded simultaneously with efforts to strengthen respect for life in other areas—the abolition of capital punishment, for example. Indeed, Callahan's major thesis is that modern moral decisions can seldom rest on a single, paramount principle; they must be made individually, after a careful weighing of the facts and all the nuances in each particular case.

The same considerations that apply to abortion would appear to apply, in principle, to decisions at the other end of the life-span. In practice, however, it has proven difficult to approach the latter decisions with quite the same degree of detachment as those involving the life and death of an unborn

embryo. It is not easy to overlook the fact that the dying patient possesses at least the remnants of a personality that developed over many decades and that involved a complicated set of interrelationships with other human beings. In the case of the embryo, such relationships are only potential, and it is easier to ignore the future than to overlook the past. It can be argued, however, that it should be easier to terminate a life whose potentialities have all been realized than to interrupt a pregnancy the future of which remains to be unfolded.

Once it is recognized that the process of dying under modern conditions is at least partially controlled by the decisions made by individual human beings, it becomes necessary to think rather more fully and carefully about what human beings should be involved and what kinds of considerations should be taken into account in making the decisions.

Traditionally it has been the physician who has made the decisions, and he has made them almost exclusively on his own view of what is best for the patient. Only under conditions of special stress, where available medical resources have been clearly inadequate to meet current needs, has the physician taken the welfare of third parties or "society" into account in deciding whether to give or withhold therapy. Until recently, such conditions were only encountered on the battlefield or in times of civilian catastrophe such as great fires, floods, or shipwrecks. Increasingly, however, the availability of new forms of therapy that depend on inherently scarce resources demands that decisions be made about distribution. In other words, the physician who is considering putting a patient on an artificial kidney may sometimes be forced to consider the needs of other potential users of the same device. The situation is even more difficult when the therapeutic device is an organ from another human being. In some communities, the burden of such decisions is shifted from a single physician to a group or committee that may contain nonmedical members.

These dramatic instances are often thought of as being special cases without much re-

[6]W. E. H. Lecky, *History of European Morals from Augustus to Charlemagne* (New York: Appleton, 1870), vol. 1.

[7]H. Sidgwick, *Outlines of the History of Ethics* (London: Macmillan, 1886; Boston: Beacon, 1960).

lationship to ordinary life and death. On the other hand, one may look upon them as simply more brilliantly colored examples of what is generally true but is not always so easy to discern. Any dying patient whose life is unduly prolonged imposes serious costs on those immediately around him and, in many cases, on a larger, less clearly defined "society." It seems probable that, as these complex interrelationships are increasingly recognized, society will develop procedures for sharing the necessary decisions more widely, following the examples of the committee structure now being developed to deal with the dramatic cases.

It is not only probable, but highly desirable that society should proceed with the greatest caution and deliberation in proposing procedures that in any serious way threaten the traditional sanctity of the individual life. As a consequence, society will certainly move very slowly in developing formal arrangements for taking into account the interests of others in life-and-death decisions. It may not be improper, however, to suggest one step that could be taken right now. Such a step might ease the way for many dying patients without impairing the sanctity or dignity of the individual life: instead, it should be enhanced. I refer here to the possibility of changing social attitudes and laws that now restrain the individual from taking an intelligent interest in his own death.

The Judeo-Christian tradition has made suicide a sin of much the same character as murder. The decline of orthodox theology has tended to reduce the sinfulness of the act, but the feeling still persists that there must be something wrong with somebody who wants to end his own life. As a result, suicide, when it is not recognized as a sin, is regarded as a symptom of serious mental illness. In this kind of atmosphere, it is almost impossible for a patient to work out with his doctor a rational and esthetically satisfactory plan for conducting the terminating phase of his life. Only rarely can a great individualist like George Eastman or Percy Bridgman[8] transcend the prevailing mores to show us a rational way out of current prejudice. Far from injuring the natural rights of the individual, such a move can be regarded as simply a restoration of a right once greatly valued by our Roman ancestors, who contributed so much to the "natural law" view of human rights. Seneca,[9] perhaps the most articulate advocate of the Roman view that death should remain under the individual's control, put the matter this way: "To death alone it is due that life is not a punishment, that erect beneath the frowns of fortune, I can preserve my mind unshaken and master of myself."

---

[8]G. Holton, *Bull. At. Sci.* 18 (No. 2), 22 (February 1962).

[9]Seneca, *Ad Marciam, de Consolatione*, XX, translated by W. E. H. Lecky, in *History of European Morals from Augustus to Charlemagne*, vol. 1, p. 228.

6

Death
as an event
LEON R. KASS

As I understand R. S. Morison's argument, it consists of these parts, although presented in different order. First: He notes that we face serious practical problems as a result of our unswerving adherence to the principle, "always prolong life." Second: Although *some* of these problems could be solved by updating the "definition of death," such revisions are scientifically and philosophically unsound. Third: The reason for this is that life and death are part of a continuum; it will prove impossible, in practice, to identify any border between them because theory tells us that no such border exists. Thus: We need to abandon both the idea of death as a concrete event and the search for its definition; instead, we must face the fact that our practical problems can only be solved by difficult judgments, based upon a complex cost-benefit analysis, concerning the value of the lives that might or might not be prolonged.

I am in agreement with Morison only on the first point. I think he leads us into philosophical, scientific, moral, and political error. Let me try to show how.

Some Basic Distinctions

The difficulties begin in Morison's beginning, in his failure to distinguish clearly among aging, dying, and dead. His statement that "dying is seen as a long-drawn-out process that begins when life itself begins" would be remarkable, if true, since it would render dying synonymous with living. One consequence would be that murder could be considered merely a farsighted form of euthanasia, a gift to the dying of an early exit from their miseries.[1] But we need not ponder these riddles, because what Morison has done is to confuse dying with aging. Aging (or senescence) apparently does begin early in life (though probably not at conception), but there is no clear evidence that it is ever the cause of death. As Sir Peter Medawar has pointed out:[2]

> Senescence, then, may be defined as that change of the bodily faculties and sensibilities and energies which accompanies aging, and which renders the individual progressively more likely to die from accidental causes of random incidence. Strictly speaking, the word "accidental" is redundant, for all deaths are in some degree accidental. No death is wholly "natural"; no one dies *merely* of the burden of the years.

[1]This calls to mind the following exchange from Shakespeare's *Julius Caesar*, immediately following Caesar's assassination (Act III, scene i, ll. 101-105): "Casca: Why, he that cuts off twenty years of life/Cuts off so many years of fearing death. Brutus: Grant that, and then is death a benefit. So are we Caesar's friends, that have abridg'd/His time of fearing death."

[2]P. B. Medawar, *The Uniqueness of the Individual* (New York: Basic Books, 1957), p. 55.

As distinguished from aging, dying is the process leading from the incidence of the "accidental" cause of death to and beyond some border, however ill-defined, after which the organism (or its body) may be said to be dead.

Morison observes, correctly, that death and life are abstractions, not things. But to hold that "livingness" or "life" is the property shared by living things, and thus to abstract this property *in thought*, does not necessarily lead one to hold that "life" or "livingness" is a thing in itself with an existence apart from the objects said to "possess" it. For reification and personification of life and death, I present no argument. For the adequacy of the abstractions themselves, we must look to the objects described.

What about these objects: living, nonliving, and dead things? A person who believes that living things and nonliving things do not differ in kind would readily dismiss "death" as a meaningless concept. It is hard to be sure that this is not Morison's view. When he says, "These objects *we elect to call* 'living things' [emphasis added]," is he merely being overly formal in his presentation, or is he deliberately intimating that the distinction between living and nonliving is simply a convention of human speech, and not inherent in the nature of things? My suspicions are increased by his suggestion that "substitutes can be devised for each of the major components [of a man], and the necessary integration can be provided by a computer." A living organism comprising mechanical parts with computerized "integration"? Morison should be asked to clarify this point: Does he hold that there is or is not a *natural* distinction between living and nonliving things? Are his arguments about the fallacy of misplaced concreteness of "death" and "life" merely secondary and derivative from his belief that living and nonliving or dead objects do not differ in kind?[3]

If there is a natural distinction between living and nonliving things, what is the proper way of stating the nature of that difference? What is the real difference between something alive and that "same" something dead? To this crucial question, I shall return later. For the present, it is sufficient to point out that the real source of our confusion about death is probably our confusion about living things. The death of an organism is not understandable because its "aliveness" is not understood except in terms of nonliving matter and motion.[4]

One further important distinction must be observed. We must keep separate two distinct and crucial questions facing the physician: (i) When, if ever, is a person's life no longer worth prolonging? and (ii) When is a person in fact dead? The first question translates, in practice, to: When is it permissible or desirable for a physician to withhold or withdraw treatment so that a patient (still alive) may be allowed to die? The second question translates, in practice, to: When does the physician pronounce the (ex)patient fit for burial? Morison is concerned only with the first question. He commendably condemns attempts to evade this moral issue by definitional wizardry. But regardless of how one settles the question of whether and what kind of life should be prolonged, one will still need criteria for recognizing the end. The determination of death may not be a very interesting question, but it is an extremely important one. At stake are matters of homicide and inheritance, of burial and religious observance, and many others.

In considering the definition and determination of death, we note that there is a difference between the meaning of an abstract concept such as death (or mass or gravity or time) and the operations used to determine or measure it. There are two "definitions" that should not be confused. There is the conceptual "definition" or meaning and the operational "definition" or mean-

---

[3]Would A. N. Whitehead himself have considered life and death as exemplifying his "fallacy of misplaced concreteness"? I seriously doubt it. See, for example, two of his essays, "Nature Lifeless" and "Nature Alive" [in *Modes of Thought* (New York: Free Press, 1968), pp. 127-147, 148-169]; and *Science and the Modern World* (New York: Mentor, 1948).

[4]For an excellent discussion of the problematic status of "life" in modern scientific thought, see H. Jonas [*The Phenomenon of Life: Toward a Philosophical Biology* (New York: Dell, 1968)], especially the first essay (pp. 7-37).

ing. I think it would be desirable to use "definition of death" only with respect to the first, and to speak of "criteria for determining that a death has occurred" for the second. Thus, the various proposals for updating the definition of death,[5] their own language to the contrary, are not offering a new definition of death but merely refining the procedure stating that a man has died. Although there is much that could be said about these proposals, my focus here is on Morison's challenge to the concept of death as an event, and to the possibility of determining it.

The Concept of Death

There is no need to abandon the traditional understanding of the concept of death: Death is the transition from the state of being alive to the state of being dead. Rather than emphasize the opposition between death and life, an opposition that invites Morison to see the evils wrought by personification, we should concentrate, for our purposes, on the opposition between death and birth (or conception). Both are transitions, however fraught with ambiguities. Notice that the notion of transition leaves open the question of whether the change is abrupt or gradual and whether it is continuous or discontinuous. But these questions about *when* and *how* cannot be adequately discussed without some substantive understanding of *what* it is that dies.

What dies is the organism as a whole. It is this death, the death of the individual human being, that is important for physicians and for the community, not the "death" of organs or cells, which are mere parts.

The ultimate, most serious effect of injury is death. Necrosis is death but with this limitation; it is death of cells or tissue *within a living organism*. Thus we differentiate between *somatic death*, which is death of the whole, and *necrosis*, which is death of the part.

From a tissue viewpoint, even when the whole individual dies, he dies part by part and at different times. For instance, nerve cells die within a few minutes after circulation stops, whereas cartilage cells may remain alive for several days. Because of this variation in cellular susceptibility to injury, it is virtually impossible to say just when all the component parts of the body have died. Death of composite whole, the organism as an *integrated* functional unit, is a different matter. Within three or four minutes after the heart stops beating, hypoxia ordinarily leads to irreversible changes of certain vital tissues, particularly those of the central nervous system, and this causes the *individual* to die.[6]

The same point may perhaps be made clearer by means of an anecdote. A recent discussion on the subject of death touched on the postmortem perpetuation of cell lines in tissue culture. Someone commented, "For all I know, I myself might wind up in one of those tissue-culture flasks." The speaker was asked to reconsider whether he really meant "I myself" or merely some of his cells.

Is Death a Discrete Event?

A proof that death is not a discrete event[7]—that life and death are part of a continuum—would thus require evidence that the organism as a whole died progressively and continuously. This evidence Morison does not provide. Instead he calls attention to the continuity of the different ages of man and to growth and decay, but he does not show that any of these changes are analogous to the transition of death. The

---

[5]The most prominent proposal is contained in the report of the ad hoc committee of the Harvard Medical School, H. K. Beecher, chairman [*J. Am. Med. Assoc.* 205, 337 (1968)].

[6]H. C. Hopps, *Principles of Pathology* (New York: Appleton-Century-Crofts, 1959), p. 78. This passage also suggests, in opposition to Morison, that the notion of death as a discrete event has a distinguished medical and scientific history and is not simply an artistic, literary, or legal fiction. The dead body that was lately alive is a concrete fact, a fact understood to some extent even by animals. One must wonder about the sort of scientific understanding of the world which tells us that the apparent change in state from a man alive to a man dead is but an illusion. If this is an illusion, then what is not?

[7]To say that something is a discrete event does not mean that it need be instantaneous. Moreover, even instantaneous events take time, for how long is an instant?

continuity between childhood and adolescence says nothing about whether the transition between life and death is continuous. He also mentions the "post-mortem" viability of cells and organs. He says that "various parts of the body can go on living for months after its central organization has disintegrated." It should be clear by now that the viability of *parts* has no necessary bearing on the question of the whole. His claim that the beginning of life is not a discrete event ("the living human being starts inconspicuously, unconsciously, and at an unknown time, with the conjugation of two haploid cells"), even granting the relevance of the analogy with death, is really only a claim that we do not see and hence cannot note the time of the event. Morison himself more than once identifies the beginning as the discrete event in which egg and sperm unite to form the zygote, with its unique chromosomal pattern.

Only in a few places does Morison even approach the question of the death of the organism as a whole. But his treatment only serves to discredit the question. ["The nervous system is, of course, more closely coupled to personality than are the heart and lungs (a fact that is utilized in developing the new definitions of death), but there is clearly something arbitrary in tying the sanctity of life to our ability to detect the electrical potential charges that managed to traverse the impedence of the skull."] Lacking a concept of the organism as a whole, and confusing the concept of death with the criteria for determining it, Morison errs by trying to identify the whole with one of its parts and by seeking a single "infallible physiological index" to human personhood. One might as well try to identify a watch with either its mainspring or its hands; the watch is neither of these, yet it is "dead" without either. Why is the concept of the organism as a whole so difficult to grasp? Is it because we have lost or discarded, in our reductionist biology, all notions of organism, of whole?[8]

Morison also attempts to discredit the

"last gasp" as indicative of death as a discrete event: "Observers of such a climactic agony have found it easy to believe that a special event of some consequence has taken place, that indeed Death has come and Life has gone away." But if we forget about reification, personification, spirits fleeing, Death coming, Life leaving—is this not a visible sign of the death of the organism as a whole? This is surely a reasonable belief, and one which, if it now seems unreasonable, seems so only because of our tinkering.

Morison credits "the constant tinkering of man with his own machinery" for making it "obvious that death is not really a very easily identifiable event. . . ." To be sure, our tinkering has, in some cases, made it difficult to decide when the moment of death occurs, but does it really reveal that no such moment exists? Tinkering can often obscure rather than clarify reality, and I think this is one such instance. I agree that we are now in doubt about some borderline cases. But is the confusion ours or nature's? This is a crucial question. If the indeterminacy lies in nature, as Morison believes, then all criteria for determining death are arbitrary and all moments of death a fiction. If, however, the indeterminacy lies in *our* confusion and ignorance, then we must simply do the best we can in approximating the time of transition.

We are likely to remain ignorant of the true source of the indeterminacy. If so, then there is absolutely no good reason for insisting that it is nature's, and at least two good reasons for blaming ourselves. (i) It is foolish to abandon or discredit nature as a standard in matters of fundamental human importance: birth, death, health, sickness, origin. In the absence of this standard, we are left to our tastes and our prejudices about the most important human matters; we can never have knowledge, but, at best, only social policy developed out of a welter of opinion. (ii) We might thereby be permitted to see how we are responsible for confusing ourselves about crucial matters, how technological intervention (with all its blessings) can destroy the visible manifestations and signs of natural phenomena, the recognition of which is indispensible to human com-

---

[8]See works by Whitehead (*3*) and by Jonas (*4*) for consideration of the problem of organism.

munity. Death was once recognizable by any ordinary observer who could see (or feel or hear). Today, in some difficult cases, we require further technological manipulation (from testing of reflexes to the electroencephalogram) to make manifest latent signs of a phenomenon, the visible signs of which an earlier intervention has obscured.

In the light of these remarks, I would argue that we should not take our bearings from the small number of unusual cases in which there is doubt. In most cases, there is no doubt. There is no real need to blur the distinction between a man alive and a man dead or to undermine the concept of death as an event. Rather, we should ask, in the light of our traditional concepts (though not necessarily with traditional criteria), whether the persons in the twilight zone are alive or not, and find criteria on the far side of the twilight zone in order to remove any suspicion that a man may be pronounced dead while he is yet alive.

Determining Whether a Man Has Died

In my opinion, the question, "Is he dead?" can still be treated as a question of fact, albeit one with great moral and social consequences. I hold it to be a medical-scientific question in itself, not only in that physicians answer it for us. Morison treats it largely as a social-moral question. This is because, as I indicated above, he does not distinguish the question of when a man is dead from the question of when his life is not worth prolonging. Thus, there is a conjoined issue: Is the determination of death a matter of the true, or a matter of the useful or good?

The answer to this difficult question turns, in part, on whether or not medicine and science are in fact capable of determining death. Therefore, the question of the true versus the good (or useful) will be influenced by what is in fact true and knowable about death as a medical "fact." The question of the true versus the good (or useful) will also be influenced by the truth about what is good or useful, and by what people think to be good and useful. But we can and should also ask, "What is the truth?" about which one of these concerns—scientific

truth or social good—is uppermost in the minds of people who write and speak about the determination of death.

To turn to Morison's essay in the light of the last question, it seems clear that his major concern is with utility. He abandons what he calls "esoteric philosophical concerns," his own characterization of his scientific discussion about death, to turn to "practical matters of great moment." Despite his vigorous scientific criticisms of the proposals for "redefining" death, he thinks they have "great practical merit," and thus he does not really oppose them as he would any other wrong idea. Am I unfair in thinking that his philosophical and scientific criticism of the concept of death is really animated by a desire to solve certain practical problems? Would the sweeping away of the whole concept of death for the unstated purpose of forcing a cost-benefit analysis of the value of prolonging lives be any less disingenuous than a redefinition of death for the sake of obtaining organs?

Morison properly criticizes those who would seek to define a man out of existence for the purpose of getting at his organs or of saving on scarce resources.[9] He points out

---

[9]Such second-party benefits are, without embarrassment, admitted to be a major (if not *the* major) reason for updating the criteria for pronouncing a man dead [See especially the opening paragraph of the Harvard committee report (5)]. In support of the new criteria, Beecher has written: "[I]t is within our power to take a giant step forward in relieving the shortages of donor material. . . . The crucial point is agreement that brain death is death indeed, even though the heart continues to beat." And again: "Thus, if these new criteria of brain death are accepted, the tissues and organs now consigned to the grave can be utilized to restore those who, although critically ill, can still be saved" [*Daedalus* (Spring 1969), p. 291 and p. 294]. Indeed, the new criteria have been so linked with transplantation that one physician has publicly referred to them as a "new definition of heart donor eligibility" [D. D. Rutstein, *Daedalus* (Spring 1969), p. 526]. It can be only regarded as unsavory and dangerous, both for medicine and for the community at large, to permit the determination of one person's death to be contaminated by a consideration of the needs of others. Having said this, however, I hasten to add that the redefiners also think that their criteria do happen to fit the

that the redefiners take unfair advantage of the commonly shared belief that a body, once declared dead, can be buried or otherwise used. His stand here is certainly courageous. But does he not show an excess of courage, indeed rashness, when he would decree death itself out of existence for the sake of similar social goods? Just how rash will be seen when his specific principles of social good are examined.

The Ethics of Prolonging Life

We are all in Morison's debt for inviting us to consider the suffering that often results from slavish and limitless attempts to prolong life. But there is no need to abandon traditional ethics to deal with this problem. The Judeo-Christian tradition, which teaches us the duty of preserving life, does not itself hold life to be the absolute value. The medical tradition, until very recently, shared this view. Indeed, medicine's purpose was originally *health*, not simply the unlimited prolongation of life or the conquest of disease and death. Both traditions looked upon death as a natural part of life, not as an unmitigated evil or as a sign of the physician's failure. We sorely need to recover this more accepting attitude toward death[10] and, with it, a greater concern for the human needs of the dying patient. We need to keep company with the dying and to help them cope with terminal illness.[11] We must learn to desist from those

useless technological interventions and institutional practices that deny to the dying what we most owe them—a good end. These purposes could be accomplished in large measure by restoring to medical practice the ethic of allowing a person to die.[12]

But the ethic of allowing a person to die is based solely on a consideration of the welfare of the dying patient himself, rather than on a consideration of benefits that accrue to others. This is a crucial point. It is one thing to take one's bearings from the patient and his interests and attitudes, to protect his dignity and his right to a good death against the onslaught of machinery and institutionalized loneliness; it is quite a different thing to take one's bearings from the interests of, or costs and benefits to, relatives or society. The first is in keeping with the physician's duty to act as the loyal agent of his patient; the second is a perversion of that duty, because it renders the physician, in this decisive test of his loyalty, merely an agent of society, and ultimately, her executioner. The first upholds and preserves the respect for human life and personal dignity; the second sacrifices these on the ever-shifting altar of public opinion.

To be sure, the physician always operates within the boundaries set by the community —by its allocation of resources, by its laws, by its values. Each physician, as well as the profession as a whole, should perhaps work to improve these boundaries and especially to see that adequate resources are made available to better the public health. But in his relations with individual patients, the physician must serve the interest of the patient. Medicine cannot retain trustworthiness or trust if it does otherwise.[13]

---

fact of death. The authors claim that they are true criteria, capable of scientific, and not simply utilitarian, justification. All the experience to date in using these criteria for pronouncing a patient dead supports the validity of this claim.

[10]More generally, modern biomedical science needs to come to terms with human mortality. With Presidents making the conquest of cancer a national goal, and with others proposing crash programs to conquer genetic disease, heart disease, stroke, and aging (to each his favorite malady), medicine will soon be called upon to do battle with death itself, as if death were just one more disease. Fortunately, such a battle will not succeed, for death is not only inevitable, but also biologically, psychologically, and spiritually desirable.

[11]E. Kübler-Ross, *On Death and Dying* (New York: Macmillan, 1969).

[12]See P. Ramsey [*The Patient as Person: Explorations in Medical Ethics* (New Haven, Conn.: Yale Univ. Press, 1970), pp. 113-164] for an excellent account of this ethic.

[13]The exceptional cases cited by Morison (battlefield or civilian catastrophes) do not provide a precedent for allowing considerations of "the welfare of third parties or 'society'" to intrude upon the doctor's treatment of his patient under ordinary circumstances. What is special about these cases is that the survival of the entire group or community, as a group or community, is in jeopardy,

On this crucial matter, Morison seems to want to have it both ways. On the one hand, he upholds the interest of the deteriorating individual himself. Morison wants him to exercise a greater control over his own death, "to work out with his doctor a rational and esthetically satisfactory plan for conducting the terminating phase of his life." On the other hand, there are hints that Morison would like to see other interests served as well. For example, he says: "It appears that parts of the dying body may acquire values greater than the whole." Greater to whom? Certainly not to the patient. We are asked to consider that "Any dying patient whose life is unduly prolonged imposes serious costs on those immediately around him and, in many cases, on a larger, less clearly defined 'society.' " But cannot the same be said for any patient whose life is prolonged? Or is Morison suggesting that the "unduliness" of "undue" prolongation is to be defined in terms of social costs? In a strictly patient-centered ethic of allowing a person to die, these costs to others would not enter—except perhaps as they might influence the patient's own judgment about prolonging his own life.

In perhaps the most revealing passage, in which he merges both the interests of patient and society, Morison notes:

> . . . the life of the dying patient becomes steadily less complicated and rich, and, as a result, less worth living or preserving. The pain and suffering involved in maintaining

what is left are inexorably mounting, while the benefits enjoyed by the patient himself, or that he can in any way confer on those around him, are just as inexorably declining. As the costs mount higher and higher and the benefits become smaller and smaller, one may well begin to wonder what the point of it all is. These are the unhappy facts of the matter, and we have to face them sooner or later.

What are the implications of this analysis of costs and benefits? What should we do when we face these "unhappy facts"? The implication is clear: We must take, as the new "moment," the point at which the rising cost and declining benefit curves intersect, the time when the costs of keeping someone alive outweigh the value of his life. I suggest that it is impossible, both in principle and in practice, to locate such a moment, dangerous to try, and dangerously misleading to suggest otherwise. One simply cannot write an equation for the value of a person's life, let alone for comparing two or more lives. Life is incommensurable with the cost of maintaining it, despite Morison's suggestion that each be entered as one term in an equation.[14]

Morison's own analogy—abortion—provides the best clue as to the likely consequences of a strict adoption of his suggestions. I know he would find these consequences as abhorrent as I. No matter what

---

not simply that they represent "conditions of special stress where available medical resources are clearly inadequate to meet current needs." There is an overriding, acknowledged single principle, the survival of the group, which justifies the practice of "triage" or "disaster medicine" under conditions of battle, great fires, floods, or shipwrecks. Those who are most able to be returned to function and most able, when functioning again, to save others are treated first. No such danger to community safety or survival is entailed by the ordinary (though by no means simple or trivial) problems that result from the usual scarcity of medical resources. See Ramsey (*12*, pp. 256-259) and P. A. Freund, *Daedalus* (Spring 1969), pp. xiii-xiv.

[14]Morison writes: "Another significant parameter will be the sanctity *accorded to* any human life [emphasis added]." Life either has sanctity or it does not. Sanctity cannot be given or taken away by human accord (indeed, "sanctity" implies and requires "the sacred" and the divine), although men can, of course, choose to deny or ignore that human life possesses it. The difficulties and dangers of the cost-benefit approach to matters of life and death would not be lessened by placing the decisions in the hands of public committees. A widely-discussed citizens' committee in Seattle, which selected, on grounds including "social worth," from many medically fit candidates those who could use the few artificial kidney machines, has been disbanded. Its members felt incapable of judging the comparative value of individual lives when life and death are at stake. The problem resides not in any deficiencies of the Seattle citizens, but in the human impossibility of their task.

one can say in favor of abortion, one can't say that it is done for the benefit of the fetus. His interests are sacrificed to those of his mother or of society at large. The analogous approach to the problem of the dying, the chronically ill, the elderly, the vegetating, the hopelessly psychotic, the weak, the infirm, the retarded—and all others whose lives might be deemed "no longer worth preserving"—points not toward suicide, but toward murder. Our age has witnessed the result of one such social effort to dispense with "useless lives."

To be fair, in the end, Morison explicitly suggests only that we make acceptable the practices of suicide and assisted suicide, or euthanasia. But in offering this patient-centered suggestion for reform, he challenges the ethics of medical practice, which has always distinguished between allowing to die and deliberately killing. Morison questions the validity of this distinction: "The intent appears to be the same in the two cases, and it is the intent that would seem to be significant." But the intent is not the same, although the outcome may be. In the one case, the intent is to desist from engaging in useless "treatments" precisely because they are no longer treatments, and to engage instead in the positive acts of giving comfort to and keeping company with the dying patient. In the other case, the intent is indeed to directly hasten the patient's death. The agent of the death in the first case is the patient's disease; in the second case, his physician. The distinction seems to me to be valuable and worth preserving.

Nevertheless, it may be true that the notion of a death with dignity encompasses, under such unusual conditions as protracted, untreatable pain, the right to have one's death directly hastened. It may be an extreme act of love on the part of a spouse or a friend to administer a death-dealing drug to a loved one in such agony. In time, such acts of mercy killing may be legalized.[15] But when and if this happens, we should insist upon at least this qualification: The hastening of the end should never be undertaken for anyone's benefit but the dying patient's. Indeed, we should insist that he spontaneously demand such assistance while of sound mind, or, if he were incapable of communication at the terminal stage, that he have made previous and very explicit arrangements for such contingencies. But we might also wish to insist upon a second qualification—that the physician not participate in the hastening. Such a qualification would uphold a cardinal principle of medical ethics: Doctors must not kill.

Summary

1) We have no need to abandon either the concept of death as an event or the efforts to set forth reasonable criteria for determining that a man has indeed died.

2) We need to recover both an attitude that is more accepting of death and a greater concern for the human needs of the dying patient. But we should not contaminate these concerns with the interests of relatives, potential transplant recipients, or "society." To do so would be both wrong and dangerous.

3) We should pause to note some of the heavy costs of technological progress in medicine: the dehumanization of the end of life, both for those who die and for those who live on; and the befogging of the minds of intelligent and moral men with respect to the most important human matters.[16]

---

[15]Strictly speaking, I doubt if we could establish the *right* to be mercifully killed. Rights imply duties, and I doubt that we can make killing the *duty* of a friend or loved one.

[16]I am genuinely grateful to R. S. Morison for his stimulating and provocative essay. He has helped me begin to see more clearly what some of the serious and important questions are.

III.
The "Naturalness"
of Death

7

The indignity
of
'death with dignity'
PAUL RAMSEY

NEVER ONE am I to use an ordinary title when an extraordinary one will do as well! Besides, I mean to suggest that there is an additional insult besides death itself heaped upon the dying by our ordinary talk about "death with dignity." Sometimes that is said even to be a human "right"; and what should a decent citizen do but insist on enjoying his rights? That might be his duty (if there is any such right), to the commonwealth, to the human race or some other collective entity; or at least, embracing that "right" and dying rationally would exhibit a proper respect for the going concept of a rational man. So "The Indignity of Death" would not suffice for my purposes, even though all I shall says depends on understanding the contradiction death poses to the unique worth of an individual human life.

The genesis of the following reflections may be worth noting. A few years ago,[1] I embraced what I characterized as the oldest morality there is (no "new morality") concerning responsibility toward the dying: the

acceptance of death, stopping our medical interventions for all sorts of good, human reasons, *only* companying with the dying in their final passage. Then suddenly it appeared that altogether too many people were agreeing with me. That caused qualms. As a Southerner born addicted to lost causes, it seemed I now was caught up in a triumphal social trend. As a controversialist in ethics, I found agreement from too many sides. As a generally happy prophet of the doom facing the modern age, unless there is a sea-change in norms of action, it was clear from these premises that anything divers people agree to must necessarily be superficial if not wrong.

Today, when divers people draw the same warm blanket of "allowing to die" or "death with dignity" close up around their shoulders against the dread of that cold night, their various feet are showing. Exposed beneath our growing agreement to that "philosophy of death and dying" may be significantly different "philosophies of life"; and in the present age that agreement may reveal that these interpretations of human life are increasingly mundane, naturalistic, antihumanistic when measured by *any* genuinely "humanistic" esteem for the individual human being.

These "philosophical" ingredients of any view of death and dying I want to make prominent by speaking of "The Indignity of 'Death with Dignity'." Whatever practical

---

[1] Paul Ramsey, "On (Only) Caring for the Dying," *The Patient as Person* (New Haven: Yale University Press, 1971).

agreement there may be, or "guidelines" proposed to govern contemporary choice or practice, these are bound to be dehumanizing unless at the same time we bring to bear great summit points and sources of insight in mankind's understanding of mankind (be it Christian or other religious humanism, or religiously-dependent but not explicitly religious humanism, or, if it is possible, a true humanism that is neither systematically nor historically dependent on any religious outlook).

Death with Dignity Ideologies

There is nobility and dignity in caring for the dying, but not in dying itself. "To be a therapist to a dying patient makes us aware of the uniqueness of each individual in this vast sea of humanity."[2] It is more correct to say that a therapist brings to the event, from some other source, an awareness of the uniqueness, the once-for-allness of an individual life-span as part of an "outlook" and "on-look" upon the vast sea of humanity. In any case, that is the reflected glory and dignity of caring for the dying, that we are or become aware of the unique life here ending. The humanity of such human caring is apt to be more sensitive and mature if we do not lightly suppose that it is an easy thing to convey dignity to the dying. That certainly cannot be done simply by withdrawing tubes and stopping respirators or not thumping hearts. At most, those omissions can only be prelude to companying with the dying in their final passage, if we are fortunate enough to share with them —they in moderate comfort—those interchanges that are in accord with the dignity and nobility of mankind. Still, however noble the manifestations of caring called for, however unique the individual life, we finally must come to the reality of death, and must ask, what can possibly be the meaning of "death with dignity"?

At most we convey only the liberty to die with human dignity; we can provide some of the necessary but not sufficient conditions. If the dying die with a degree of nobility it will be mostly their doing in doing their own dying. I fancy their task was

easier when death as a human event meant that special note was taken of the last words of the dying—even humorous ones, as in the case of the Roman Emperor who said as he expired, "I Deify." A human countenance may be discerned in death accepted with serenity. So also there is a human countenance behind death with defiance. "Do not go gentle into that good night," wrote Dylan Thomas. "Old age should rage and burn against the close of day; Rage Rage against the dying of the light." But the human countenance has been removed from most modern understandings of death.

We do not begin to keep human community with the dying if we interpose between them and us most of the current notions of "death with dignity." Rather do we draw closer to them if and only if our conception of "dying with dignity" encompasses—nakedly and without dilution—the final indignity of death itself, whether accepted or raged against. So I think it may be profitable to explore "the indignity of 'death with dignity'." "Good death" (euthanasia) like "Good grief!" are ultimately contradictions in terms, even if superficially, and before we reach the heart of the matter, there are distinctions to be made; even if, that is to say, the predicate "good" still is applicable in both cases in contrast to worse ways to die and worse ways to grieve or not to grieve.

"Death is simply a part of life," we are told, as a first move to persuade us to accept the ideology of the entire dignity of dying with dignity. A singularly unpersuasive proposition, since we are not told what sort of part of life death is. Disease, injury, congenital defects are also a part of life, and as well murder, rapine, and pillage.[3] Yet there is no campaign for accepting or doing those things with dignity. Nor, for that matter, for the contemporary mentality which would enshrine "death with dignity" is there an equal emphasis on "suffering with dignity," suffering as a "natural" part of life, etc. All those things, it seems, are enemies and violations of human nobility while death is not, or (with a few changes) need not be. Doctors did not invent the fact that death is an

---

[2]Elisabeth Kübler-Ross, *On Death and Dying* (New York: Macmillan, 1969), p. 247.

[3]Schopenhauer's characterization of human history: if you've read one page, you've read it all.

enemy, although they may sometimes use disproportionate means to avoid final surrender. Neither did they invent the fact that pain and suffering are enemies and often indignities, although suffering accepted may also be ennobling or may manifest the nobility of the human spirit of any ordinary person.

But, then, it is said, death is an evolutionary necessity and in that further sense a part of life not to be denied. Socially and biologically, one generation follows another. So there must be death, else social history would have no room for creative novelty and planet earth would be glutted with humankind. True enough, no doubt, from the point of view of evolution (which—so far—never dies). But the man who is dying happens not to be evolution. He is a part of evolution, no doubt: but not to the whole extent of his being or his dying. A crucial testimony to the individual's transcendence over the species is man's problem and his dis-ease in dying. Death is a natural fact of life, yet no man dies "naturally," nor do we have occasions in which to practice doing so in order to learn how. Not unless the pursuit of philosophy is a practice of dying (as Plato's *Phaedo* teaches); and that I take to be an understanding of the human being we moderns do not mean to embrace when we embrace "death with dignity."

It is small consolation to tell mortal men that as long as you are, the death you contribute to evolution is not yet; and when death is, you are not—so why fear death? That is the modern equivalent to the recipe offered by the ancient Epicureans (and some Stoics) to undercut fear of death and devotion to the gods: as long as you are, death is not; when death is, you are not; there's never a direct encounter between you and death; so why dread death? Indeed, contrary to modern parlance, those ancient philosophers declared that death is *not a part of life;* so, why worry?

So "death is not a part of life" is another declaration designed to quiet fear of death. This can be better understood in terms of a terse comment by Wittgenstein: "Our life has no limit in just the way in which our visual field has no limit."[4] We cannot see beyond the boundary of our visual field; it is

more correct to say that beyond the boundary of our visual field *we do not see.* Not only so. Also, we do not see the boundary, the limit itself. There is no seeable bound to the visual field. *Death is not a part of life* in the same way that the boundary is not a part of our visual field. Commenting on this remark by Wittgenstein, James Van Evra writes: "Pressing the analogy, then, if my life has no end in *just the way* that my visual field has no limit, then it must be in the sense that I can have no experience of death, conceived as the complete cessation of experience and thought. That is, if life is considered to be a series of experiences and thoughts, then it is impossible for me to experience death, for to experience something is to be alive, and hence is to be inside the bound formed by death."[5] This is why death itself steadfastly resists conceptualization.

Still, I think the disanalogy ought also to be pressed, against both ancient and contemporary analytical philosophers. That notion of death as a limit makes use of a visual or spatial metaphor. Good basketball players are often men naturally endowed with an unusually wide visual field; this is true, for example, of Bill Bradley. Perhaps basketball players, among other things, strive to enlarge their visual fields, or their habitual use of what powers of sight they have, if that is possible. But ordinarily, everyone of us is perfectly happy within the unseeable limits of sight's reach.

Transfer this notion of death as a limit from space to time as the form of human perception, from sight to an individual's inward desire, effort and hope, and I suggest that one gets a different result. Then death as the temporal limit of a life-span is something we live toward. That limit still can never be experienced or conceptualized; indeed death is *never* a part of life. Moreover, neither is the boundary. Still it is a limit we conative human beings know we live *up against* during our life-spans. We do not live toward or up against the side-limits of our visual-span. Instead, within that acceptable visual limit (and other limits as well) as channels we live toward yet another limit which is death.

Nor is the following analogy for death as

[4]Wittgenstein, *Tractatus,* 6.4311.

[5]James Van Evra, "On Death as a Limit," *Analysis* 31 [5] (April, 1971), 170-76.

a limit of much help in deepening understanding. "... The importance of the limit and virtually *all* of its significance," writes Van Evra, "derives from the fact that the limit serves as an ordering device"—just as absolute zero serves for ordering a series; it is not *just* a limit, although nothing can exist at such a temperature. The analogy is valid so far as it suggests that we conceive of death not in itself but as it bears on us while still alive. As I shall suggest below, death teaches us to "number our days."

But that may not be its only ordering function for conative creatures. Having placed death "out of our league" by showing that it is not a "something," or never a part of life, and while understanding awareness of death as awareness of a limit bearing

T hen death as the temporal limit of a life-span is something we live toward. That limit still can never be experienced or conceptualized; indeed death is *never* a part of life. Moreover, neither is the boundary. Still it is a limit we conative human beings know we live *up against* during our life-spans.

upon us only while still alive, one ought not forthwith to conclude that this understanding of it "exonerates death as the purported snake in our garden." Death as a limit can disorder no less than order the series. Only a disembodied reason can say, as Van Evra does, that "the bound, not being a member of the series, cannot defile it. The series is what it is, happy or unhappy, good or bad, quite independently of any bound as such." An Erik Erikson knows better than that when writing of the "despair and often unconscious fear of death" which results when "the one and only life cycle is not accepted as the ultimate life."

Despair, he observes, "expresses the feeling that the time is short, too short for the attempt to start another life and to try out alternate roads to integrity."[6]

It is the temporal flight of the series that is grievous (not death as an evil "something" within life's span to be balanced, optimistically or pessimistically, against other things that are good). The reminder that death is *not a part of life,* or that it is only a boundary never encountered, is an ancient recipe that can only increase the threat of death on any profound understanding of human life. The dread of death is the dread of oblivion, of there being only empty room in one's stead. Kubler-Ross writes that for the dying, death means the loss of every loved one, total loss of everything that constituted the self in its world, separation from every experience, even from future possible, replacing experiences—nothingness beyond. Therefore, life is a time-intensive activity and not only a goods-intensive or quality-intensive activity. No matter how many "goods" we store up in barns, like the man in Jesus' parable we know that this night our soul may be required of us (Luke 12: 13-21). No matter what "quality of life" our lives have, we must take into account the opportunity-costs of used time. Death means the conquest of the time of our lives —even though we never experience the experience of the nothingness which is natural death.

"Awareness of dying" means awareness of *that;* and awareness of that constitutes an experience of ultimate indignity in and to the awareness of the self who is dying.

We are often reminded of Koheleth's litany: "For everything there is a season, and a time for every matter under heaven: a time to be born and a time to die; a time to plant, and a time to pluck up what is planted," etc. (Eccles. 3:1,2). Across those words of the narrator of Ecclesiastes the view gains entrance that only an "untimely" death should be regretted or mourned. Yet we know better how to specify an untimely death than to define or describe a "timely" one. The author of Genesis tells us that, at 180 years of age, the patriarch Isaac

---

[6]Erik Erikson, "Identity and the Life Cycle," *Psychological Issues,* I, [1] (New York: International University Press, 1959).

"breathed his last; and he died and was gathered to his people, old and full of years ..." (Gen. 35:29). Even in face of sacred Scripture, we are permitted to wonder what Isaac thought about it; whether he too knew how to apply the category "fullness of years" *to himself* and agreed his death was nothing but timely.

We do Koheleth one better and say that death cannot only be timely; it may also be "beautiful." Whether such an opinion is to be ascribed to David Hendin or not (a "fact of life" man he surely is, who also unambiguously subtitled his chapter on euthanasia "Let There Be Death"),[7] that opinion seems to be the outlook of the legislator and physician, Walter Sackett, Jr., who proposed the Florida "Death with Dignity" Statute. All his mature life his philosophy has been, "Death, like birth, is glorious— let it come easy."[8] Such was by no means Koheleth's opinion when he wrote (and *wrote* beautifully) about a time to be born and a time to die. Dr. Sackett also suggests that up to 90 percent of the 1,800 patients in state hospitals for the mentally retarded should be allowed to die. Five billion dollars could be saved in the next half century if the state's mongoloids were permitted to succumb to pneumonia, a disease to which they are highly susceptible.[9] I suggest that the physician in Dr. Sackett has atrophied. He has become a public functionary, treating taxpayers' pocketbooks under the general anesthesia of a continuous daytime soap opera entitled "Death Can Be Beautiful!"

"Death for an older person should be a beautiful event. There is beauty in birth, growth, fullness of life and then, equally so, in the tapering off and final end. There are analogies all about us. What is more beautiful than the spring budding of small leaves; then the fully-leaved tree in summer; and then in the beautiful brightly colored autumn leaves gliding gracefully to the ground? So it is with humans." Those are words from a study document on Euthanasia drafted by the Council for Christian Social Action of the United Church of

Christ in 1972. An astonishing footnote at this point states that "the naturalness of dying" is suggested in funeral services when the minister says "God has called" the deceased, or says he has "gone to his reward," recites the "dust to dust" passage, or notes that the deceased led a full life or ran a full course!

Before that statement was adopted by that Council on Feb. 17, 1973, more orthodox wording was inserted: "Transformation from life on earth to life in the hereafter of the Lord is a fulfillment. The acceptance of death is our witness to faith in the resurrection of Jesus Christ (Rom. 8). We can rejoice." The subdued words "we can rejoice" indicate a conviction that *something* has been subdued. The words "acceptance of death" takes the whole matter out of the context of romantic naturalism and sets it in a proper religious context—based on the particular Christian tenet that death is a conquered enemy, to be accepted in the name of its Conqueror. More than a relic of the nature mysticism that was so luxurient in the original paragraph, however, remains in the words, "Death for an older person should be a beautiful event. There is beauty in birth, growth, fullness of life and then, *equally so,* in the tapering off and final end." (Italics added.) I know no Christian teaching that assures us that our "final end" is "equally" beautiful as birth, growth and fullness of life. Moreover, if revelation disclosed any such thing it would be contrary to reason and to the human reality and experience of death. The views of our "pre-death morticians" are simply discordant with the experienced reality they attempt to beautify. So, in her recent book, Marya Mannes writes "the name of the oratorio is euthanasia." And her statement "dying is merely suspension within a mystery," seems calculated to induce vertigo in face of a fascinating abyss in prospect.[10]

No exception can be taken to one line in the letter people are being encouraged to write and sign by the Euthanasia Societies of Great Britain and America. That line states: "I do not fear death as much as I fear the indignity of deterioration, dependence and hopeless pain." Such an exercise

---

[7]David Hendin, *Death as a Fact of Life* (New York: W. W. Norton, 1973).

[8]Reported in *ibid.,* p. 89.

[9]*The Florida Times-Union,* Jacksonville, Fla., Jan. 11, 1973.

[10]Marya Mannes, *Last Rights* (New York: William Morrow, 1973), p. 6, (cf. 80, 133).

in analyzing *comparative indignities* should be given approval. But in the preceding sentence the letter states: "Death is as much a reality as birth, growth, maturity, and old age—it is the one certainty." That logically leaves open the question what sort of "reality," what sort of "certainty," death is. But by placing death on a parity with birth, growth, maturity—and old age in many of its aspects—the letter beautifies death by association. To be written long before death when one is thinking "generally" (i.e. "rationally"?) about the topic, the letter tempts us to suppose that men can think generally about their own deaths. Hendin observes in another connection that "there is barely any relation between what people think that they think about death and the way they actually feel about it when it must be faced."[11] Then it may be that "the heart has its reasons that reason cannot know" (Pascal)—beforehand —and among those "reasons," I suggest, will be an apprehension of the ultimate (noncomparative) indignity of death. Talk about death as a fact or a reality seasonally recurring in life with birth or planting, maturity and growth, may after all not be very rational. It smacks more of whistling before the darkness descends, and an attempt to brainwash one's contemporaries to accept a very feeble philosophy of life and death.

Birth and death (our *terminus ad quo* and our *terminus ad quem*) are not to be equated with any of the qualities or experiences, the grandeur and the misery, in between, which constitutes "parts" of our lives. While we live toward death and can encompass our own dying in awareness, no one in the same way is aware of his own birth. We know that we were born in the same way we know *that* we die. Explanations of whence we came do not establish conscious contact with our individual origin; and among explanations, that God called us from the womb out of nothing is as good as any other; and better than most. But awareness of dying is quite another matter. That we may have, but not awareness of our births. And while awareness of birth might conceivably be the great original individuating experience (if we had it), among the race of men it is awareness of

dying that is uniquely individuating. To encompass one's own death in the living and dying of one's life is more of a task than it is a part of life. And there is something of indignity to be faced when engaging in that final act of life. Members of the caring human community (doctors, nurses, family) are apt to keep closer company with the dying if we acknowledge the loss of all worth by the loss of him in whom inhered all worth in his world. Yet ordinary men may sometimes nobly suffer the ignobility of death.

By way of contrast with the "A Living Will" framed by the Euthanasia Society, the Judicial Council of the AMA in its recent action on the physician and the dying patient had before it two similar letters. One was composed by the Connecticut Delegation:

To my Family, my Physician
my Clergyman, my Lawyer—

If the time comes when I can no longer actively take part in decisions for my own future, I wish this statement to stand as the testament of my wishes. If there is no reasonable expectation of my recovery from physical or mental and spiritual disability, I, ..., request that I be allowed to die and not be kept alive by artificial means or heroic measures. I ask also that drugs be mercifully administered to me for terminal suffering even if in relieving pain they may hasten the moment of death. I value life and the dignity of life, so that I am not asking that my life be directly taken, but that my dying not be unreasonably prolonged nor the dignity of life be destroyed. This request is made, after careful reflection, while I am in good health and spirits. Although this document is not legally binding, you who care for me will, I hope, feel morally bound to take it into account. I recognize that it places a heavy burden of responsibility upon you, and it is with the intention of sharing this responsibility that this statement is made.

A second letter had been composed by a physician to express his own wishes, in quite simple language:

To my Family, To my Physician—

Should the occasion arise in my lifetime when death is imminent and a decision is to

[11]Hendin, *Death as a Fact of Life*, p. 103.

be made about the nature and the extent of the care to be given to me and I am not able at that time to express my desires, let this statement serve to express my deep, sincere, and considered wish and hope that my physician will administer to me simple, ordinary medical treatment. I ask that he not administer heroic, extraordinary, expensive, or useless medical care or treatment which in the final analysis will merely delay, not change, the ultimate outcome of my terminal condition.

A comparison of these declarations with "A Living Will" circulated by the Euthanasia Society reveals the following signal

All concerned take the wrong turn in trying either to "thing-ify" death or to beautify it. The dying have at least this advantage, that in these projects for dehumanizing death by naturalizing it the dying finally cannot succeed, and death makes its threatening visage known to them before ever there are any societal or evolutionary replacement values or the everlasting arms or Abraham's bosom to rest on.

differences: neither of the AMA submissions engages in any superfluous calculus of "comparative indignities";[12] neither associates the reality of death with such things as birth or maturation; both allow death to be simply what it is in human experience; both are in a general sense "pro-life" statements,

in that death is neither reified as one fact among others nor beautified even comparatively.[13]

Everyone concerned takes the wrong turn in trying either to "thing-ify" death or to beautify it. The dying have at least this advantage, that in these projects for dehumanizing death by naturalizing it the dying finally cannot succeed, and death makes its threatening visage known to them before ever there are any societal or evolutionary replacement values or the everlasting arms or Abraham's bosom to rest on. Death means *finis*, not in itself *telos*. Certainly not a telos to be engineered, or to be accomplished by reducing both human life and death to the level of natural events.

"Thing-ifying" death reaches its highest pitch in the stated preference of many people in the present age for *sudden* death,[14] for death from unanticipated internal collapse, from the abrupt intrusion of violent outside forces, from some chance occurrence due to the natural law governing the operation of automobiles. While for a comparative calculus of indignities sudden *unknowing* death may be preferred to suffering knowingly or unknowingly the indignity of deterioration, abject dependence, and hopeless pain, how ought we to assess in human

---

[13]I may add that while the House of Delegates did not endorse any particular form to express an individual's wishes relating prospectively to his final illness, it recognized that individuals have a right to express them. While it encouraged physicians to discuss such matters with patients and attend to their wishes, the House nevertheless maintained a place for the conscience and judgment of a physician in determining indicated treatment. It did not subsume every consideration under the rubric of the patient's right to refuse treatment (or to have refused treatment). That sole action-guide can find no medical or logical reason for distinguishing, in physician actions, between the dying and those who simply have a terminal illness (or have this "dying life," Augustine's description of all of us). It would also entail a belief that wishing or autonomous choice makes the moral difference between life and death decisions which then are to be imposed on the physician-technician; and that, to say the least, is an ethics that can find no place for either reason or sensibility.

[14]Cf. the report of a Swedish survey by Gunnar Biörck, M.D., in *Archives of Internal Medicine*, October, 1973; news report in *The New York Times*, Oct. 31, 1973.

---

[12]What, after all, is the point of promoting, as if it were a line of reasoning, observations such as that said to be inscribed on W. C. Field's tombstone: "On the whole I'd rather be here than in Philadelphia"?

terms the present-day absolute (noncomparative) preference for sudden death? Nothing reveals more the meaning we assign to human "dignity" than the view that sudden death, death as an eruptive natural event, could be a prismatic case of death with dignity or at least one without indignity. Human society seems about to rise to the moral level of the "humane" societies in their treatment of animals. What is the principled difference between their view and ours about the meaning of dying "humanely"? By way of contrast, consider the prayer in the Anglican prayer book: "From perils by night and perils by day, perils by land and perils by sea, and *from sudden death,* Lord, deliver us." Such a petition bespeaks an age in which dying with dignity was a gift and a task (*Gaube und Aufgaube*), a liberty to encompass dying as a final act among the actions of life, to enfold awareness of dying as an ingredient into awareness of one's self dying as the finale of the self's relationships in this life to God or to fellowman—in any case to everything that was worthy.

Man Knows that He Dies

Before letting Koheleth's "a time to be born and a time to die" creep as a gloss into *our* texts, perhaps we ought to pay more attention to the outlook on life and death expressed in the enchantment and frail beauty of those words,[15] and ask

---

[15]In the whole literature on death and dying, there is no more misquoted sentence, or statement taken out of context, than Koheleth's "time to be born and a time to die"—unless it be "Nor strive officiously to keep alive." The latter line is from an ironic poem by the nineteenth century poet Arthur Hugh Clough, entitled "The Latest Decalogue":

"Thou shalt not kill; but need'st not strive
   Officiously to keep alive.
Do not adultery commit;
Advantage rarely comes of it:
Thou shalt not steal; an empty feat,
When it's so lucrative to cheat:
Bear not false witness; let the lie
Have time on its own wings to fly:
Thou shall not covet; but tradition
Approves all forms of competition.
The sum of all is, thou shalt love
If anybody, God above:
At any rate, shalt never labor
More than thyself to love thy neighbor."

whether that philsophy can possibly be a proper foundation for the practice of medicine or for the exercise of the most sensitive care for the dying.

That litany on the times for every matter under heaven concludes with the words, "What gain has the worker from his toil?" (Eccles. 3:9). In general, the author of Ecclesiastes voices an unrelieved pessimism. He has "seen everything that is done under the sun," in season and out of season. It is altogether "an unhappy business that God has given to the sons of men to be busy with"—this birthing and dying, planting and uprooting; "all is vanity and seeking after wind" (Eccles. 1:3b, 14). So, he writes with words of strongest revulsion, "I hated life, because what is done under the sun was grievous to me"; "I hated all my toil and gave myself up to despair . . ." (Eccles. 2:17, 18a, 20).

After that comes the litany "for everything there is a season"—proving, as Kierkegaard said, that a poet is a man whose heart is full of pain but whose lips are so formed that when he gives utterance to that pain he makes beautiful sounds. Koheleth knew, as later did Nietzsche, that the eternal recurrence of birth and death and all things else was simply "the spirit of melancholy" unrelieved, even though there is nothing else to believe since God died.[16] (The Pope knows: he was at the bedside.)

"Death with dignity" because death is a "part" of life, one only of its seasonal realities? If so, then the acceptable death of all flesh means death with the same signal indignity that brackets the whole of life and its striving. Dying is worth as much as the rest; it is no more fruitless.

"For the fate of the sons of men and the fate of the beasts is the same; as one dies so dies the other. They all have the same breath, and man has no advantage over the beasts; for all is vanity" (Eccles. 3:19). "Death with dignity" or death a part of life based on an equilibration of the death of a man with the death of a dog? I think that is not a concept to be chosen as the foundation of modern medicine, even though both dogs and men are enabled to die "humanely."

---

[16]Nietzsche, *Thus Spake Zarathustra,* especially XLVI and LXVI.

Or to go deeper still: "death with dignity" because the dead are better off than the living? "I thought the dead who are already dead," Koheleth writes in unrelieved sorrow over existence, "more fortunate than the living who are still alive; and better than both is he who has not yet been, and has not seen the evil deeds that are done under the sun" (Eccles. 4:2,3). Thus the book of Ecclesiastes is the source of the famous interchange between two pessimistic philosophers, each trying to exceed the other in gloom: First philosopher: More blessed are the dead than the living. Second philosopher: Yes, what you say is true; but more blessed still are those who have never been born. First philosopher: Yes, wretched life; but few there be who attain to that condition!

But Koheleth thinks he knows some who have attained to the blessed goal of disentrapment from the cycles in which there is a time for every matter under heaven. "... An untimely birth [a miscarriage] is better off [than a living man], for it [a miscarriage] comes into vanity and goes into darkness, and in darkness its name is covered, moreover it has not seen the sun or known anything; yet it finds rest rather than he [the living]" (Eccles. 6:3b, 4,5). So we might say that death can have its cosmic dignity if untormented by officious physicians, because the dying go to the darkness, to Limbo where nameless miscarriages dwell, having never seen the sun or known anything. Thus, if dying with dignity as a part of life's natural, undulating seasons seems not to be a thought with much consolation in it (being roughly equivalent to the indignity besetting everything men do and every other natural time), still the dying may find rest as part of cosmic order, from which, once upon a time, the race of men arose to do the unhappy business God has given them to be busy with, and to which peaceful darkness the dying return.

Hardly a conception that explains the rise of Western medicine, the energy of its care of the dying, or its war against the indignity of suffering and death—or a conception on which to base its reformation! Dylan Thomas' words were directed against such notions: "The wise men at their end know dark is right,/Because their words had forked no lightning."

There is finally in Ecclesiastes, however, a deeper strand than those which locate men living and dying as simply parts of some malignly or benignly neglectful natural or cosmic order. From these more surface outlooks, the unambiguous injunction follows: Be a part; let there be death—in its time and place, of course (whatever that means). Expressing a deeper strand, however, Koheleth seems to say: Let the natural or cosmic order be whatever it is; men are different. His practical advice is: Be what you are, in human awareness apart and not a part. Within this deeper understanding of the transcendent, threatened nobility of a human life, the uniqueness of the individual human subject, there is ground for awareness of death as an indignity yet freedom to encompass it with dignity.

Now it is that Koheleth reverses the previous judgments he decreed over all he had seen under the sun. Before, the vale of the sunless not-knowing of a miscarriage having its name covered by darkness seemed preferable to living; and all man's works a seeking after wind. So, of course, there was "a time for dying." But now Koheleth writes, "... there is no work or thought or knowledge or wisdom in Sheol, to which you are going" (Eccles. 9:10b). While the fate of the sons of men and the fate of the beasts are the same, still "a living dog is better than a dead lion"; and to be a living man is better than either, because of what Koheleth means by "living." "He who is joined with all the living has hope" (Eccles. 9:4), and that is hardly a way to describe dogs or lions. Koheleth, however, identifies the grandeur of man not so much with hope as with awareness, even awareness of dying, and the misery of man with the indignity of dying of which he, in his nobility, is aware. "For the living know that they will die," he writes, "but the dead know nothing..." (Eccles. 9:5). Before, the dead or those who never lived had superiority; now, it is the living who are superior precisely by virtue of their awareness of dying and of its indignity to the knowing human spirit.

Therefore, I suggest that Koheleth probed the human condition to a depth to which more than twenty centuries later Blaise Pascal came. "Man is but a reed, the feeblest in nature, but he is a thinking reed. ... A vapour, a drop of water, is sufficient to slay him. But were the universe to crush him, man would still be nobler than that which kills him, for *he knows that he dies,* while the universe knows nothing of the advantage it has over him. Thus our whole dignity consists in thought."[17] (Italics added.)

So the grandeur and misery of man are fused together in the human reality and experience of death. To deny the indignity of death requires that the dignity of man be refused also. The more acceptable in itself death is, the less the worth or uniqueness ascribed to the dying life.

True Humanism and the Dread of Death

I always write as the ethicist I am, namely, a Christian ethicist, and not as some hypothetical common denominator. On common concrete problems I, of course, try to elaborate analysis at the point or on a terrain where there may be convergence of vectors that began in other ethical outlooks and onlooks. Still one should not pant for agreement as the hart pants for the waterbrooks, lest the substance of one's ethics dissolve into vapidity. So in this section I want, among other things, to exhibit some of the meaning of "Christian humanism" in regard to death and dying, in the confidence that this will prove tolerable to my colleagues for a time, if not finally instructive to them.

In this connection, there are two counterpoised verses in the First Epistle of St. John that are worth pondering. The first reads: "Perfect love casts out fear" (which being interpreted means: Perfect care of the dying casts out fear of one's own death or rejection of their dying because of fear of ours). The second verse reads: "Where fear is, love is not perfected" (which being interpreted means: Where fear of death and dying remains, medical and human care of the dying is not perfected). That states nothing so much as the enduring dubiety and ambiguity of any mortal man's care of another through his dying. At the same time there is here applied without modification a standard for unflinching care of a dying fellowman, or short of that of any fellow mortal any time. That standard is cut to the measure of the perfection in benevolence

I always write as the ethicist I am, namely, a Christian ethicist, and not as some hypothetical common denominator. On common concrete problems I, of course, try to elaborate analysis at the point, or on a terrain, where there may be convergence of vectors that begin in other ethical outlooks and onlooks. Still one should not pant for agreement as the hart pants for the waterbrooks, lest the substance of one's ethics dissolve into vapidity.

believed to be that of our Father in Heaven in his dealings with mankind. So there is "faith-ing" in an ultimate righteousness beyond the perceptible human condition presupposed by those verses that immediately have to do simply with loving and caring.

Whatever non-Christians may think about the *theology* here entailed, or about similar foundations in any religious ethics, I ask that the notation upon or penetration of the human condition be attended to. Where and insofar as fear is, love and care for the dying cannot be perfected in moral agents or the helping professions. The religious traditions have one way of addressing that problematic. In the modern age the problematic itself is avoided by various forms and degrees of denial of the tragedy of death which proceeds first to reduce the unique worth and once-for-all-ness of the individual life-span that dies.

Perhaps one can apprehend the threat posed to the dignity of man (i.e. in an easy and ready dignifying of death) by many modern viewpoints, especially those dominating the scientific community, and their superficial equivalents in our culture gen-

---

[17]Pascal, *Pensées*, p. 347.

erally, by bringing into view three states of consciousness in the Western past.

The burden of the Hebrew Scriptures was man's obedience or disobedience to covenant, to Torah. Thus sin was the problem, and death came in only as a subordinate theme; and, as one focus for the problematic of the human condition, this was a late development. In contrast, righteousness and disobedience (sin) was a subordinate theme in Greek religion. The central theme of Greek religious thought and practice was the problem of death—a problem whose solution was found either by initiation into religious cults that promised to extricate the soul from its corruptible shroud or by belief in the native power of the soul to outlast any number of bodies. Alongside these, death was at the heart of the pathos of life depicted in Greek tragical drama, against which, and against the flaws of finitude in general, the major character manifested his heroic transcendence. So sin was determinative for the Hebrew consciousness; death for the Greek consciousness.

Consciousness III was Christianity, and by this, sin and death were tied together in Western man's awareness of personal existence. These two foci of man's misery and of his need for redemption—sin and death—were inseparably fused. This new dimension of man's awareness of himself was originally probed most profoundly by St. Paul's Letter to the Romans (5-7). Those opaque reflections, I opine, were once understood not so much by the intellect as along the pulses of ordinary people in great numbers, in taverns and market places; and it represents a cultural breakdown without parallel that these reflections are scarcely understandable to the greatest intelligences today. A simple night school lesson in them may be gained by simply pondering a while the two verses quoted above from St. John's Epistle.

The point is that according to the Christian saga the Messiah did not come to bring boors into culture. Nor did he bear epilepsy or psychosomatic disorders to gain victory over them in the flesh before the interventions of psychoneurosurgery. Rather is he said to have been born *mortal* flesh to gain for us a foretaste of victory over sin and death where those twin enemies had taken up apparently secure citadel.

Again, the point for our purposes is not to be drawn into agreement or disagreement with those theological affirmations, and it is certainly not to be tempted into endless speculation about an after-life. Crucial instead is to attend to the notation on the human condition implied in all that. Death is an enemy even if it is the last enemy to be fully conquered in the Fulfillment, the eschaton; meanwhile, the sting of death is sin. Such was the new consciousness-raising that Christianity brought into the Western world. And the question is whether in doing so it has not grasped some important experiential human realities better than most philosophies, whether it was not attuned to essential ingredients of the human condition vis-a-vis death—whatever the truth or falsity of its theological address to that condition.

The foregoing, I grant, may be an oversimplification; and I am aware of needed corrections more in the case of Hebrew humanism than in the case of Greek humanism. The New Testament word, "He will wipe away every tear from their eyes, and death shall be no more, neither shall there be mourning nor crying nor pain any more, for the former things have passed away," (Rev. 21:3,4) has its parallel in the Hebrew Bible: "He will swallow up death forever, and the Lord God will wipe away tears from all faces . . ." (Isa. 25:8). Again, since contemplating the Lord God may be too much for us, I ask only that we attend to the doctrine of death implied in these passages: it is an enemy, surely, and not simply an acceptable part of the natural order of things. And the connection between dread of death and sin, made most prominent in Christian consciousness, was nowhere better stated than in Ecclesiastes: "This is the root of the evil in all that happens under the sun, that one fate comes to all. Therefore, men's minds are filled with evil and there is madness in their hearts while they live, for they know that afterward —they are off to the dead!"

One can, indeed, ponder that verse about the source of all evil in the apprehended evil of death together with another verse in Ecclesiastes which reads: "Teach us so to number our days that we may apply our hearts unto wisdom." The first says that death is an evil evil: it is experienced as a threatening limit that begets evil. The second says that death is a good evil: that experience also begets good. Without death, and death perceived as a threat, we would also have no reason to "number our days" so as to ransom the time allotted us, to receive life as a precious gift, to drink the wine of gladness in toast to every successive present moment. Instead, life would be an endless boredom and boring because end-

Some there are who number their days so as to apply their hearts unto eating, drinking, and being merry—for tomorrow we die. Some there are who number their days so as to apply their hearts unto wisdom—for tomorrow we die. Both are life-spans enhanced in importance and individuation under the stimulus of the perceived evil of death.

less; there would be no reason to probe its depths while there is still time. Some there are who number their days so as to apply their hearts unto eating, drinking and being merry—for tomorrow we die. Some there are who number their days so as to apply their hearts unto wisdom—for tomorrow we die. Both are life-spans enhanced in importance and in individuation under the stimulus of the perceived evil of death. Knowledge of human good or of human evil that is in the slightest degree above the level of the beasts of the field are both enhanced because of death, the horizon of human existence. So, debarment from access to the tree of life was on the horizon and a sequence of the events in the Garden of Paradise; the temptation in eating the fruit of the tree of knowledge of good and evil was because that seemed a way for mortal creatures to become like gods. The punishment of that is said to have been death; and no

governor uses as a penalty something that anyone can simply choose to believe to be a good or simply receive as a neutral or dignified, even ennobling, part of life. So I say death may be a good evil or an evil evil, but it is perceived as an evil or experienced indignity in either case. Existential anxiety or general anxiety (distinguishable from particular fears or removable anxieties) means anxiety over death toward which we live. That paradoxically, as Reinhold Niebuhr said, is the source of all human creativity and of all human sinfulness.

Of course, the sages of old could and did engage in a calculus of comparative indignities. "O death, your sentence is welcome," wrote Ben Sira, "to a man worn out with age, worried about everything, disaffected and beyond endurance" (Ecclus. 41:2,3). Still death was a "sentence," not a natural event acceptable in itself. Moreover, not every man grows old gracefully in the Psalms; instead, one complains:

> Take pity on me, Yahweh,
> I am in trouble now.
> Grief wastes away my eye,
> My throat, my inmost parts.
> For my life is worn out with sorrow,
> My years with sighs;
> My strength yields under misery,
> My bones are wasting away.
> To every one of my oppressors
> I am contemptible,
> Loathsome to my neighbors,
> To my friends a thing of fear.
> Those who see me in the street
> Hurry past me.
> I am forgotten, as good as dead, in their hearts,
> Something discarded. (Ps. 31:9-12)

What else is to be expected if it be true that the madness in men's hearts while they live, and the root of all evil in all that happens under the sun, lies in the simple fact that every man consciously lives toward his own death, knowing that afterward he too is off to the dead? Where fear is—fear of the properly dreadful—love and care for the dying cannot be perfected.

Unless one has some grounds for respecting the shadow of death upon every human countenance—grounds more ultimate than perceptible realities—then it makes good sense as a policy of life simply to try to outlast one's neighbors. One can, for example, *generalize,* and so attenuate our neighbors' irreplaceability. "If I must grieve whenever the bell tolls," writes Carey McWilliams, "I am never bereft: some of my kinsmen will remain. Indeed, I need not grieve much—even, lest I suggest some preference among my brethren, should not grieve much—for each loss is small compared to what remains."[18] But that solace, we know, is denied the dead who have lost everything making for worth in this their world. Realistic love for another irreplaceable, non-interchangeable individual human being means, as Unamuno wrote, care for another "doomed soul."

In this setting, let us now bring into consideration some empirical findings that in this day are commonly supposed to be more confirmatory than wisdom meditated from the heart.

In the second year anatomy course, medical students clothe with "gallows humor" their encounter with the cadaver which once was a human being alive. That defense is not to be despised; nor does it necessarily indicate socialization in shallowness on the students' part. Even when dealing with the remains of the long since dead, there is special tension involved—if I mistook not a recent address by Renée Fox—when performing investigatory medical actions involving the face, the hands, and the genitalia. This thing-in-the-world that was once a man alive we still encounter as once a communicating being, not quite as an object of research or instruction. Face and hands, yes; but why the genitalia? Those reactions must seem incongruous to a resolutely biologizing age. For a beginning of an explanation, one might take up the expression "carnal knowledge"—which was the best thing about the movie bearing that title—and behind that go to the expression "carnal *conversation,*" an old, legal term for adultery, and back of both to the Biblical word "knew" in "And Adam *knew* his wife and begat. . . ." Here we have an entire anthropology impacted in a word, not a squeamish euphemism. In short, in those reactions of medical students can be discerned a sensed relic of the human being bodily experiencing

and communicating, and the body itself uniquely speaking.

Notably, however, there's no "gallows humor" used when doing or observing one's first autopsy, or in the emergency room when a D.O.A. (Dead on Arrival) is brought in with his skull cleaved open. With regard to the "newly dead" we come as close as we possibly can to experiencing the incommensurable contrast between life and death. Yet those sequential realities—life and death—here juxtaposed never *meet* in direct encounter. So we never have an impression or experience of the measure and meaning of the two different worlds before which we stand in the autopsy and the emergency room. A cadaver has over time become almost a thing-in-the-world from which to gain knowledge of the human body. While *there* a little humor helps, to go about acquiring medical knowledge from autopsies requires a different sort of inward effort to face down or live with our near-experience of the boundary of life and death. The cleavage in the brain may be quite enough and more than enough to *explain* rationally why this man was D.O.A. But, I suggest, there can be no gash deep enough, no physical event destructive enough to account for the felt difference between life and death that we face here. The physician or medical student may be a confirmed materialist. For him the material explanation of this death may be quite sufficient rationally. Still the heart has its reasons that the reason knows not of; and, I suggest, the awakening of these feelings of awe and dread should not be repressed in anyone whose calling is to the human dignity of caring for the dying.

In any case, from these empirical observations, if they be true, let us return to a great example of theological anthropology in order to try to comprehend why death was thought to be the assault of an enemy. According to some readings, Christians in all ages should be going about bestowing the gift of immortality on one another posthaste. A distinguished Catholic physician, beset by what he regarded as the incorrigible problems of medical ethics today, once shook his head in my presence and wondered out loud why the people who most believe in an after-life should have established so many hospitals! That seems to require explanation, at least as against silly

[18]Wilson Carey McWilliams, *The Idea of Fraternity in America* (Berkeley: University of California Press, 1973), p. 48.

interpretations of "otherworldliness." The answer is that none of the facts or outlooks cited ever denied the reality of death, or affirmed that death ever presents a friendly face (except comparatively). The explanation lies in the vicinity of Christian anthropology and the Biblical view that death is an enemy. That foundation of Western medicine ought not lightly to be discarded, even if we need to enliven again the sense that there are limits to man's struggle against that alien power.

Far from the otherworldliness or body-soul dualism with which he is often charged, St. Augustine went so far as to say that "the body is not an extraneous ornament or aid, but a part of man's very nature."[19] Upon that understanding of the human being, Augustine could then express a quite realistic account of "the dying process":

> Wherefore, as regards bodily death, that is, the separation of the soul from the body, it is good to none while it is being endured by those whom we say are in the article of death [dying]. For the very violence with which the body and soul are wrenched asunder, which in the living are conjoined and closely intertwined, brings with it a harsh experience, jarring horribly on nature as long as it continues, till there comes a total loss of sensation, which arose from the very interpenetration of flesh and spirit.[20]

From this Augustine correctly concludes: "Wherefore death is indeed . . . good to none while it is actually suffered, and while it is subduing the dying to its power. . . ." His ultimate justifications attenuate not at all the harshness of that alien power's triumph. Death, he only says, is "meritoriously endured for the sake of winning what *is* good. And regarding what happens after death, it is no absurdity to say that death is good to the good, and evil to the evil."[21] But that is not to say that death as endured in this life, or as life's terminus, is itself in any way good. He even goes so far as to say:

> For though there can be no manner of doubt that the souls of the just and holy lead lives in peaceful rest, yet so much better would it be for them to be alive in healthy, well-conditioned bodies, that even those who hold the tenet that it is most blessed to be quit of every kind of body, condemn this opinion in spite of themselves.[22]

Thus, for Biblical or later Christian anthropology, the only possible form which human life in any true and proper sense can take here or hereafter is "somatic." That is the Pauline word; we today say "psycho-somatic." Therefore, for Christian theology death may be a "conquered enemy"; still it was in the natural order—and as long as the generations of mankind endure will remain—an enemy still. To pretend otherwise adds insult to injury—or, at least, carelessness.

There are two ways, so far as I can see, to reduce the dreadful visage of death to a level of inherently acceptable indifference. One way is to subscribe to an interpretation of "bodily life" that reduces it to an acceptable level of indifference to the person long before his dying. That—if anyone can believe it today, or if it is not a false account of human nature—was the way taken by Plato in his idealized account of the death of Socrates. (It should be remembered that we know not whether Socrates' hands trembled as he yet bravely drank the hemlock, no more than we know how Isaac experienced dying when "fullness of years" came upon him. Secondary accounts of these matters are fairly untrustworthy.)

Plato's dialogue *The Phaedo* may not "work" as a proof of the immortality of the soul. Still it decisively raises the question of immortality by its thorough representation of the incommensurability between mental processes and bodily processes. Few philosophers today accept the demonstration of the mind's power to outlast bodies because the mind itself is not material, or because the mind "plays" the body like a musician the lyre. But most of them are still wrestling with the mind-body problem, and many speak of two separate languages, a language for mental events isomorphic with our language for brain events. That's rather like saying the same thing as Socrates (Plato) while claiming to have gone beyond him (Soren Kierkegaard).

I cite *The Phaedo* for another purpose:

---

[19]Augustine, *City of God,* Book I, Chapter XIII.
[20]*Ibid.,* Book XIII, Chapter VI.
[21]*Ibid.,* Book XIII, Chapter VIII.

[22]*Ibid.,* Book XIII, Chapter XIX.

to manifest one way to render death incomparably welcomed. Those who most have mature manhood in exercise—the lovers of wisdom—have desired death and dying all their life long, in the sense that they seek "in every sort of way to dissever the soul from the communion of the body"; "thought is best when the mind is gathered into herself and none of these things trouble her—neither sounds nor sights nor pain nor any pleasure—when she takes leave of the body...." That life is best and has nothing to fear that has "the habit of the soul

Whenever these two escapes are simultaneously rejected—if the "bodily life" is neither an ornament nor a drag but a part of man's very nature; and if the "personal life" of an individual in his unique life-span is accorded unrepeatable, noninterchangeable value—then it is that Death the Enemy again comes into view. Conquered or Unconquerable.... I suggest that it is better to have the indignity of death on our hands and in our outlooks than to "dignify" it in either of these two possible ways. Then we ought to be much more circumspect in speaking of death with dignity, and hesitant to—I almost said—thrust that upon the dying!

gathering and collecting herself into herself from all sides out of the body." (Feminists, note the pronouns.)

Granted, Socrates' insight is valid concerning the self's transcendence, when he says: "I am inclined to think that these muscles and bones of mine would have gone off long ago to Megara and Boeotia—by the dog, they would, if they had been moved only by their own idea of what was best...." Still Crito had a point, when he feared that the impending dread event had more to do with "the same Socrates who has been talking and conducting the argument" than Socrates is represented to have believed. To fear the loss of Socrates, Crito had not to fancy, as Socrates charged, "that I am the other Socrates whom he will soon see, a dead body." Crito had only to apprehend, however faintly, that there is not an entire otherness between those two Socrates *now,* in this living being; that there was unity between, let us say, Socrates the conductor of arguments and Socrates the gesticulator or the man who stretched *himself* because his muscles and bones grew weary from confinement.

The other way to reduce the dreadful visage of death is to subscribe to a philosophy of "human life" that reduces the stature, the worth, and the irreplaceable uniqueness of the individual person (long before his dying) to a level of acceptable transiency or interchangeability. True, modern culture is going this way. But there have been other and better ways of stipulating that the image of death across the human countenance is no shadow. One was that of Aristotelian philosophy. According to its form-matter distinction, reason, the formal principle, is definitive of essential humanity. That is universal, eternal as logic. Matter, however, is the individuating factor. So when a man who bears a particular name dies, only the individuation disintegrates—to provide matter for other forms. Humanity goes on in other instances. Anything unique or precious about mankind is not individual. There are parallels to this outlook in Eastern religions and philosophies, in which the individual has only transiency, and should seek only that, disappearing in the Fulfillment into the Divine pool.

These then are two ways of denying the dread of death. Whenever these two escapes are *simultaneously* rejected—i.e., if the "bodily life" is neither an ornament nor a drag but a part of man's very nature; and if the "personal life" of an individual in his unique life-span is accorded unrepeatable, noninterchangeable value—then it is that

Death the Enemy again comes into view. Conquered or Unconquerable. A true humanism and the dread of death seem to be dependent variables. I suggest that it is better to have the indignity of death on our hands and in our outlooks than to "dignify" it in either of these two possible ways. Then we ought to be much more circumspect in speaking of death with dignity, and hesitant to—I almost said—thrust that upon the dying! Surely, a proper care for them needs not only to know the pain of dying which human agency may hold at bay, but also care needs to acknowledge that there is grief over death which no human agency can alleviate.

8

The dignity of the inevitable and necessary

ROBERT S. MORISON

Paul Ramsey suggests that anyone unable to speak as a Christian ethicist must do so as some "hypothetical common denominator." Maybe so, but for the present I will think of myself as a latter-day (not very animistic) pagan. I will also remind you that I tend to look upon death as a process and therefore regard the phrase *"death* with dignity" as essentially equivalent to *"dying* with dignity." Paul Ramsey's essay seems to follow no consistent line on this issue. Sometimes he seems to be talking simply about dying and how to do it or be helped to do it. At other times, he rages with Dylan Thomas about death as an arbitrary, wholly unacceptable event descending from God-knows-where to take away one's own very special and unique gift of life. I will try to talk separately and successively about these two views although I recognize that in between these extremes are a number of other interpretations and nuances that must be neglected for the present.

Undignified Prolongation of Life

In the first place, then, let us talk about the process of dying and whether or not it can be carried out with dignity. I take it that it is this question that most occupies those numerous individuals who are proposing an increasing flood of legislation, composing letters of intent to their physicians, or simply appearing on television programs under the title "Death with Dignity."

To approach the subject somewhat from the back door, I will start by saying that, together with a number of other people, I hold that at a certain stage in the process of dying, it is basically *un*dignified to continue casting desperately about for this or that potion, philter, or device to prolong some minor sign of life, after all reasonable chance for the reappearance of its major attributes has disappeared. Admittedly, this is an instinctive, possibly purely pagan reaction on my part. I simply find something offensive about this frantic search for some last remedy, some magic wire to hook up merely to postpone the inevitable.

Actually, as Paul Ramsey would agree, his behavior and mine would ordinarily differ very little at the bedside of such a patient. What goes on in our heads may, however, be quite different. To put the difference in its most extreme form: He might be saying to himself "Death is an undignified matter at best, and I feel that the appropriate treatment for this stage of this patient's illness is to withdraw active efforts to prolong life and thus allow God to decide, unimpeded by human intervention, how to get this undignified business over with as quickly as possible. Even if I give the patient some morphine to ease his pain, and even though I know that this will slow his respiration and reduce his interest in coughing, I will in no way be causing his death because this is simply a secondary or incidental effect of my actions."

I might be saying to myself, on the other hand: "To be candid about it, the trajectory of this patient's life has now reached its final stage of decline. Virtually everything that once made his life a pleasure to himself, a delight to his friends, and an asset to society has now disappeared, never to return. All that remain are the least dignified of his interchanges with the environment, and even these in their least dignified form. I am sure from previous conversations that this man would not wish to remain in this subhuman condition, and I will therefore withdraw all treatments that would prolong life and continue only those that will prevent restlessness and pain, fully recognizing that such measures will also hasten the end. By thus fulfilling the wishes of my friend and patient, I restore to him the dignity of controlling, to the extent possible, the circumstances under which he returns to an inanimate state."

There is an implicit indignity in the conception of the meaning of human life revealed by overvigorous efforts to maintain its outward, visible, and entirely trivial signs. It is not breathing, urinating, and defecating that makes a human being important even when he can do these things by himself. How much greater is the indignity when all these things must be done for him, and he can do nothing else. Not only have means thus been converted into ends; the very means themselves have become artificial. It is simply an insult to the very idea of humanity to equate it with these mechanically maintained appearances.

The Examined Death

Clearly, then, the omission of what are so oddly referred to as *heroic* means can spare us at least in part from death with indignity. Does such restraint at the same time convert the process into death *with dignity,* or are we simply left with a blank sheet of paper, a soul wandering about in limbo perhaps, free of the ultimate indignity but unable to attain dignity?

Here Paul Ramsey himself may inadvertently have given us a clue to improving matters. In the first place, he speaks with contempt of those who wish for sudden death. His grounds are that, to be appreciated, death must be experienced, if not indeed thought carefully about in advance. He quotes with approval Pascal's observation that man's nobility lies in the fact that he knows that he dies. He also notes that the Book of Common Prayer includes sudden death among various other perils from which the Lord is especially petitioned to deliver us. Obviously, the pagan will agree, and it is in just this spirit that latter-day pagans are thinking about their deaths well in advance. Indeed, against all current custom and in some discordance with existing legislation, they are endeavoring to prepare not only themselves, but their friends and physicians, to cooperate with them in their wish to face death with dignity.

A particularly interesting example of divine cooperation with the human desire not to die suddenly and unprepared, but only after calm reflection in one's study is provided by the pagan philosopher Seneca in his comment on the suicide of Cato the Younger.

In it he quotes Cato as scorning to die in hand-to-hand combat (as two of his young officers had chosen to die) on the grounds that "it were as ignoble to beg death from any man as to beg life." He then goes on to describe the deliberation with which he arranged for the escape of his followers, spent an evening in his usual studies, and then attempted suicide by stabbing himself in the abdomen. He did not die immediately and apparently was attended by a surgeon who sutured the wound, which Cato tore open at the next opportunity. This double effort causes Seneca to make the following memorable comment:

> His virtue was held in check and called back that it might display itself in a harder role; for to seek death needs not so great a soul as to reseek it. Surely the gods looked with pleasure upon their pupil as he made his escape by so glorious and memorable an end! Death consecrates those whose end even those who fear must praise.

It seems from what we have said so far that Ramsey, with his respect for Pascal, and

I, with my respect for Seneca, are really not so far apart on the possibility of carrying out the final process of dying with dignity.

We turn, then, to the contention that the very fact of death, the inevitability that the individual human life must always end, is an indignity in some sort of universal sense.

I am not sure that I fully understand Ramsey's bitter hostility against those who, on the contrary, attempt to see a certain dignity in death as an inevitable, indeed as an essential, part of life as we know it. I shall begin my comment, however, with an attempt to establish a positive case for the view and then to go on to comment on some of Paul Ramsey's strictures about Koheleth, the Preacher.

In the first place, let me say that I find something basically undignified in a failure to accept the inevitable logic or the empirically demonstrable structure of the natural world. Whatever else may be said about him, Dostoievski's antihero in the "Notes from Underground," who rails against the fact that two plus two make four, is not a *dignified* figure. Conversely, for most of us, Job gains in dignity when he finally accepts the way that God has decided to run things. Much the same spirit activated Milton when he intoned, "Just are the ways of God and justifiable to man." Seneca wrote his little essay on Providence in part to "reconcile" a friend to the ways of God. Such individuals seem far closer to my conception of what is meant by human dignity than Paul Ramsey's curious choice of Dylan Thomas, whom he commends for raging "against the close of day."

Biological Necessities

In other essays and presentations I have often stressed the basic biological necessities that set up a constant tension betwen the individual man and his society. In his recent book, *The Tyranny of Survival,* Daniel Callahan has reviewed the same evidence in connection with his discussion of the generally pessimistic thoughts expressed by Freud in *Civilization and Its Discontents.* Incidentally, the German title is somewhat to be preferred—*Das Unbehagen in der Kultur*—since, following Spengler and others, one tends to think of civilization as a relatively late human development, whereas "the uneasiness of culture" dates back to man's earliest days as a human being.

After all, Freud is not really concerned with such modern discontents as waiting in line for some gasoline, but with the much more profound sacrifices every human being must make because he is at the same time an individual and a member of society. Much of man's basic physiology is designed to ensure his survival in strictly individual terms. He eats, he drinks, he fights or runs away at the command and with the help of this complex, highly individual apparatus. Many of these activities are accompanied by intense subjective experiences and drives. Nevertheless, his survival equally depends upon his interactions with his group, tribe, society, or *Kultur.* As Freud and many others pointed out, this dependence on the group demands certain painful sacrifices as an individual, but, as Willard Gaylin recently remarked, "Not everyone finds these sacrifices as painful as Freud did since we are also provided with additional physiological machinery which helps bind us to others and gives us at least some pleasure in doing something for them."

It is, of course, well known that in other animals reproductive behavior from courting to weaning is under rather strict endocrine and genetically determined nervous control. It is probable that human beings cannot entirely escape this, although the learned or cultural element is much larger, as La Rochefoucauld recognized when he remarked that few people would fall in love if they hadn't read about it. However determined, man's social interdependence is a fact, and he derives from it satisfaction, as well as pain. Sometimes, perhaps more often than not, the pain and the satisfaction are closely intermingled. The limiting case may be that of the young man, so often praised by both poet and politician, who lays down his life for his country.

But in a larger and deeper sense, every human death is ultimately for the good of the group. It is, at least in biological terms, the most fundamental of creative acts. For an audience such as this, it is scarcely necessary to review all the facts that attest to the role of selective death in the evolutionary process. It must be equally, or perhaps even more, obvious that cultural evolution also relies on death not only to select the "fittest," but simply to make room and to give more opportunity for the bearers of new ideas and novel life styles. If Ponce de León and his colleagues had ever found the Fountain of Eternal Youth, it would have soon shown itself a pool of stagnation.

Discontent, or the slightly more uncomfortable German *Unbehagen*, may be rather weak words to describe the obligation to die, as well as to sublimate for one's culture. Indeed, it is possible to find not only dignity, but a certain grandeur in the concept. To rage with Dylan Thomas and other rebellious Celts at the injustice of it all, is to rage at the very process which made one a human being in the first place. It is all these things that the pagan biologist has in mind when he says that death is part, parcel, and process of life and not some absurd event tacked on at the end out of divine spite or, worse still, as a punishment for sin.

Indeed, it is in their reading of the book of Genesis that the pagan finds it hardest to follow the Christians. The idea that death was laid upon us as a punishment for original sin is so foreign to the pagan biologist that he must make a constant effort to remind himself that other people really do believe it, and that it is this belief that colors so much of their thinking on other issues.

It is not that we do not believe in sin, because of course many of us do, and we all believe in death. We simply don't see much connection between the two. Furthermore, the whole business of being saved from sin by having salvation bestowed on us in the twinkling of an eye in the form of immortality seems bizarre in the extreme. But perhaps this is another story.

The "Preacher" comes much closer to the biological position and is even regarded by some as a pagan himself. At any rate, in words which even Paul Ramsey has to admit have a certainty beauty, he reflects helpfully on the cyclical and seasonal character of life. It seems clear from the context that he regarded these regularities as "fitting and proper." What made him sad and pessimistic was not the regularity of sowing and reaping, but the inexplicable *ir*regularities and perversities within the system—the fact that the race was not always to the swift or riches to the wise, but that time and chance happens to them all—in other words, there ain't no justice under the sun. Also

and furthermore, men tend to look for the wrong things. All these human failings bothered the Preacher, but I see nothing in his remarks to suggest that he found indignity in death. Indeed, he mentions death only very rarely, most notably in Chapter 7, where he says,

> A good name is better than precious ointment and the day of death than the day of one's birth. It is better to go into the house of mourning than to go into the house of mirth.... The heart of the wise is in the house of mourning, but the heart of the fool is in the house of mirth.

Good Grief

Incidentally, this passage may also serve as a text for commenting on Paul Ramsey's summary dismissal of "good grief" as a contradiction in terms. Even in its simplest terms, grief is recognized by every physician and by such nonprivy counselors as Ann Landers as not only a good, but the best therapy. Indeed, the inability to experience grief is the sign of the worst of all human detachments—pathognomonic, as we doctors would say, of schizophrenia.

Like every other good thing, the Greeks had a word for it: *catharsis*. What, indeed, are the tragedies of the house of Atreus but exercises in good grief? Not very long ago, some of us gained wisdom by entering into the house of mourning with Creon and Eurydice on Public Television while fools twisted their dials to the houses of mirth.

In the midst of his discussion of the Preacher, Paul Ramsey admits, citing Kierkegaard, that the Preacher was a poet and that as a poet his heart was full of pain but his lips were so formed that when he gives utterance to that pain he makes beautiful sounds. Alfred Kazin put the matter more succinctly when he said that art is the fusion of suffering with form. One might pursue the thought a little further and observe that "Death with Dignity" is simply the title of the last poem, in which the end of life is given its proper form. But perhaps this is a view that appeals only to pagans and stoics, who sometimes seem to have regarded the whole business of life as the study of how to give form and dignity to suffering.

9

Averting one's eyes, or facing the music? —on dignity and death

LEON R. KASS

THE THESIS of Paul Ramsey's chapter, "The Indignity of 'Death with Dignity,'" is that current campaigns to naturalize, romanticize, beautify, or dignify death—which he collects together as campaigns for "death with dignity"—heap added insults and indignities upon dying people. This thesis rests on two foundations. First, Ramsey believes that many adherents of "death with dignity" have an impoverished and shrunken view of the meaning and dignity of human life which, in turn, leads them to an impoverished and insensitive view of the meaning of death for dying individuals and their near ones. Second, Ramsey believes that death itself—even an easy and painless death coming in old age to a human being who has lived a worthy and happy life—is inherently an indignity, and one which cannot be over-

This essay is dedicated to the memory of Gerhard Emil Otto Meyer, teacher and friend, who died at the age of seventy in December, 1973, three weeks after completing a thirty-six-year career in undergraduate teaching at the University of Chicago. He lived the way he thought he should, and the way he thought he should coincided with the way he wanted. He will remain for many of us a touchstone of human dignity.

come or even mitigated. There are then two themes—"The Indignity of 'Death with Dignity,'" and "The Indignity of Death"—and the first theme rests upon the second, as Ramsey himself admits, discussing his title in his opening paragraph: "So 'The Indignity of Death' would not suffice for my purposes, even though *all* I shall say *depends* on understanding the contradiction death poses to the unique worth of an individual human life." (Emphasis added.)

This commentary will deal almost exclusively with the question of the "indignity of death." My purpose is to expose some of the roots of Ramsey's argument and thus to open up and join on some questions that need further and more serious attention. I shall also point to some alternative ways of thinking about our subject, though I am fully aware that I discuss none of them adequately, and perhaps some of them even incorrectly. Though I hesitate to start a quarrel I am unable to finish, I hope others may profit from this beginning.

I hesitate to make public my sharp disagreement with Ramsey on this matter because I happen to share some of his concerns regarding our current and future practices toward the dying. I worry that the accelerating drive to compensate for previous excessive denial and avoidance of death may, on an equally distant swing, lead us past the sensible mean to a weakened respect for life. I see a real danger that the combination of our general zeal to rectify wrongs all at once, our swelling and not unjustified revulsion at some results of senseless (but also of sensible) efforts to prolong life at all costs, our delight in debunking myths and in shedding taboos, our prejudices against the old and "useless," and, in some cases, our simply crass and selfish interests, sometimes masquerading as compassion, may lead to grave excesses. I am therefore reluctant to give any comfort to the insensitively zealous by attacking one of their most articulate and intelligent critics. Yet if close attention be paid, it will be seen that my criticism of Ramsey's principles contains a criticism also of some of those he confronts.

For yet more personal reasons do I hesitate to present the following comments. While much of the early part of his chapter is a punch and jab critique of the fuzzy opinions of others, Ramsey later reveals that it is by the light and with the fists of a Christian teaching that he has been in combat. Am I not foolish to engage this Goliath of a Christian thinker and pugilist, and on the very subject of his profoundest beliefs? My task is made yet more difficult because I respect and admire this Christian gentleman, owe much of my current career to his encouragement, and regard him as my friend. Yet I think he might not mind —and I hope not merely feel the need to turn the other cheek—if I proceed in the spirit of a remark made by a wise man of old, who, faced with a similar dilemma but with a far more imposing challenge than mine, said:

> Yet it would perhaps seem to be better and even necessary, for the sake of safeguarding the truth, even to destroy the things of our own, especially as we are lovers of wisdom; for while both are dear, it is fitting to prefer the truth.

The Title

The same wise man has also said, "The beginning is more than half the whole." Let me begin then at the beginning, with the title: "The Indignity of 'Death with Dignity.'" This is a clever, paradoxical, and hence enticing title. We do not yet know what it means, and therefore, whether as a proposition it is true. But it serves im-

mediately to raise questions about the meaning of the phrase "death with dignity" and about the possibilities and limits of such a death, whatever the phrase turns out to mean. More radically, it points to questions about the meaning of *"dignity,"* about the existence of *"human dignity,"* and about whether and how any such dignity is attained or lost, conferred or withdrawn.

This preference for the extraordinary use of words—a confessed addiction of the author—is, however, a risky business generally, and here in particular. Though it can dramatically call attention to a question hitherto relatively ignored, extraordinary

Crudely speaking, we might say that the *possibility* of a humanly dignified facing of death can be destroyed from without (and, of course, from within), but the *actualization* of that possibility depends largely on the soul, the character, the bearing of the dying man himself—i.e., on things *within*.

usage can distort the terms in which the question is posed and discussed. An extraordinary title may indeed succeed in prolonging the life of a question but only at the price of reducing or disfiguring its character —and also—if ignorance may be said to be one form of "suffering"—of prolonging suffering. This, as I will try to show, is here the case. Would that Ramsey had adhered to his own medico-moral teaching about eschewing extraordinary means.

The difficulty to which I refer concerns the nature of human dignity and the relation of death to any such dignity. The opinions which lie behind my critique are that dignity is something that belongs to a human being and is displayed in the way he lives, and hence something not easily taken away from him; therefore, that death is, at the very least, neutral with respect to dignity; that, further, human mortality may even be the necessary condition for the display of at least *some* aspects of a human being's dignity; and, finally, that human dignity is more dependent on the exercise of those generic human qualities rather than on those things which make him Ramsey and me Kass. These individuating differences may be pleasing and may make life more "interesting," but there is more dignity in our common effort to understand each other and to understand the meaning of human life, or in our parallel efforts to live fully human lives, than in any of our unique, distinctive, and idiosyncratic features.[1]

Before proceeding to the discussion, we need to disentangle the questions and clarify some terms.

What is the Question?

The slogan "death with dignity," whatever its difficulties, stands partly for the proposition: "There are more and less dignified ways to face death or to die." Ramsey and I would agree with this proposition, and so, I think, should anyone; numerous examples could be cited that would draw common assent. The *possibility* of dying with dignity can be diminished, undermined, or even eliminated by many things in many ways, for example, by coma or senility, unbearable pain, madness, sudden death, denial, depravity, ignorance, cowardice, isolation, destitution, as well as by excessive and impersonal medical and technological intervention—and even, as Ramsey rightly points out, by the imposition of a false or exploitative or insensitive or shallow doctrine of "death with dignity."

On this last point, the primary surface theme and target of Ramsey's essay, I hasten to add my agreement. Ramsey and I agree, on the one hand, that excessive efforts to prolong life and the impersonal institutional arrangements and callous treatments these efforts tend to foster can be an affront to dying patients, their families and friends, indeed, to all of us. But Ramsey and I also agree, on the other hand, that it can be equally insensitive and insulting to do battle with these excesses under a slogan that implies that dignity will reign if only we can push back officious doctors, machinery, and hospital administrators. Moreover, I suspect that Ramsey might even agree with me in holding that an inadequate or partial notion of human dignity informs both the excessive efforts to prolong life *and* some of the current efforts to curb these excesses.

A death with dignity—which may turn out to be something rare or uncommon, even under the best of circumstances, like a life with dignity, on which a death with dignity may most often depend[2]—entails

---

[1]Indeed, I would suggest that Ramsey's predicament of finding himself in bed with too many partners may stem in part from the fact that both he and they give too much emphasis to "uniqueness," to the subjective, to the individual human soul in its "individuation." Could it be that the stress on the "unique worth of the individual" connects together the mainstream of today's secular thought and its severed theological source, from which Paul Ramsey still takes his watering?

[2]Consider Cephalus' answer to Socrates' question about whether old age is a hard time of life. See Plato, *Republic* 1. trans. by Allan Bloom (New York: Basic Books, 1968), p. 5:

" 'By Zeus, I shall tell you just how it looks to me, Socrates,' he said. 'Some of us who are about the same age often meet together and keep up the old proverb. Now then, when they meet, most of the members of our group lament, longing for the pleasures of youth and reminiscing about sex, about drinking bouts, and feasts and all that goes with things of that sort; they take it hard as though they were deprived of something very important and had then lived well but are now not even alive. Some also bewail the abuse that old age receives from relatives, and in this key they sing a refrain about all the evils old age has caused them. But, Socrates, in my opinion these men do not put their fingers on the cause. For, if this were the cause, I too would have suffered these same things insofar as they depend on old age and so would everyone else who has come to this point in life.... But of these things and of those that concern relatives, there is one certain cause: not old age, Socrates, but the character of the human beings. If they are balanced and good-tempered, even old age is only moderately troublesome; if they are not, then both age, Socrates, and youth alike turn out to be hard for that sort.' "

more than the absence of external indignities. Dignity in the face of death cannot be given or conferred from the outside—at least not by other men—but requires a dignity of soul in the human being who faces it. This, despite the many claims to the contrary, neither the partisans of "death with dignity" nor the myriad servants of mankind, from the Department of Welfare to departments of medicine or psychiatry, can supply—though they can, perhaps, offer some assistance. On these matters I think Ramsey and I agree, and we need no longer tarry over them, except perhaps to note a useful distinction. Crudely speaking, we might say that the *possibility* of a humanly dignified facing of death can be destroyed from without (and, of course, from within), but the *actualization* of that possibility depends largely on the soul, the character, the bearing of the dying man himself—i.e., on things *within*. This distinction may bear also on the later and more crucial question of whether it is true that *death as such* is an "ultimate indignity" or an indignity at all—i.e., whether there is truth in this proposition which Ramsey admits is the one on which *all* he has to say depends.

But first, what is meant here by "death"? "Death," as Ramsey uses the term in this paper, suffers from frequent personification and reification: "Death is an enemy," "Death means the conquest of the time of our lives," "The dreadful visage of death," "The shadow of death on every human countenance," and "The sting of death is sin," to cite but a few examples. More serious and confusing is Ramsey's failure to distinguish among (1) the state of *"being" dead,* i.e., of nonbeing, (2) the "final" *transition,* whether process or event,[3] between the state of being alive and the state of being dead, (3) the process, often drawn out, of *"being dying,"* to borrow from Cassell[4], and (4) *the fact of human mortality,* of human finitude. All of these Ramsey calls simply "death." Yet it is the

fourth sense, "death" as *mortality,* that Ramsey must mean when he speaks of the "contradiction *death* poses to the unique worth of an individual human life." Thus Ramsey's "The Indignity of Death" I take to mean "The Indignity of Human Mortality."

From this clarification, two others follow. First, we are not here talking about the dignity or indignity of *premature* death or *painful* death or *violent* death or *untimely* death, that is, of the death of a young child by drowning or of an elderly widow with disseminated cancer or of a middle-aged President killed by an assassin or of a composer in the midst of writing his greatest symphony. We are talking only about the fact that we must die. Indeed, another way of stating Ramsey's claim is to say that there is no such thing as a timely death, as a death in season, because the "contradiction" of our mortality means that there never is a right time to die. Second, if mortality is an indignity, so are aging and senescence. The waning of the light, no less than its inevitable extinction, must come under Ramsey's charge of "indignity," as must everything which diminishes or jeopardizes human vitality and ripeness.

A second cause of confusion, as perplexing as his imprecision in the use of the term "death," is Ramsey's frequent weaving back and forth between (1) a subjective perspective on a *particular* "death" in its "individuality"—including some identified particular "deaths"—and its implications for the dying man, his loved ones, or a disinterested observer, and (2) an objective perspective on human mortality itself, and on the implications for each of us as human beings of the fact that death is (in this sense) a necessary and inescapable condition of human life.

Now Ramsey's essay is, admittedly, presented in the context of current discussions of "allowing to die" and "medical mercy killings"; his remarks are therefore addressed to people who will think less about human mortality in general and more about how to care for particular dying human beings. Were he writing mainly to the philosophical and theological questions he might have written differently. Yet never before, even when addressing practical men

[3]Robert S. Morison, "Death: Process or Event?" and Leon R. Kass, "Death as an Event: A Commentary on Robert Morison."

[4]Eric J. Cassell, "Being and Becoming Dead," *Social Research* 39 (Autumn, 1972), 528-42.

and their practical problems, have I known Ramsey to detach himself from the normative questions—to the annoyance of some and the delight of others, including myself. Though he enjoys good anecdotes and can conjure cases better than most, the particular cases are for the sake of the generic and, ultimately, the normative. He usually would be the first to call attention to the difference between what men *do* and what they *should do*—even men like Isaac and Socrates about whom he here fishes for empirical evidence that they acted other than we know. Thus, I invite him to join me in his usual question: How *should* Socrates or Isaac or Ramsey or Kass or any human being regard —now and when we are dying—the fact that we must each and all die? Who *should* we take as our model: Socrates, his wife, Crito, Ivan Ilych, Joan of Arc, Dr. Sackett, a Kamikaze pilot, Dylan Thomas' old man, Isaac upon the altar or at the end of his days, Achilles facing Hector, Shakespeare's Caesar or Brutus or Antony or Cleopatra, the Eskimo elder walking off to freeze, or Zarathustra? We may not be able to emulate fully our model, either now or in the face of our own "being dying," but this in no way detracts from the importance of the question. On the contrary, we may find our own stance toward our mortality, now and then, *improved* as a result of thinking through the truth about the questions, "How should we regard the fact that we must die?" "Is our mortality an indignity?"

To be sure, this question may be dealt with differently—or even ignored—by different people. The doctor, the death-bed confessor, the general, and the philosopher may, and perhaps must, adopt different perspectives, according to their different works. Yet there can be and usually are prevailing opinions and outlooks which inform these perspectives. Further, there may even be a *truth* about these matters which might be in conflict with these prevailing opinions, and which, if we could discern or approach it, could conceivably reform and improve these opinions, or at least free us from certain harmful superstitions. (Do we not implicitly, even if unwittingly, make just such assumptions when we engage in serious discussion about this—or any subject?) But, on the other hand—and here I at least must pause —it is possible that certain opinions, even

so-called superstitions, may be more beneficial than the unvarnished truth or than that portion of the truth which may be accessible to us. This, I submit, may be the case here.

Let us consider what course we should follow on the assumption that there is a tension between "the true" and "the useful." Are we and should we be interested in fostering opinions which could possibly be popularly embraced and which could give comfort and solace, regardless of whether or not they are true? Or are we and should we be interested in pursuing the truth, allowing the chips to fall where they may?

Ramsey and I agree, I think, at least in this instance, on the superiority of the latter course, though we may soon thereafter part company on where to look in our pursuit of what is true. And since we have not yet shown that the truth about death is deadly, or is likely to be, I am willing to venture to inquire into what is true about the meaning of the fact that human beings die and the relationship of this fact to the dignity of human life.

Formally, there are at least three positions on our question about the dignity or indignity of death itself: (1) That men must die is inherently an indignity or an affront to human dignity which cannot be overcome, no matter how dignified one's stance toward death; (2) That men must die is inherently part of human dignity; and (3) That men must die is neutral with respect to dignity, dignity or indignity in dying, as in living, depending only on the actions of the human being involved. These formal alternatives stated, we can make no material progress toward an answer unless and until we know what we mean by dignity. The failure to provide an analytic of "dignity" is, I hold, a major weakness in Ramsey's chapter. Had he explored this question, I suspect—and I will try to show why—he would have been sorry he saddled himself with these terms.

Toward an Analytic of Dignity

The English word "dignity" derives from the Latin *dignitas,* which, according to the *White and Riddle Latin-English Dictionary,* means (1) a being worthy, worthiness, merit, desert, (2) dignity, greatness, grandeur, authority, rank, and (3) (of inanimate things) worth, value, excellence. The noun·is cognate with the adjective *dignus* (the root *DIC,* related to the Sanskrit *DIC* and the Greek *DEIK,* means "to bring to light," "to show," to point out"), literally, "pointed out" or "shown," and hence, "worthy" or "deserving" (of persons), and "suitable," "fitting," "becoming," or "proper" (of things).

"Dignity," in the *Oxford English Dictionary,* is said to have eight meanings, the four relevant ones I reproduce here: (1) The quality of being worthy or honourable; worthiness, worth, nobleness, excellence (for instance, "The real dignity of a man lies not in what he *has,* but in what he *is,*" or "The dignity of this act was worth the audience of kings"); (2) Honourable or high estate, position, or estimation; honour; degree of estimation, rank (for instance, "Stones, though in dignitie of nature inferior to plants," or "Clay and clay differs in dignity, whose dust is both alike"); (3) An honourable office, rank, or title; a high official or titular position (for instance, "He ... distributed the civil and military dignities among his favorites and followers"); (4) Nobility or befitting elevation of aspect, manner, or style; becoming or fit stateliness, gravity (for instance, "A dignity of dress adorns the Great").

The central notion, in both Latin and English, is that of worthiness, elevation, honor, nobility, height—in short, of excellence. In all its meanings, it is a term of distinction; dignity is not something which, like a navel or a nervous system, is to be expected or to be found in every living human being. Dignity is, in principle, aristocratic—this is inescapable, quite apart from however one might specify the *content* of excellence or distinction.

Certain qualifications should be noted. First, honor and rank are, of course, problematic. Though they are meant to be signs of worth, they often depend more on those who bestow them than on those who receive them. For example, the lasting honor and glory of Achilles depends on the greatness of Homer, that of Pericles on Thucydides and Plutarch. More generally, the worth and tastes and opinions of the bestowers will be decisive for determining what is honored.

Esteem is given not always for excellence, and excellence is not always esteemed. Esteem and honor can be withdrawn, whereas dignity, in the sense of worthiness, excellence, and nobility, is something not easily taken from a man. Nevertheless, despite elements of relativity and the possibilities of error, the simple fact that human beings do bestow praise and blame, and *point out* by these means examples of worthiness, acknowledges the existence of various human excellences that bring themselves to light. This is also attested to by the great pains men often take to bring their judgments of worthiness in line with some standards of what is indeed noble and excellent.

Second, one can, of course, seek to democratize the principle; one can argue that "excellence," "being worthy" is a property of *all* human beings, say, for example, in comparison with animals or plants, or with machines that may perform certain tasks as well as human beings. This, I take it, is what is meant by *"human* dignity." This is also what is implied when it is asserted that much of the terminal treatment of dying patients is dehumanizing, or that attachments to catheters, pacemakers, monitors, respirators, suction tubes, intravenous tubes, and oxygen masks destroy or hide the human countenance and thereby insult the dignity of the dying. This view is not without some merit. Yet on further examination this universal attribution of dignity to human beings pays tribute to human potentiality, to the *possibilities* for human excellence. The human countenance is expressive of the presence of the human soul and of the possibilities of its excellences. *Full* dignity, or dignity properly so-called, would depend on the *realization* of these possibilities.

Moreover, to speak of dignity as predicable of all human beings, say in contrast to animals, is to tie dignity to those distinctively human features of human animals, such as thought, image-making, the sense of beauty, freedom, friendship, and the moral life, and not the mere presence of life itself. *Among* human beings, there would still be, on any such material principle, distinctions to be made—unless one evacuates the meaning of the term, and the predicate "dignity" is held to add nothing to "born of woman." Thus even if one were to accept the rather attenuated notion of dignity implied in Pascal's "Our whole dignity consists in thought" (by which he means preeminently self-consciousness and awareness of mortality), one would have to wonder about the relative ranking of those who think more and less, that is, are more or less self-conscious. Or, to take another possible ground of human dignity, while each human being can be said to have a moral life in that everyone faces moral choices, *dignity* would seem to depend on having a *good* moral life, that is, on choosing well. Clearly, we do not want to say that there is dignity—or much dignity—in the life of a paid killer, a slave-dealer, or a prostitute, or that they compare in dignity with Ghandi, Abraham Lincoln, or Joan of Arc. And is there not more dignity in courage than in cowardice, in moderation than in self-indulgence, in righteousness than in wickedness?[5]

A brief look at *indignity,* again from the *Oxford English Dictionary.* "Indignity" is "any action toward another which manifests contempt for him," "an offense against personal dignity," "incivility," "unmerited contemptuous treatment," in short, an *affront.*

It is important to note that dignity, in the sense of worth and worthiness, is not precisely or even mainly the opposite of indignity. Dignity does not consist merely in the absence of indignity, and indignity is not itself merely the absence of dignity. Dignity and indignity seem to be two separate "things," each of which one can "possess" more or less or not at all. Thus, the more accurate meaning of "death with dignity," when used as a slogan against excessive medical intervention, is really "death without further or additional indignity."

Death and Dignity

Without *further* or *additional* indignity? Additional to what? To death itself? We have come at last to our question. In what sense can death (mortality) be an indignity? Is it an "action toward another"—and if so, whose? Or "an offense against personal dignity" or "unmerited contemptuous treatment" or an affront? I think not. Only if dignity were synonymous or coextensive with life itself could we even begin to make such a case.[6]

And yet, though merely to live is not yet to live excellently or with dignity, to die is to put an end to all further possibility of dignity. Human life is a necessary condition of there being any human dignity, and one ought—even on this ground alone—to respect it and respect it highly. My previous argument appears to need some qualification. Could we not call death or mortality "an indignity" because it "destroys" or limits the conditions of dignity, even though the conditions as such—life—are not by themselves sufficient to produce dignity or worthiness? (Here we may have an analogy to the distinction drawn above in my discussion of more and less dignified ways to die, where it was noted that "external" conditions could make a so-called "dignified death" difficult if not impossible.) Could it be said, then, that death is in this sense "the ultimate indignity," just as murder is perhaps the ultimate personal crime—ultimate precisely because, by destroying the foundations, it makes impossible the entire edifice, right up to the crown?

I think not. Death *may* be a great evil,

---

[5]This is not necessarily to say that one should treat other people, including those who eschew dignity, as if they lacked it. This is a separable question. It may indeed be salutary to treat people on the basis of their capacities to live humanly, despite even great falling short or even willful self-degradation. Yet this would, in the moral sphere at least, require that we expect and demand of people that they behave worthily. One cannot, without self-contradiction, both attribute moral dignity to everyone and then excuse a man's crimes and moral failings by blaming them on his toilet training, his poverty, or "The System." Moral dignity without the presumption of responsibility and accountability is impossible, and to assert it is ludicrous.

[6]Ramsey in fact adopts a view very close to this, in locating dignity in the once-and-for-all, never-to-be-repeated, unique living-toward-death that is, for him, the "definition" of a human life. Man's *worldly* dignity, for Ramsey, stems from the perceived threat of death which, he implies, is ever present with every man so long as he lives. This strikes me as a most misanthropic view of dignity. Moreover, death, which Ramsey claims to be an ultimate indignity, paradoxically emerges on his own view as the "great individualizer," and hence as the source of all worldly dignity. (I am indebted to William F. May for this last insight.)

but it should not be considered *in itself* an "indignity."[7] I offer several suggestions that might be developed into full-blown arguments. *First,* looking to our common sense ways of speaking and feeling, for all that we may fear death, we do not react as if death were an indignity to Picasso or Stravinsky or DeGaulle, each of whom died full of days after a rich and worthy life. We may miss them, but do we regard their death as an affront to them? Do we even regard it as an evil?

Second, as many instances of heroism or martyrdom show, death can be for some human beings the occasion for the display of dignity, indeed of their greatest dignity, for example, in the laying down of one's life for one's friend, one's country, or one's beliefs. Far from undermining their worth, their death—like the life it terminates— is a necessary condition for their display of dignity. Consider, for example, the Athenians eulogized by Thucydides' Pericles in the famous Funeral Oration:

> Thus choosing to die resisting, rather than to live submitting, they fled only from dishonor, but met danger face to face, and after one brief moment, while at the summit of their fortune, escaped, not from their fear, but from their glory....
>
> Comfort, therefore, not condolence, is what I have to offer to the parents of the dead who may be here. Numberless are the chances to which, as they know, the life of man is subject; but fortunate indeed are they who draw for their lot a death so glorious as that which has caused your mourning, and to whom life has been so exactly measured as to terminate in the happiness in which it has been passed.[8]

And this need not only be true of heroes. Take the case of Tolstoi's unheroic Ivan Ilych. It has been argued that with the insight the dying Ilych gets into the meaninglessness of his (former) life,

the man grows far beyond himself in the last hours of his life; he attains an inner greatness which retroactively hallows all of his previous life—in spite of its apparent futility—and makes it meaningful.... Not only the sacrifice of one's life can give life meaning; life can reach nobility even as it founders on the rocks.[9]

Though I think the claim made here for Ivan Ilych is excessive, the general point is worth pondering.

Third, to expand this point, it has been argued that human mortality is a necessary spur, throughout all of one's life, to the pursuit of excellence and the acquisition of dignity, and that immortal life, even without senescence, could not be lived with seriousness or with passion.[10] Ramsey himself notes that without death "life would be an endless boredom, and boring because endless; there would be no reason to probe its depths while there is still time." And so, when Ramsey says that "death may be a good evil," I think he means to acknowledge the importance of mortality for at least some aspects of human worthiness. I myself have doubts about the full adequacy of this view, and seriously question the notion of human life as "living-toward-death." In this connection, I suggest we consider the alternative outlooks implied either in the life of Socrates, as Plato presents it, or in the possibly apocryphal story about St. Francis who, while in the garden planting onions, was asked, "What would you do if you learned that you were to die tomorrow?" and who supposedly answered, "I would continue planting onions." And yet, if we consider the statesman, the warrior, the athlete, the painter, the poet, the actor, the architect, the teacher, or the lover, we can see the importance of not having world enough and time.

Fourth, as Hans Jonas has pointed out, death may not only be the necessary spur to our numbering our days, but also the condition of the possibility of renewed life and youth and hope:

---

[7]As the above analysis of the relation between "dignity" and "indignity" suggests, to show that mortality is not an indignity would say nothing about whether it is "beautiful" or "full of dignity"; for these excessive claims I hold no brief.

[8]*The Complete Writings of Thucydides: The Peloponnesian War,* trans. by Richard Crawley, Modern Library Edition (New York: Random House, 1934), pp. 107-08.

[9]Viktor E. Frankl, *The Doctor and the Soul* (New York: Vintage Books, 1973), p. 106.

[10]See, for example, Eric J. Cassell, "Death and the Physician," *Commentary,* June, 1969, pp. 73-79.

With their ever new beginning, with all their foolishness and fumbling, it is the young that ever renew and thus keep alive the sense of wonder, of relevance, of the unconditional, of ultimate commitment, which (let us be frank) goes to sleep in us as we grow older and tired. It is the young, not the old, that are ready to give their life, to die for a cause[11]—

and I would add, it is the cycle of birth answering death that brings the ever renewable possibility of a concern for excellence and dignity.

Death as Natural

Yet I think I would emphasize a fifth and final reason why death cannot be regarded as an indignity, or I might even add, as an ultimate evil. I return, without romanticism but with a sober appreciation of what I think is true, to the fact that *death is natural and necessary and inextricably tied to life.* To live is to be mortal; death is the necessary price for life. To decline and to die are necessary parts of the *life cycle,* whether fully and *consciously* experienced or not. (I admit freely that "one's own nonbeing" cannot be experienced—it is an impossibility—though I am not certain that it cannot be imagined.) Already Aristotle notes that living things have in themselves a principle of growth *and decay.* Decay and decline are not "affronts from outside," but are natural processes *built into* the principle that causes life.

Ramsey's personification of death is at least partly responsible for his failure to appreciate this point. "Death is an enemy," and his other personifications all treat "death" as an external agent. Ramsey is thus easily led to the view that death is always an assault from outside, and, even when timely, so-to-speak "violent." Even his more neutral formulations of "living-toward-death" and "living toward a limit" also externalize mortality and fail to acknowledge the degree to which that limit is set *within.*

Modern biology has in no fundamental way altered Aristotle's view; the maximum life-span of a species is governed from within, the result of processes that are genetically determined—that is, natural—and encoded in the genome that "contains the information" for the other processes of life. How can death be an indignity if it is the natural and necessary accompaniment of life itself? When we "buy" life we "buy" death. Is there thus not even some indignity—some childish desire to cheat, or to eat one's life and keep it—in the suggestion that death is a contradiction to the *worth* of a human life? Is there really dignity in attempting the impossible or in railing against the inevitable? Is there not more dignity in facing up to such things and in facing them nobly and bravely? Consider the following passages from Aristotle's *Ethics.* After acknowledging that "death is the most terrible of all things; for it is the end, and nothing is thought to be any longer either good or bad for the dead," Aristotle concludes his discussion of courage:

> Death and wounds will be painful to the brave man and against his will, but he will face them because it is noble to do so or because it is base not to do so. And the more he is possessed of virtue in its entirety and the happier he is, the more he will be pained at the thought of death; for life is best worth living for such a man, and he is knowingly losing the greatest goods, and this is painful. But he is none the less brave, and perhaps all the more so, because he chooses noble deeds of war at that cost.[12]

Against the view that mortality is a "part of life" Ramsey has urged that "disease, injury, congenital defects are also a part of life, and as well murder, rapine, and pillage." But are any of these as natural, necessary, and inextricably bound up with life as are death or decay? The closest case would be disease; but whereas both disease and decline have "natural" causes, much disease is caused at least in part by external agency, and the body responds to disease by "attempting" to heal itself, to make itself healthy, to make itself whole. In this sense, disease is *fought* by nature working within, whereas decline is *produced* by

---

[11]Hans Jonas, "Contemporary Problems in Ethics From a Jewish Perspective," *Journal of Central Conference of American Rabbis* (January, 1968), 27-39; reprinted in *Judaism and Ethics,* ed. by D. J. Silver (New York: Ktav Publishing Company, 1970).

[12]W. D. Ross translation.

nature working within. This is, of course, oversimplified and crude, but nevertheless adequate enough to suggest that, unlike all those other things which *occur* in life, decline and death are a *part* of life, an integral part which cannot be extruded without destroying the whole.

Against this view Ramsey has also urged the empirical argument that although "death is a natural fact of life yet no man dies 'naturally,' nor do we have occasions in which to 'practice' doing so in order to learn how." Maybe most men don't, but some men do. Maybe not always eagerly—if that is what he means by "naturally"—but often willingly, or at least not unwillingly. And if he means by "naturally" something like "spontaneously" or "not without training," it is simply not true that there is *no* occasion to practice doing so; there is more occasion to practice dying—indeed, a nightly occasion—than to practice child-bearing or child-rearing.

There are many things which human beings do "by nature," by virtue of capacities and possibilities that are inborn in them as human beings, but which nevertheless require training and habituation. Man is by nature an animal that speaks, but each one of us must be taught a language. According to Aristotle, man is by nature a *polis*-animal, that is, an animal that lives in cities, yet he also adds that the man who *discovered* the *polis* was a great benefactor of mankind. More generally, habit is regarded as a kind of second nature; and while our habits do not come to us "naturally," at birth, still our *capacity to form habits,* and good habits, is itself inborn. And while it is true that, unlike speech and the civic and philosophical lives it makes possible, death is not an end or purpose of human life (*telos*) but merely its termination (*finis*), it is nevertheless possible for us to educate ourselves about the role and meaning of mortality, and thereby to habituate our sentiments and feelings, so that we may live properly before it, without undue fear or anxiety. For this, more important than the experience of sleeping may be the experience of the lives and deaths of those who have gone before, whether in fact or in myth, experience accessible to us if we study the lives of some great human beings and if we carefully read and think

about the great literature of our tradition. And even if we have not studied, and even if we never saw anyone die, we could still, in principle, learn something about how *we ought* to stand toward death—and not only how most of us do—if we reflect on the fact that we were once not here and that we will again not be here, and that this is the way things are and must be. If we are really to eschew whistling in the dark, let us come fully into the light and see nature as it is.

Ramsey's paper fails to give nature her due. Though what nature is is a great mystery and a long question, she deserves more respect than Ramsey gives her. He complains that certain modern "interpretations of human life are increasingly mundane, naturalistic, antihumanistic when measured by *any* genuinely 'humanistic' esteem for the individual human being." Here we come close to fundamentals. Ultimately, though not in this paper, we shall have to ask whether the "esteem" for the "individual human being" is tied first and most to what is *individuated* or to what is *human*—that is, generic—about that *particular* human being. Ramsey speaks briefly to this question, and nods to Aristotle, at the end of his paper. But he presents little if any argument. He intimates that there are few adherents of Plato and Aristotle around today, as if that constituted a valid

Is death an evil or a good, or a good *evil* or an evil *good?* . . . For Ramsey, the genus of mortality is ineradicably *evil,* even though for some of us it may be a good evil. . . . In contrast, Maimonides and Rabbi Meir seem to say that death is an evil good. This latter view seems to me correct.

argument against them, and concludes, why I do not know, that *"a true humanism and the dread of death seem to be dependent variables."* (Emphasis added.) A true humanism or a true humanitarianism? In either case, does he mean "true," or merely "more comforting"? And he adds, again I know not why, "I suggest that it is better to have the indignity of death on our hands and in our outlooks than to 'dignify' it in either of these two possible ways." Why and how *better*? But I digress—this is for another day.

For the present, I note from the above passage only how Ramsey has demoted the world and nature, and thereby also man insofar as he is (merely) natural and worldly. What are the opposites of "mundane, naturalistic, antihumanistic," if not "other-worldly, unnaturalistic, humanistic"?

To the First Things and the Origin of Death

Ramsey's critique of a view of death as natural and hence acceptable is a critique which rests not on his reason but in his faith. He speaks as if the really *proper* condition for a being such as man is immortality, that man fell to a merely mortal, merely natural condition. He speaks as if man had a chance for immortality but squandered it. (That Ramsey is not a pessimist stems from his unstated belief that men—though not as worldly men—have not really lost immortality.) Notice where dignity lies on Ramsey's view of nature and man. Man, the mortal sinner, has only an alien dignity bestowed upon him by God, who out of His infinite love became man and was crucified, and who thus redeems man and offers him salvation from sin and the conquest of death. Ramsey's view of death as an indignity rests upon his belief in "the Fall of Man," as recounted in Genesis, but not called "the Fall of Man" in Genesis, or, as far as I know, anywhere else in the Hebrew tradition. (I checked the latest edition of the *Encyclopedia Judaica* and found between Falkowitsch, Joel Baerisch, and Falticeni, Rumania, only Fall River, Massachusetts.)

This may perhaps be an appropriate place to mention that I have serious questions about the adequacy of Ramsey's treatment of the Hebrew sources or tradition on this topic. It is a simplification, and I think a gross distortion, to say as he does that "sin was determinative for the Hebrew consciousness" (so too, "death for the Greek consciousness"). Even at this simplistic formulaic level, what about "covenant" or "sanctification" or "love of God"? Also, Ramsey's interpretation of Ecclesiastes is at variance in some important respects with the few Hebrew commentators I have read,[13] and I myself would dispute whether the book shows "an unrelieved pessimism," and whether "the practical advice" of Koheleth isn't more akin to "Live joyously; do not toil in vain or seek wisdom," than to Ramsey's formulation, "Be what you are, in human awareness apart and not a part," which makes Koheleth too much like Pascal to be Koheleth. And, concerning the critical passage, "Everything has its appointed time," etc. (Eccles. 3: 1-9), while it is clear from the overall context that these

---

[13]See, for example, Robert Gordis, *Koheleth: The Man and His World: A Study of Ecclesiastes* (New York: Schocken, 1967) and *Midrash Rabbah Ecclesiastes,* trans. by Rev. A. Cohen (London: Soncino Press, 1961). Consider, as one example, how differently from Ramsey one Midrash interprets the verse, "A good name is better than precious oil, and the day of death better than the day of birth" (7:1):

"When a person is born all rejoice; when he dies all weep. It should not be so; but when a person is born there should be no rejoicing over him, because it is not known in what class he will stand by reason of his actions, whether righteous or wicked, good or bad. When he dies, however, there is cause for rejoicing if he departs with a good name and leaves the world in peace. It is as if there were two ocean-going ships, one leaving the harbor and the other entering it. As the one sailed out of the harbor all rejoiced, but none displayed any joy over the one which was entering the harbor. A shrewd man was there and he said to the people, 'I take the opposite view to you. There is no cause to rejoice over the ship which is leaving the harbor because nobody knows what will be its plight, what seas and storms it may encounter; but when it enters the harbor all have occasion to rejoice since it has come in safely.' Similarly, when a person dies all should rejoice and offer thanks that he departed from the world with a good name and in peace. That is what Solomon said, *And the day of death [is better] than the day of one's birth.*"

lofty verses do not constitute simply a paean of praise but also something of a complaint, it seems that the complaint is for man's ignorance of God's purpose in arranging things thus, rather than for change and death. The real "conclusion" of the litany may not be "What profit then has the worker in his toil?" (Eccles. 3: 9), but rather the sequel:

> I know the concern which God has given men to be afflicted with. Everything He has made proper in its due time, and He has also placed the love of the world in men's hearts, except that they may not discover the work God has done from beginning to end.
> I know that there is no other good in life but to be happy while one lives. Indeed, every man who eats, drinks and enjoys happiness in his work—that is the gift of God. I know that whatever God does remains forever—to it one cannot add and from it one cannot subtract, for God has so arranged matters that men should fear Him. What has been, already exists, and what is still to be, has already been, and God always seeks to repeat what has gone by.[14]

In any event, the Book of Ecclesiastes is perplexing and resists simple formulation and I am not yet prepared to say much more than I think the matter needs more study. There are numerous problems of exegesis and interpretation, not to speak of difficulties caused by translators who have tried to "improve" upon the original. I understand too that there has long been controversy about the Jewishness of this Jewish book, and that it is probably not the best source for the many Jewish teachings on the subject of death.

A better one may be the minor and late Talmudic Tractate "Mourning" (generally referred to by its euphemistic title Semahot, "Rejoicings"; that it is a minor tractate, compared with major tractates on Benedictions or Sabbath or Marriage or property damage and personal injury or sacrifices, may say something about the place of death in Jewish thought). From here comes the following passage on the theme of timely and untimely death:

[14]Trans. by Robert Gordis, in Gordis, The Wisdom of Ecclesiastes (New York: Behrman House, 1945).

> Whosoever dies before he is fifty has been cut down before his time.
> At the age of fifty-two: this is the death of Samuel the Ramathite.
> At the age of sixty: this is the death of which Scripture speaks, for it is said: Thou shalt come to thy grave in ripe age, like a shock of corn cometh in its season. (Job 5:26)
> At the age of seventy: this is the death of divine love, for it is said: The days of our years are threescore and ten. (Ps. 90:10)
> At the age of eighty: this is the death of 'strength,' for it is said: Or even by reason of strength of fourscore years. (Ps. 90:10)
> Similarly, Barzilai said to David: I am this day fourscore years old, can I discern between good and bad? (2 Sam. 19:36)
> After this, life is anguish.

Let me return with Paul Ramsey to the Garden of Eden. Ramsey, ultimately, cannot accept the view that death is "natural," because he follows the teaching about original sin and its wage: "Wherefore, as by one man sin entered into the world, and death by sin; and so death passed upon all men, for that all have sinned" (Rom. 5:12). To be sure, there is Hebrew Biblical support for this view, and one strand of Jewish thought also attributes man's mortality to disobedience (but probably more to each man's disobedience than to Adams'), grounding this view on Genesis 3: 22-24. But the most traditional Jewish view on the necessity of death traces not to the expulsion from the Garden, and not even to disobedience. Death is held to be part of the order of the world since creation. God made man from the dust of the earth, and to dust he must return (Gen. 2:7 and 3:19). Even the account of Genesis 1, with the creation of two sexes and the first commandment to "Be fruitful and multiply, and replenish the earth," already implies the "creation" of mortality. At the completion of creation of the world God saw "everything He had made, and behold, it was very good." The sage Rabbi Meir commenting on this verse says, "it was very good, that is 'death was good,'" which comment Maimonides later cites approvingly in a section of The Guide of the Perplexed, which, at least on the surface, teaches that *everything which is is good*: "Even the existence of this inferior matter, whose manner of being it is to be a concomitant of privation entailing death and all evils, all this is also *good* in view of the perpetuity of generation and the permanence of being through succession."[15]

This last passage permits me to open up a question that goes beyond the dignity or indignity of death. Is death an evil or a good, or a good *evil* or an evil *good?* The passage from Maimonides, while acknowledging that death is an evil (or, at least, is to be grouped with "all evils"), asserts death to be a good. As already noted, Ramsey has made an analogous concession, stating that *awareness* of death can be the cause of a virtuous life if it teaches us to number our days. But for Ramsey, the genus of mortality is ineradicably *evil,* even though for some of us it may be a good evil: "So I say death may be a good evil or an evil evil, but it is perceived as an evil or experienced indignity in either case." In contrast, Maimonides and Rabbi Meir seem to say that death is an evil good. This latter view seems to me correct. The following are some elements of an argument.

First, even though an evil, death is and ought to be preferred to some greater evils. If to lay down one's life under some circumstances is noble, and to continue to live under others is base, then death cannot be an ultimate or worst evil. This does not yet show, of course, that death is a good.

Second, mortality is an evil for the individual—though an evil that is, I repeat, part and parcel of the good which is his life, or more precisely, of the bitter-sweet bargain which is mortal life, as well as, perhaps, the mother of certain strivings toward the good and the beautiful—but it is necessary for the group, be the group defined as the political community or the species. Death is necessary not just in the sense of "unavoidable," which it is also for the individual, but in the sense of "indispensable." Mortality, like taxation, is both certain *and indispensable* for the common good, and the common good is, needless to say, a good from which each individual benefits.

---

[15]Maimonides, *The Guide of the Perplexed,* trans. by Shlomo Pines, Vol. III (Chicago: Univ. of Chicago Press, 1963), Chap. 10.

Third, the evil which death is for us as individuals—for instance, in the sense of the earlier passage from Aristotle in which he calls death the most terrible of all things—becomes good because of generation, continuity, and renewal, that is, "in view of the perpetuity of generation and the permanence of being through succession." The secret is to transcend one's selfish attachments and to shun the view which preaches the "dread of death" as "the dread of oblivion, of there being only empty room in one's stead." Rather one should harken to transmission and regeneration, and to the view which sees in death the presence of one's children and one's grandchildren in one's stead.

Finally, I add an empirical test of Ramsey's view. If death is indeed an irreducible evil, then he should, it seems to me, be willing *in principle* (that is, setting aside other compelling arguments about boredom and about the possible disrupting social consequences) to embrace current biochemical research which aims to retard the process of aging and greatly extend our life expectancy. On *his* principles, were he to find the fountain of youth, he should drink. But knowing Ramsey's other writings, I suspect he would, on principle, refuse. His heart may know the reasons why he should not drink and why, indeed, "There is a time to be born and a time to die," but his reason's reasons—at least those given in this paper—would not tell him or us why not.

To pull together some threads, though there is no Biblical word for "nature," it seems that we can say that death, on the Jewish view, no less than on the Aristotelian or the modern scientific view, is "natural" or "proper to a man." The Christian view—or at least Paul Ramsey's view of the Christian view, which he seems to rest largely on the teachings of St. Paul—disputes this. There are, of course, other Christian views. For example, with St. Thomas Aquinas' efforts to hold together Aristotelian nature and the Gospels, "death as natural" and "Nature as a standard" acquired a permanent place in Christian thought. But whether it is really possible to reconcile Aristotle's elevated nature and natural death with the Pauline view of nature as base and death as the wages of sin I do not know.

These are matters about which I am largely ignorant. I raise these points only to suggest that the "true humanism" dependent on the "dread of death" may turn out to be only one variety of Christian humanism—or rather humanitarianism—though, nevertheless, still possibly true. Also, it is possible that the hyphen needs to be removed from the Judaeo-Christian traditions, at least on this fundamental matter.

But however true the metaphor of the Garden of Eden may be for displaying man's inherent moral weakness or for making intelligible the presence of suffering in the world, can we regard the story as *literally* true? What is the truth about nature and man's place in it? Is nature the prison to which man has fallen or the home out of which he has risen? And more specifically, what is the truth about the origins of human mortality?

We cannot honestly think about the origin of mortal man without facing up to the theory of evolution. In part, Ramsey should be pleased by this move. For never has there been a scientist whose theory so resonates with what Ramsey claims to be the Christian outlook on the world as Darwin: Evolution by natural selection; everything is sin and separation—albeit the only sin is the failure to be fruitful and multiply. Whether the "special theory of evolution," that is, the theory of natural selection, can fully account for the rise of man, or mutation for the appearance of large evolutionary novelties, is a long question. But that man has not always been, and was not specially created *as he now is,* is beyond dispute. Man never was immortal or capable of bodily immortality. He is mortal because his prehuman ancestors were mortal, because each living being is and has always been mortal. He has come to be as a result of birth and death, emerging gradually, via other living forms, out of potentialities that must have been present even in pre-animate matter. That there should be life at all is the greatest "miracle" and wonder, and that through a process blind but perhaps not dumb an intelligent being came to be who considers where he comes from and how he is to live, who sees beauty in nature and who imitates it in his works, who is capable of so much that is excellent—and also so much that is

base—here lies a being and a process with dignity.

In Darwin's view, this rise of man and the higher animals was the result of selective death. Here is how he concludes *The Origin of Species*:

> Thus, from the war of nature, from famine and death, the most exalted object which we are capable of conceiving, namely, the production of the higher animals, directly follows. There is grandeur in this view of life, with its several powers, having been originally breathed into a few forms or into one; and that, whilst this planet has gone cycling on according to the fixed law of gravity, from so simple a beginning endless forms most beautiful and most wonderful have been, and are being, evolved.[16]

To the Last Things?

And yet, to come back a little bit toward Ramsey, and to restore the ecumenical spirit, I must add this final qualification. We now know that "the perpetuity of generation and the permanence of being through succession," which enabled Maimonides to deem death a good, is itself not guaranteed, neither by theory nor in practice. Evolution merely means change, not necessarily "progress," and extinction of species is the general rule. If the death of the individual is an evil for him and a loss to his survivors, the death or extinction of the human species would be far more than that. Man is, regardless of how he came to be, the only being which, though only a part of the whole, can think of, appreciate, and care for the whole. The extinction of man would rob the world of its dignity.

Given our current predicaments, for which we are ourselves largely to blame, perhaps we should begin to pray that there is indeed a providential hand that will not let it happen.

---

[16]For those who may wonder about the adequacy of Darwin's views about the ultimate origin of life, and for those who think the above passage is meant to support a quarrel between science and religion, it is perhaps worth noting that, beginning with the second and continuing through the sixth and last edition of the *Origin,* that is, long after there would be any need to appease religious objectors, Darwin inserted "by the Creator" into the above passage, between "breathed" and "into."

10

The counsels
of finitude

H. TRISTRAM ENGELHARDT, JR.

IN THIS chapter, I will contend that death is a natural event in the course of human life. If I am correct, there is something strange if not perverse in the very notion that such an argument need be made. There is hardly any event as universal as death. How could such an ingredient element of human history be regarded as anything but natural? What would be the need of arguing that death is natural? What would be at issue in such a dispute? What sort of problem is in need of solution?

The issue is a somewhat vague one—a set of loosely bound presuppositions of modern Western culture which lead to an implicit cultural judgment: that death is unnatural. Western thinkers have developed a way of seeing the condition of individuals such that their death is not only regretted but seen as adventitious. It is as if humans were naturally immortal and death an accidental entry into human history. Such an appreciation of death makes it an event to be denied and opposed at all costs, rather than anticipated and articulated in one's anticipation of the future, as ingredient to human life, providing in part for the shape and character of life.

First, I want to make clear that I do not intend to propose an argument against individual immortality, except to suggest that

an argument for immortality cannot succeed. Yet, even if one cannot demonstrate immortality, its possibility is not excluded. I do hope, though, to suggest that immortality would be gratuitous, by the grace of God, not of human nature. However, this chapter will not offer arguments, at least not in any strict sense. My attempt, rather, will be to sketch the lineaments of a view of man in which death can be seen as natural. I will suggest that such a view can allow us to deal better with our finitude, to live better with death and our own dying, hoping to show, thereby, the plausibility of taking counsel from our finitude.

1. Plato, St. Paul, and Charles Hartshorne

Plato's view of death draws heavily on a dualism of mind and matter which was developed on the basis of important epistemological and ontological assumptions. Verging on the brink of dangerous oversimplification, one could say that Plato wished to distinguish a realm of unchanging ideas or essences from matter, the realm of the changing which has significance only through participation in the significance of the ideas. Plato held the mind to have the same status as the ideas it knows. In this regard, his argument for immortality in the *Phaedo* is illustrative. This dialogue portrays Socrates at the time of his death, reviewing arguments concerning death, immortality, and the implications that one's views concerning such issues should have for one's style of life. Plato has Phaedo state, "Socrates, no one but a fool is entitled to face death with confidence, unless he can prove that the soul is absolutely immortal and indestructible" (*Phaedo* 88b).[1] In the course of the dialogue Socrates offered a number of arguments for the immortality of the soul.

Most, if not all, of the arguments in the *Phaedo* turn on the distinction between ideas and matter.[2] Moreover, the argument is in terms of conceptual distinctions which are taken to be material distinctions. Plato has Socrates complete his final argument in this fashion:

> So whenever soul takes possession of a body, it always brings life with it?
> Yes, it does.
> Is there an opposite to life, or not?
> Yes, there is.
> What?
> Death.
> Does it follow, then, from our earlier agreement, that soul will never admit the opposite of that which accompanies it? . . .
> Very good. And what do we call that which does not admit death?
> Immortal.
> And soul does not admit death?
> No.
> So soul is immortal. . . .
> If what is immortal is also imperishable, it is impossible that at the approach of death soul should cease to be. It follows from what we have already said that it cannot admit death, or be dead—just as we said that three cannot be even, nor can odd; nor can fire be cold, nor can the heat which is in the fire (*Phaedo, 105d, e, 106b*).

Plato thus concludes that the mind is as perduring as the ideas it knows, in fact that

individual minds (souls) have the enduring character of ideas. From this Plato wishes as well to argue that the body only obscures mental life, rather than also making it possible (*Phaedo* 79-80).

Such arguments concerning the mind (soul) became a part of Western tradition especially through the reflections of the Middle Ages on the question of the soul and mortality. Saint Thomas Aquinas's arguments for the immortality of soul turn similarly on the contention that the intellectual soul is subsistent: that it acts independently of the body. It is worthwhile noting that in his argument Saint Thomas draws on Aristotle's opinion that understanding, intellectual appreciation of ideas, is performed independently of corporeal organs.[3]

Such views of the mind and its operation collide with actual experience. Not only does the body not impede the mind, it allows and enables its function. The body reveals itself in experience as the physical locus of mind. When one is tired, a cup of coffee can allow the mind to function again, while a few martinis too many can obscure mental function. One thinks, perceives, and acts in and through one's body and under its conditions. Even understanding, as modern neurophysiology has shown, has its organ. With better or worse cerebral function, there is better or worse understanding. Understanding has an organ in a way analogous to the way the sense of sight has the eye as its organ.

In part, the notion that mind is separable from the body turns on confusing distinguishability with separability. Mind and its functions are distinguishable from the body and its functions. Also, there is a failure to distinguish objects of the mind from mental operations. Even if the objects of pure thought are universal and eternal, it does not follow that the knowings of such objects must be. On the contrary, even if there are eternal ideas to know, the knowings thereof occur in a particular space and time, have a history and geography which are that of the

[1]All quotations of Plato's writings are taken from *The Collected Dialogues of Plato*, ed. Edith Hamilton and Huntington Cairns (Princeton: Princeton University Press, 1961).
[2]Plato gives many arguments, including one from a consideration of knowledge to a doctrine that conceptual knowledge is a recollection of ideas acquired in a past life, thereby concluding to a doctrine of preexistence.

[3]Saint Thomas Aquinas, *Summa Theologica*, Part I, Q 75, Article 3; Aristotle, *De Anima* III, 4 (429a24).

embodiment of the mind in question. One always knows and acts in the where and when of one's body. The finitude of human existence is the condition of one's physical presence in the world, a fact that senility and its effect on the brain, and thus on the mind (soul), only too clearly demonstrate.

To attempt to talk about the mind (soul), to use scholastic terms, as not naturally corruptible is to conceive of the mind (soul) as a thing, not as a distinct process possessed only by certain entities, as my analysis would suggest.[4] Or to put it a bit more practically, talking in dualistic fashion about humans tempts one to think that the mind could prosper independently of the body because it can be conceptually distinguished from the body. But the intimate connection of mind and body suggest, if anything, that mind and body are distinct inseparables, distinguishable aspects of one entity, not two separable entities. However, if one does hold that the mind is not only distinguishable but separable as well, then one makes man in his essence, or in his most enduring reality, something other than a part of nature's usual cycles and seasons. He becomes a spirit to be freed of the chains of the body (*Phaedo* 67).

Again, the sequence of inferences in my argument may be less than strict. Yet, even if loose, it suggests that dualistic conceptions of humans lead to thinking of them as naturally possessing an infinite future. It would be as if humans naturally had no seasons, or at least no fall and winter of the mind (soul). Within such viewpoints, human life is thought of as existing apart from the general constraints and rhythms of nature.

The view of the mind as naturally noncorruptible was complemented by a view of the body as corrupted due to human error, human sin. Christianity and its doctrine of original sin, which accounted for the temptations and waywardness of the flesh, supported the view that even the decline and death of the body was itself due to a historical accident. By the sin of Adam, Saint Paul held, "death passed upon all men."[5] Intended or not, such a view of the human condition tended to discount as unnatural, if not perverse, the vicissitudes of nature which bind human life. This is not to argue that death should be appreciated as a moral good, only that the Pauline position suggested that death was not only an unnatural limit, but an unnatural evil resulting from moral evil.

In order to appreciate the significance of this view, it is useful to consider the contrasting position that death is a natural event. There have been a number of persons in Western culture, from the author of Ecclesiastes (Chapter 3) to Stoics such as Marcus Aurelius, who have argued simply that death and disease are as natural to humans as life. "Why should a man feel any dread of the change and dissolution of all his elements? For it is as nature wills it, and nothing is evil which nature wills."[6] In the modern period Charles Hartshorne has given one of the best developments of the logic of such viewpoints through an analysis of the meaning of human finitude and an appeal to a principle of aesthetic richness. Hartshorne's basic thesis is that "to be finite or limited in time is no more an injury than to be finite in space."[7] Moreover, temporal finitude is, he contends, requisite in order to prevent monotony in the world. His argument is thus frankly an aesthetic one, and a great deal of his argument turns on his notion of God as the ultimate appreciator and preserver of the aesthetic value of the universe, which gives a special accent to the significance of the aesthetic over the ethical. "Birth and death are the solutions to the aesthetic problem of unity in contrast, the synthesis of the expected and unexpected, the familiar

---

[4]H. Tristram Engelhardt, Jr., *Mind-Body: A Categorical Relation* (The Hague: Martinus Nijhoff, 1973), pp. 39-55.

[5]Romans 5:12.

[6]Marcus Aurelius, *Meditations*, in *Marcus Aurelius and His Times*, trans. George Lona (Roslyn, New York: Walter J. Black, 1945), II, 17, p. 25.

[7]Charles Hartshorne, "A Philosophy of Death," to appear in *Philosophical Aspects of Thanatology*, ed. F. H. Hetzler, J. Gutman, and A. H. Kutscher (New York: The Foundation of Thanatology), manuscript p. 1.

and the novel."[8] Death in this view is necessary to terminate lives which if prolonged indefinitely would be boring, as well as to allow for the replacement of those who have died by new generations.

This view of Hartshorne's involves appreciating the finitude of humans as natural, that "mortality as such . . . [is] in no proper sense inappropriate or evil, but essentially appropriate and good."[9] This is perhaps best understood as an attempt to indicate the significance of the obvious—that humans, as all other contingent beings, can of necessity not last forever. Further, it involves an important distinction among three different questions: Why humans in general are mortal, why particular people die at a particular time, and why particular people die in a particular manner. The first question is the one that has been under discussion here. The second question is raised, for example, when someone dies in childhood, or in his prime; and one is moved to ask about what is surely an evil for that person. The third is the sort of question raised about the evil in someone's having a painful death. In short, it is one thing to come to terms with the general issue of human mortality, to accept human finitude and mortality, and another thing to want to live to an old age and die a painless death.[10]

2. Some Disquietudes with Finitude

Distinguishing these three questions and answering the first in terms of the naturalness of death implies an interplay between the individual and the community. Even if death is natural and beneficial to the community by making room for new members, early death and painful death are evils for the individual. There results a tension between the community and the individual, a tension drawn from the very essence of the human condition: mortality. The mediator of the tension is often, if only in part, medicine, the response sine qua non of a technological society to the vicissitudes of disease and

death. Medicine is customarily seen as a battle against death, and death as medicine's enemy. Casting medicine and death in these roles obscures the different significances they have on the one hand for society and on the other for the individual. It is one thing to conceive the enemy of medicine to be death as such, and another to conceive the enemy to be an untimely or painful death. To conceive of medicine as focused on the elimination of the causes of death is not only to embark on an absurdity but to obscure the character of medicine's care for individuals in the absence of hope for cure. Moreover, to seek stubbornly the elimination of causes of death as such may lead one to place the accent upon the quantity of life, at the expense of the quality of life.

A disclaimer is in order if the above is not to be misunderstood. What I wish to suggest is not an abandonment of the attempt to curtail death caused by heart disease, cancer, etc., but to stress the obvious, that what is involved is a postponement of death by heart disease, cancer, etc., or the replacement of these causes by others. It is a question of accent, but not one without consequences in a secular society where aspirations to immortality are bereft of a religious context. That is, when there is a presupposition that humans should have been immortal and that death is evil, the consequence in a secular society is a view of death as something to be eradicated. Such views make death an ultimate evil both for society and the individual, rather than a good for society, that is, a means to allow room for new and vigorous members and an evil for individuals only when it is untimely or painful.

Twentieth century reflections on the human condition often have shown such a failure to recognize human finitude. Camus' Doctrine of the Absurd can in part be viewed as an example: "My appetite for the absolute and for unity and [its] impossibility . . . [is the] hell of the present, . . . [man's] Kingdom at last."[11] Heidegger's concept of anx-

---

[8]*Ibid.*, p. 4.
[9]*Ibid.*, pp. 2-3.
[10]*Ibid.*, p. 2.

[11]Albert Camus, *The Myth of Sisyphus and Other Essays*, trans. Justin O'Brien (New York: Alfred Knopf, 1961), pp. 51-52.

iety or dread also makes individual death an ultimate point of reference for human existence, and thus accents individual death over against the social significance of death. Death and, consequently, life are viewed in solitary terms: "Thrownness into death reveals itself to *Dasein* [Being-there] in a more primordial and impressive manner in that state-of-mind which we have called 'anxiety.' Anxiety in the face of death is anxiety 'in the face of' that potentiality-for-Being which is one's ownmost, non-relational, and not to be outstripped."[12] For Heidegger, "freedom towards death" is effected only through release from "lostness in the they-self."[13] In the individual's being-toward-death, the individual lives over against his death as an individual and ultimate limit which, in the end, separates him from others. Such notions define human existence in terms of an individual rebellion against or anxiety over death, and suggest a covert desire for existence of non-finite proportions. Moreover, such anxiety is asocial if not antisocial. It fails to place death with regard to the general value of individual life and death for the community.

Such issues of human finitude and the significance of the community structure the transactions of medicine. The general disquietude concerning the role of medical technology as it centers on questions of controlling life and death turns in part upon the realization that such means are finite in availability and effect.[14] The disquietude reflects a conflict between the individual and society with regard to human finitude. If society is to prevent death at any cost, and if there are not sufficient funds to provide expensive life-saving treatment to everyone, the moral problem of developing social mechanisms for choosing just some persons for such treatment becomes acute. Cryonic suspension (deep freezing at death to preserve individuals until a later date when their

diseases would be curable) provides a flamboyant example of the pursuit to avoid death without regard for the profound social consequences which would be raised by circumventing the usual limits of life.[15] One need only think of the problems of the population pressure given a general resurrection of a large cryonically suspended population, to perceive that the accent of such technology is on individual human life (quantity of life of an individual), in isolation from social concerns or the counsels of finitude (quality of life of the individual and the community). Even action based on maxims or clichés of preserving individual human life at any cost results in similar ethical paradoxes. The possibility of extending almost everyone's life to some extent, albeit only briefly, with little positive quality and ultimately at very high cost, provides a material reductio ad absurdum of the maxim. The cost of extending individual life thus raises the issue of revaluing human life in less than absolute terms.

To resolve these conceptual and practical difficulties, some have thought that it will be necessary to "violate and ultimately destroy the Western ethic with all that this portends,"[16] in particular with regard to the evaluation of human life. The realization that energies and resources are finite raises issues about the extent to which societies or individuals should be committed to the eradication of disease and the deferment of death. That is, since there is an indefinite possible future to be given any individual, and since the resources for the prolongation of that future (his life) are finite, the preservation of human life *ad indefinitum* for humans generally is an absurdity.

Now medicine at first glance appears to be an attempt to resolve individual needs in opposition to society's need for regeneration through the replacement of old members; there is an apparent tension between the

---

[12]Martin Heidegger, *Being and Time*, trans. John Macquarrie and Edward Robinson (New York: Harper & Row, 1962), p. 295.

[13]*Ibid.*, p. 311.

[14]Kenneth Vaux (ed.), *Who Shall Live?* (Philadelphia: Fortress Press, 1970).

[15]Curtis Henderson and Robert Ettinger, "Cryonic Suspension and the Law," *UCLA Law Review*, 15 (February, 1968), pp. 414-419.

[16]Editorial, "A New Ethic for Medicine and Society," *California Medicine*, 113 (September, 1970), p. 68.

goals of medicine and the individual, on one side, and society on the other. The investing of resources and energies in the prolongation of the life and death of the terminally ill not only results in death occurring in the strange and alien environment of the hospital, but also denies energy and resources to the living. This expresses itself in a central quandary of medical technology: how should one, or can one, talk of natural bounds to human life? Or to put the issue more narrowly: How can one decide to what extent life should be prolonged in terminal illness? To resolve this, one needs access to a broader notion of the relationship of modern medical science and technology to the humane values of society. One needs a dialectic mediating between individual and communal needs, resolving the antithesis between the goals of individual self-realization and the general needs of society. That is, one needs a language of finitude, a way of talking decently about the limits of human life, a way of saying why and under what circumstances death is natural. Moreover, since death touches society and the individuals in different ways, one needs to place the significance of death with regard to both. Here, though, I can give only a sketch of how an answer to such questions would begin from an appreciation of the naturalness of death.

3. Hegel: Suggestions Concerning Death, the Individual, and Society

Hegel can aid us in considering these issues, for he offers an understanding of disease as an essential expression of general human limitations and as an integral dimension of the relation between the individual and the human community at large. His treatment of disease, death, and medical science in his *Philosophy of Nature* is of mixed quality.[17] But the enduring importance of Hegel's discussion rests in his attempt to bring the issues of disease, death, and medicine into the broader context of the relationship between individual finitude and the needs of the human community. As one would expect from Hegel, he attempts to give a rationale for reality, a way of understanding our actual state of affairs. In the case at hand this is very useful insofar as one wants at least a plausible way of considering human finitude. Hegel suggests a language, a rationale in terms of which death, human finitude, individual humans, and the general human community can be related. I will briefly present Hegel's view as a way of further developing Hartshorne's reflections on death and human finitude.

Hegel held an ecological view of death. He suggested that disease is contextual or ecological in nature, that it is essentially a function of limitation or finitude. Since the quality of the life of individuals is dependent upon "the external universal life of nature," its environmental context,[18] the well-being of particular animals is fortuitous. In its mere particularity an animal (including humans) is a function of nature, and the quality of the animal's life is a dependent variable. "The life of the animal shares in the vicissitudes of this universal life, and, consequently, it merely alternates between health and disease. . . . [the milieu of external contingency] is continually subjecting animal sensibility to violence and the threat of dangers. . . ."[19] For Hegel, the life of the animal is far from the ideal, good-natured state of Eden. Disease and illness are integral to animal life. "Consequently, the general life of the animal appears as a life of illness, and the animal's feelings are those of *insecurity, anxiety*, and *misery*."[20] And this state of affairs was, for Hegel, not merely accidental, but the true and proper state of an animal. To be an animal is to be a contingent being and that is a precarious business. That is, to be a contingent (not necessary) being is to be dependent upon the changing

---

[17]Citations from *Hegel's Philosophy of Nature* are taken from Vol. 3 of M. J. Petry's translation (London: George Allen and Unwin, 1970). They will be indicated by section number (#) plus page of Petry's translation. Where reference is to a *Zusatz*, this will be indicated by "Z" following the section number.

[18]#370, p. 179.
[19]*Ibid.*
[20]*Ibid.*

states of nature and, therefore, necessarily to be destined to die over the long run. Expectations of physical immortality are, given such a view, an absurdity.

Hegel's formulation of the role of death and disease is in this sense post-Christian. It is unlike the Christian position in which death and disease enter as abnormalities, as departures due to sin, from the original state of the Garden of Eden.[21] For Hegel, "The original disease of the animal, and the inborn germ of death, is its being inadequate to universality. . . . The organism can recover from disease, but it is because it is diseased from its very nature, that death is a necessity. . . ."[22] Death for Hegel is part and parcel of animal life; it is normal and natural and to be accepted as such. Further, he argued that, when it occurred in old age, death served a social function. Hegel saw old age as naturally approaching death. In the stereotypical life of old age, no longer able to respond in an innovative fashion to the environment about him, the senile person begins, so Hegel suggested, to mirror in his inactivity the stability of dead matter. In his lectures shortly before his own death, Hegel described senility as already mirroring death. "Old people settle down within themselves . . . steadily becoming . . . less aware of anything particular; as a result of this . . . they are satisfied with this habitude devoid of process. [This] lack of opposition . . . constitutes the stillness of dead being, and the repose of death overcomes the inadequacy of disease, which was therefore the primary origin of death."[23] In short, Hegel contends that old age involves a loss of vitality which culminates naturally in death— a point not unlike that of Marcus Aurelius. "Do not despise death, but be well content with it, since this too is one of those things which nature wills. For such it is to be young and to grow old . . ."[24] Hegel argues in addition that old age involves a lack of creativity and ability to innovate, character-

istics he holds necessary to the community.

This is not to argue that old age should not be postponed or that people should not live longer, but rather that even to life there must be a limit. Hartshorne's reflections supplement this through his aesthetic argument that the indefinite life of a finite being would in the end be boring: "Look at elderly people, then look at children. For the first the world is all too familiar . . . Monotony is an aesthetic, not an ethical, category; and it is a great evil. Beyond certain limits it makes life impossible."[25] The moral here is one of the bounds of finitude, even if one were to expand the compass of human life: a reminder that for a finite being there are only a finite number of ways he can achieve novelty and beauty.[26]

Hegel's resolution of the issue of human finitude turns, finally, on his argument that the enduringly human is trans-individual. On one hand, achieving and preserving mere particular existence becomes self-defeating. Any finite being has its term. Health for the individual human involves his own self-realization. But in his own particularity, an individual only imperfectly and in a one-sided and partial fashion achieves the values of humanity. He is only one human over against other and different humans who will succeed him. Any one particular human, as only one particular human, points ahead to other and different individuals who will succeed him, thus presupposing his own death to ensure continued progress. Death in this context becomes a singular indication of the importance of the community, the common life of spirit. Death, as Hegel puts it, "constitutes the sublation of the singular, and is therefore the proceeding forth of the genus, of spirit."[27] In what might seem obscure

---

[21]Romans 5:12 and 1 Corinthians 15:21-22.

[22]#375 Z, p. 209.

[23]#375 Z, p. 210.

[24]*Marcus Aurelius and His Times*, pp. 92-93.

[25]Hartshorne, "A Philosophy of Death," pp. 3, 6.

[26]It is worth noting that for Hartshorne this is not just an empirical thesis concerning the world (e.g., that generally the old lose creativity) but a theological point. For Hartshorne the world exists for the aesthetic pleasure of God. Hartshorne is contending that finite life when protracted beyond a reasonable scope would lose proportion, fail to be aesthetically pleasing to God.

[27]#376 Z, p. 212.

language, Hegel was suggesting that the death of individuals invokes a recognition that individual contingent beings are transient but that that transience itself indicates the perduring significance of trans-individual social unities and values. That is, though individuals do not and cannot last forever, the spiritual, non-idiosyncratic value of human individuals can and should. Humans, though transitory, seek and achieve enduring values—not for themselves, or only for themselves—by seeking to let trans-individual values be achieved generally. The pain of an individual's death, the fact that one dies though his goals may be enduring, can only be resolved (at least in this world) in terms of that which can be at least relatively enduring: the community of man.

Hegel is suggesting a balance. On the one hand, an attempt to prolong indefinitely the life of an individual for Hegel would have been a flagrant example of the bad infinite:[28] a vain search for satisfaction on one level where satisfaction on a higher level is possible, a failure to see that a reconceptualization could give broader compass and a more complete view of the values and issues involved. Life has its due measure, and medical technology functions properly in guarding that measure. Attempts to prolong and preserve life simply for life's sake would for Hegel have been a commitment to the bad infinite and a failure to acknowledge the due measure of life and the significance of human finitude. On the other hand, death indicates that enduring trans-individual values are to be found in the community and the world of the mind which transcends and overarches any particular individual. This for Hegel is the good infinite. That is, one becomes interested in the depth of the value of spirit (for example, art, philosophy) not in the quantity of time any particular individual or set of individuals would have to pursue those values. One seeks rather in general the continued life of the mind, the community of the spirit. Further, insofar as that

community needs new members, disease and death are not only normal and natural processes, they are prerequisites for progress both biological and societal. It is only by "proceeding from this dead husk, [that] there rises the finer nature of spirit."[29] The transitory nature of individuals for Hegel is itself an indication of the perduring significance of that community of men dedicated to values of the spirit: state, art, religion, philosophy.

In contrast, the anxiety which Heidegger indicates as evoked by death corresponds to Hegel's concept of animal anxiety, the anxiety ingredient in animal existence.[30] Although Heidegger's notion of "freedom towards death" presupposes a quality of consciousness and authenticity accessible only to humans, it is still essentially a response to the animal predicament without the context of a community. Humans, unlike animals, can know and decide to live for values that can be sustained in and by a community. Hegel's suggestion is to go beyond that predicament and to revalue the issues in terms of the transcendent values of the genus or society and ultimately the value of the community of philosophers. This difference is reflected in Heidegger's concept of "they." Rather than appreciating the "they" as a community overarching and giving meaning to the life and death of the individual, Heidegger sees the "they" as oppressive, alienating, and conducive to inauthenticity. Heidegger fails to appreciate the "they" in terms of a category of social unity, and thus of a higher significance capable of endowing the death of the individual with meaning, while Hegel resolved the tragedy of death in terms of the overriding values of, and in, society. In particular, Hegel would see such enduring value to be found in the community of thinkers more or less on the analogue of the community of scientists where such community indicates a unity of commitment to the pursuit of certain values (that is, truth, knowledge), not a particular society. One might think here of

[28]G. W. F. Hegel, *Sämtliche Werke*, Vol. 8, *System der Philosophie 1: die Logik* (Stuttgart: Frommann Verlag, 1964), #94, pp. 222-224.

[29]#376 Z, p. 211.
[30]#370, p. 179.

suggestions along this line by such modern thinkers as Jacques Monod.[31]

Hegel thus offered a view of death and disease, placing these within the context of the long-range goals of the human community. Individual finitude for Hegel was not to be transcended in the person of the individual, but was to be resolved through the values of the community of rational animals, which outlives the individual. Though Hegel acknowledged that health for an individual is his self-realization, still society's progress presupposes the death of the individual in old age. Hegel realized that this dialectic between individual and societal realization requires individual disease and death as much as it requires individual self-realization. Individual life and self-realization are values, but they are clearly not absolute, nor are they to be sought in cryonic suspension, or desperate and expensive extensions of the process of dying. Rather, they find their "higher truth" in values which perdure beyond any particular individual and which give perspective to the value of preserving individual life. The resolution of the dialectic of disease and death is in terms of social self-realization, transcending and complementing the self-realization of the individual: the progress of society presupposes the finitude of the individual and yet overcomes it in society's transcendence of these limits. The value of the mere extension of existence through technological means can be assessed, therefore, only in the context of the quality of life it ensures for society.

In particular, investment in medical research and treatment commits resources which could have been given to the pure sciences, to the arts and humanities, which for Hegel are the higher truth, the goals of man. To make the mere extension of life the goal, rather than the flourishing of cultural life, is to choose the bad infinite. Most importantly, the attempt to secure physical immortality is likely to obscure the legitimate goal of humanity, the pursuit of a rich but finite life. Considering the large amount of

energy expended in medical research and treatment, the issue of balance is unavoidable. One must remember that one prolongs the length of life so that certain values can be realized, not for the mere prolongation itself. The merit of any prolongation of life, especially through societal investment, must be measured in terms of the values such prolongation achieves or precludes. Thus, to render Hegel's point contemporary, the issue of the quantity versus the quality of life has an essentially social dimension, one that is raised in terms of the general realization of a cultural life, the life of spirit.

4. Some Hesitant Conclusions

Hegel and Hartshorne are arguing for the obvious: that humans are finite though their expectations are not, that they must die though the values which they cherish are as such enduring, living in the appreciation of whatever community of rational animals achieves them. Further, any one individual human achieves as *a* particular human only *a* particular grasp of such values. Thus societal progress depends on both new and energetic members embodying and achieving those enduring values in new ways. In so arguing, Hegel and Hartshorne presuppose two crucial premises: first, that the amount of energy and resources is finite so that if one extended the human life span one would be forced to decrease the percentage of young persons in the population; and second, that a certain fairly high percentage of young persons is necessary if a society is to be dynamic. Hartshorne and Hegel presume in addition that old age itself is, in and of itself, encumbered by a certain monotony born out of the decrease in novel experiences. I have not explicitly examined those premises, but have rather displayed some of their consequences.

They are, though, not unlikely premises. The first, what may be called the finite resources premise, has some cogency when pushed all the way. If humans achieve physical immortality and if resources are finite for the support of a population, then new

[31]Jacques Monod, *Chance and Necessity* (New York: Alfred Knopf, 1971), pp. 179-180.

members could not be added. The second premise, the youth-is-creative premise, is probably the more problematic—but probably only over the short run. That is, it might be the case that extending the human life span to one hundred and fifty or two hundred years might not have a profound effect on the tenor of society or prove a burden to those who lived such long lives. But the premise is that somewhere there must be a limit and that surely within the present bounds of senility, that limit comes before any such extended longevity.

Thus, on one hand, there are few, if any, practical, immediate consequences to this view. These reflections say nothing, for example, about what a reasonable human life span should be, about what a reasonable investment in prolonging the life of an elderly person would be, or about how one chooses between particular investments of societal resources in prolonging life. But on the other hand, there are general implications which can in the end be drawn. Or at least, the foregoing suggests certain ways in which the relation of medicine to death can be viewed. In particular, it is plain that death is not the enemy of medicine.

We are, in short, given a sense in which death is natural: death is natural to humans in that they are contingent beings. Since each particular human being is not a necessary being, that person could possibly cease to exist and over the long run therefore surely will die. Further, an infinite life span for a finite being may be difficult if not boring prospect, as Hartshorne suggests. Thus to the question of why humans are mortal, the answer is that they are contingent, finite beings, and therefore dependent on an indefinite number of possible variables which could cause their deaths. But, though physical immortality is an absurdity, it does make sense to see a painful death or a premature death (less than the usual life span) as "unnatural" in the sense of violating a reasonable human hope—for a painless death and an average life span. Painful and premature deaths are properly the enemies of medicine, not death itself.

One can conclude with a fairly common-sense moral: if death is natural it follows that it is not medicine's enemy. At the most it is untimely death or painful death which stand out to be conquered by societal investment in medicine. As a consequence, in establishing societal priorities for the control of the causes of death, the accent should fall on the control of those causes which result in painful or untimely death. The latter has been accomplished in great measure through the control of infectious diseases. But when, for example, considering a choice between investing resources in curtailing fatal diseases of old age groups versus those of younger and not on merely utilitarian grounds. The choice would reflect the fact that in the second case death occurred before the values open to those persons could have been achieved, values to which they could reasonably claim a right.

One should be careful here. The usual age at which death occurs in old age could change when and if the aging process could be slowed. Again, such slowing, if it were possible, would have to be done with serious thought concerning the values being balanced: the scope in time adequate to a rich, full life; the effect on the ability to add new members to the human community in which postponing death would result; the effect of the investment of resources in the prolongation of life upon the resources available to support the general quality of life. The latter in particular must be an object of scrutiny, otherwise one will forget about achieving the purposes of life and society while frenetically attempting to prolong life. One will confuse ends with means, one will think that the goods which make the goodness of life are merely life, and forget that, as Seneca remarked, "The wise man . . . lives as long as he should, not as long as he can."[32] Or, to put it another way, if one seeks primarily to save his life, he is likely to forget the purposes of life.

Finally, these solutions to the problem of mortality are not very edifying. Hartshorne asks one to live for the enduring aesthetic

[32]Seneca, *Letter Seventy: Suicide*, in *The Stoic Philosophy of Seneca*, trans. Moses Hadas (New York: W. W. Norton & Co., 1958), p. 202.

pleasure of God, not for oneself. Hegel is even more restrained, but after all it was he who warned that philosophy "must beware of wishing to be edifying."[33] Hegel simply argues that some things which humans labor for are of enduring value and constitute the fellowship of all rational beings. It is not as if one lived for this fellowship as a particular group, or for the future members of that group, but for the values that could only live in such a group. In short, values *are* valuable, and they live in the life of the community of minds which cherishes them. In that sense the fact that any or all particular communities of rational animals would itself finally die out, would not count against that position, at least as Hegel presents it in the *Encyclopedia*. It is enough that the community is always a possibility and sometimes an actuality. As an overarching, enduring way of achieving values, it provides for Hegel a way at least to understand the death of particular individuals as a service to the life of the community of rational animals in particular, and thus rationality generally. Again, that is not meant to be edifying, but the best counsel or rationale one can draw from the fact of our finitude.

---

[33]G. W. F. Hegel, *The Phenomenology of Mind*, trans. James Baillie (London: Allen & Unwin, 1964), p. 74.

And in the end, such a moral is a useful one. Though these reflections are at best very general, they suggest an overview of the human condition which at least begins with an acceptance of the naturalness of death. They suggest that we look for the counsels of finitude, ways in which we can live with the condition of being human, that is, with being mortal. It is at the very least an injunction to avoid the hubris associated with seeing death itself as the enemy of medicine. And this is only proper, for if anything medicine is our way of living with our finitude. In fact, if anything should teach us the counsels of finitude, the reasonable hopes and assumptions of humans, it should be medicine. Even if this general view does not provide particular priorities for health care, it does suggest a rubric for establishing such priorities: act always to ensure that the general achievement of cultural values by humans is not precluded by the investment of resources and energies in postponing death. The ways in which health and disease can effect such achievement of value is a question properly and best addressed by medicine, but yet it is always addressed in terms of finite goals: the elimination of painful or premature deaths, never death itself. Death itself is even more natural to us than medicine.

IV.
Death, Deciding,
and Mourning

11

On letting some babies die
DAVID H. SMITH

THE OCTOBER 25, 1973, issue of *The New England Journal of Medicine* contained two articles and one editorial dealing with the death of defective newborns. One author cited the following case:

Baby B was referred to ... [the MD] at the age of 36 hours with duodenal obstruction and signs of Down's syndrome. His young parents had a ten-year-old daughter, and he was the son they had been trying to have for ten years; yet, when they were approached with the operative consent, they hesitated. They wanted to know beyond any doubt whether the baby had Down's syndrome. If so, they wanted time to consider whether or not to permit the surgery to be done. Within 8 hours a geneticist was able to identify cells containing 47 chromosomes in a bone-marrow sample. Over the next three days the infant's gastrointestinal tract was decompressed with a nasogastric tube, and he was supported with intravenous fluids while the parents consulted with their ministers, with family physicians in their home community, and with our geneticists. At the end of that time, the B's decided not to permit surgery. The infant died three

days later after the withdrawal of supportive therapy.[1]

This tragic history reveals a set of difficulties faced by physicians, other members of the helping professions, parents, babies and by our culture generally. I should like to comment in a rather rough and ready way about some of these problems.[2]

As I do this I shall make two assumptions, each of which is open to question. First, I shall assume that we are dealing with newborn human beings who are human persons. While I do *not* assume that each and every product of the human womb is such a person,[3] I do assume here that those scholars who suggest that a "self-concept" (presumably involving some level of self-

[1] Anthony Shaw, M.D., "Dilemmas of Informed Consent in Children," *The New England Journal of Medicine* 289 (October 25, 1973), p. 886. This sensitive article is invaluable for study of the problems discussed in this paper.

[2] An earlier version of this chapter was read at a colloquium sponsored by the Committee on the Humanities at Indiana University. I am very grateful to the Committee, and its chairman, Professor Robert Byrnes, for the invitation. Since then, helpful suggestions have been made by André Hellegers, Richard McCormick, S.J., David C. McCullough, and LeRoy Walters. Of course, none of these persons is to be held responsible for the views I express.

[3] As an example of a problematical case, I would cite the anencephalic child.

consciousness) is a necessary ingredient of human personhood, are wrong. If I am incorrect in this assumption, of course, the problem is simplified and obligations to the newborn, although not eliminated, become indistiguishable from those to subhuman beings.[4]

Second, I shall assume that we all accept, at least as a prima facie obligation, the prohibition on killing human beings. The problem, of course, is whether the prohibition applies in the newborn situation; I do not mean to settle that issue by definitional fiat. I do mean to note that no problem arises unless one starts out with a rejection of killing. A prohibition on killing might be justified in any one of a number of ways. My own theory would involve, in part, theological rationale beginning with the biblical poetry about human nature, about persons made in the image of God. But here I should like to move beyond that issue and consider a specific kind of case in which the limits of the prohibition on killing are tested.

I shall consider two issues in a little detail. These are: (1) procedural questions of who should make decisions of this kind and (2) substantive questions of what criteria should be used in making the decisions. In conclusion I will discuss one implication of my views, views which are rather conservative.

II

Professor Paul Ramsey argues that procedural questions, questions about *who* should make decisions, are not the only questions of importance in medical ethics.[5] I grant that, but it does not follow that procedural questions are unimportant. I shall consider them before, but more briefly than, questions of substance.

When the family, described in the case with which I began, decided to refuse permission for an operation on their baby, they were, obviously, deciding to shorten his life. That is, they decided for euthanasia. This term (euthanasia) has been used in any number of ways, and it has been linked with various qualifiers (for example, passive vs. active, direct vs. indirect). I use it here in its most general and least technical sense, as meaning a decision for a comfortable death.

The reason that euthanasia on the newborn is an especially interesting case is that there is no possibility that the baby can consent to the procedure. This may be true of any proposed mercy killing of a child, although with older children the issue becomes less sharp. But it is clear that it is nonsense to speak of the consent of a thirty-six-hour-old baby. Thus euthanasia on the newborn would always be *involuntary* euthanasia.[6] The decision about the shortening of his life must be made by others. While this makes the case hard on a human and personal level, it may simplify somewhat the theoretical problems involved.

It would be possible and plausible to move from this procedural point to a conclusion on the substance. That is, one could argue that given the impossibility of patient consent, all possible means to prolong life must be utilized. Since consent is impossible to obtain in this case, no limitation of treatment could be legitimate. If the patient's life is to be shortened, the logical thing to do is to nurture him until he can make that decision himself.

Such an argument is well intentioned, but stated this simply it is inconclusive because it rests on the assumption that prolongation of life is always in the interest of the child. The possibility that shortened life might be in the interest of the child is excluded without discussion. In other words, acceptance of this "procedural" argument as conclusive would involve a failure to see that what follows from the impossibility of consent is not an obligation to maximize length of life but an obligation to act in the best interest of the child. This may or may not involve the maximization of length of life.

---

[4]A brilliant and well-qualified statement of an alternative view is Michael Tooley, "Abortion and Infanticide," *Philosophy and Public Affairs* 2 (Fall, 1972), pp. 37-65.

[5]Robert Veatch, Willard Gaylin and Councilman Morgan (eds.), "The Nature of Medical Ethics" in *The Teaching of Medical Ethics* (Hastings-on-Hudson, N.Y.: Institute of Society, Ethics and the Life Sciences, 1973), pp. 18-19.

[6]This point is very well made in LeRoy Walters, "Ethical Concepts and Attitudes Toward Passive Euthanasia" (unpublished manuscript). My great debt to Professor Walters is here, in a token way, acknowledged.

Allow me to try to put the issue another way. The "procedural" argument is unassailable, if consent is a necessary condition for euthanasia, and if newborns are persons. Given these premises, an absolute prohibition on euthanasia on the newborn will follow. I have conceded the premise about newborn personhood, but the premise about the necessity of consent as a prerequisite to euthanasia is not certain in circumstances where it would have been impossible to get consent. We must distinguish the more frequently discussed cases where the possibility of euthanasia could have been considered by the patient from cases in which it is obviously impossible for the patient to have made a decision on the matter. Conceding (for purposes of argument) that consent is a necessary condition for euthanasia on the adult, it does not follow from this that it is necessary in the case of the newborn. What we can say about the newborn is that in the absence of consent we may never define his interest in some idiosyncratic way. We must always act with an eye to his interest, plausibly construed. I shall return to this issue in part IV.

If decision-making power cannot rest with the patient, where should it reside? The two obvious possibilities are the family of the patient and the relevant physicians. How should power be balanced between these groups? Physicians have great power by virtue of their technical knowledge and social location, but it is not clear that they should exercise as much power as they sometimes do. One writer says that, when the question of who should decide is raised, the answer is:

...the child's doctor, for who else is in a similarly pivotal position to make sure that the proper medical consultation has been obtained in ascertaining the hopeless condition of the patient, that the parents receive sympathetic and thorough explanation, and that they are exposed to broadly based advice? Who else can lead all those involved to a decision, and who else is more responsible for consoling after decision has been reached? Society, ethics, institutional attitudes and committees can provide the broad guidelines, but the onus of decision making ultimately falls on the doctor in whose care the child has been put.[7]

Another author has written that the role of the parent's input into such decisions "will be primarily emotional."[8]

Against this tendency it is essential to assert the importance of family input. There are various reasons why this is true. For one thing the actual decision involved is not, in the narrow sense, a medical decision. The physician is an expert on diagnosis and therapy. His technical competence extends to both identification of pathology and decision about the relative merits of various ways of correcting the pathology. He can describe the likely course of life of patients with certain afflictions. This does not, however, make him an expert on such questions as whether a life lived with a serious handicap is "worth living." Answers to such questions involve decisions about values and their relative priorities. While I am far from thinking that such decisions are irrational, I see no reason to regard physicians as experts about them.[9]

On the other hand, we must be on guard against suggesting that physician power is demonic. Many individuals and teams of physicians dealing with children born with birth defects go to great lengths to insure the meaningful involvement and input of the patient's family.[10] Professionals may also find it difficult to get families really to weigh options and take responsibility. While professionals may become jaded and block out certain considerations, they also may be

[7]F. J. Ingelfinger, M.D., "Bedside Ethics for the Hopeless Case," *The New England Journal of Medicine* 289 (October 25, 1973), p. 914. Why do the parents require "advice" if "the onus of decision-making" rests with the physicians?

[8]John M. Freeman, M.D., "To Treat or Not to Treat: Ethical Dilemmas of Treating the Infant with a Myelomeningocele," *Clinical Neurosurgery* 20 (1973), p. 141.

[9]Robert M. Veatch has discussed this issue in many places. See especially "Generalization of Expertise," *The Hastings Center Studies* 1 [2] (1973), pp. 29-40.

[10]Cf. Dr. Shaw's article, previously cited as well as Raymond S. Duff, M.D., and A. G. M. Campbell, M.D., "Moral and Ethical Dilemmas in the Special-Care Nursery," *The New England Journal of Medicine* 289 (October 25, 1973), pp. 890-94; also, Mary D. Ames, M.D. and Luis Shut, M.D., "Results of Treatment of 171 Consecutive Myelomeningoceles—1962-1968," *Pediatrics* 50 (September, 1972), pp. 466-70.

able to compensate for this and present the forecast with clarity that only experience allows. Moreover, it is questionable—on general principles—to handle problems of power by pious exhortations to the powerful. Demands that physicians surrender power will be counterproductive, *if* they serve to shift attention away from the problem of how the physician should use the power which he or she inevitably will possess.

That said, it remains essential that a considerable amount of this particular power— over the life and death of an infant—be relinquished by physicians because the real issue involved is not a technical one over which physicians are professionally competent. It is rather a personal one concerning the family in and through which the child will live. I do not mean to suggest that the family should operate in a vacuum or unchecked. But I do mean that responsibility for this decision must be meaningfully shared and that the family (the group who will serve, enjoy, and in large part create the child) is the appropriate locus of primary decisional power.

At this point, however, we must turn to the substance of the issue. What decisions should be made about Baby B, and others more or less severely handicapped?

III

Many arguments are used to justify bringing a quick and painless end to the lives of defective infants. Such practices were well known in ancient times and received the approval of famous philosophers. The modern arguments tend to take two forms. Some argue that euthanasia on the defective child is justifiable for his own sake; others argue that it is justified for the sake of others: the family, community, or even the human race. I shall consider both these types of argument, beginning with the latter.

One argument for the quick and easy death of defective children assumes essentially the following form. The child represents a threat to the life or well-being of others. Therefore, he or she may be killed in order to *protect* these "others." This *type* of argument persuaded the early Christians to give up their pacifism and it has found recurrent form in various versions of the

Just War theory. As presented there it has the following ingredients: although killing in self-defense is unjustified, people have obligations to protect others. This *obligation to protect* can override the prohibition on killing, if the person against whom action is taken is threatening the life of someone to whom one is obliged. Other and less serious ways of stopping the killer must have been attempted, if available. In the case of action by collectives, the justified killing must have been approved by the legitimate authority, i.e., the war must have been declared by the sovereign. Finally, for some versions of the theory, the justice of a particular cause had to be pronounced by an acknowledged and impartial arbiter.[11]

Doubtless it seems a long way from the nice distinctions of philosophers and theologians to the intensive-care nursery of twentieth-century Western culture. But it may be that this paradigm of reasoning has some relevance to the issue at hand. These categories were not meant to be a way of outlawing all war; neither were they meant to be simply rationalizations which were compatible with any war which the sovereign might choose to declare. Rather, they represented a way of analyzing this most marginally moral of human activities, the taking of human life. This analysis schematized the questions which must be asked, and answered affirmatively, if a particular war were to be justified.

Let us try to see how these questions might apply to the case of the defective baby, such as Baby B. The maintenance of that baby obviously will drain the resources of his family and various health-care institutions and professionals. Resources of both family and community could be used for other purposes. Among these legitimate purposes is the protection and preservation of other people who now, or may in the future, live in his family or community. No amount of extra or palliative surgery will remove the child's mongolism and so this drain will continue no matter what is done. His death is the only alternative to living with the problem. This verdict may be well known to

[11]My formulation of this is dependent on Paul Ramsey, *War and the Christian Conscience* (Durham, N.C.: Duke University Press, 1961) and Paul Ramsey, *The Just War* (New York: Charles Scribner, 1968).

parents, the physician, and any relevant legal authorities. Thus the baby represents a serious threat to lives, a threat which cannot be removed in any other way. Once this verdict is impartially pronounced, an act destroying the child is justifiable infanticide rather than murder.

I do not think that this form of argument will fail in absolutely all cases, but there are serious problems with it. As stated above, it would prove far too much, for it would justify the killing of anyone, of any age, who in some way is a social liability. As a check against this abuse, the Just War theorists insisted that the only person who might be directly killed was the combatant, i.e., the person who was actually functioning as a killer.[12] While they did not insist that the person to be killed must be at fault or guilty in some juridical sense, they did insist that this person's social function be that of an active threatener. His victims had to be identifiable and their prospective possible deaths had to be the results of something he brought about.

How could the defective newborn possibly fit these criteria? While it is obvious— and very relevant to our overall understanding of the problem—that resources used to care for him could be used in other ways, it does not follow from this that he is personally threatening anyone. If one tries to make the most plausible possible case for threat, that is, that care for him will destroy the person (if not the life) of mother, siblings or father, one quickly runs up against the question of last resort. There are many ways in which the family can be saved, short of the death of the baby. The child can be institutionalized. One might argue of course that institutionalized life is not worth living, but then one has shifted the terms of the argument and is raising a question of the best interest of the child. Furthermore, the whole reason that this issue is a problem is that we lack a recognized sovereign who can adjudicate questions of this kind.

I am not prepared to say that there are no cases in which the argument could be made. I only say that one will have to show

actual threat to very particular people (which means family members), absence of alternative possibilities for action, and a procedure which accords the infant some semblance of due process. In fact, in our society these conditions will preclude justifications of infanticide using this type of argument.

Moreover, I believe that we can draw another conclusion from the argument from protection and our procedural considerations. Sometimes it may be suggested that the defective newborn, whose parents are missing, is a more proper candidate for euthanasia than the baby whose parents accept responsibility for decision making. And it is suggested that the reason this is true is that this deserted baby not only will lack the advantages of a home; he will also represent an unusually serious drain on society's resources.

The striking thing however about such a deserted newborn is that there is no community of which he is a part. There is no family either to represent his interests or to be threatened by him. Thus it will be impossible to show his direct threat to specific other individuals or to accord him something like due process. Consequently, the deserted, defective newborn is precisely the child who may never be killed for the sake of others. This does not, of course, settle

Society could conclude that it is inappropriate to subject a deserted child to all *possible* treatment and he may, in consequence, live a shorter time than technology now makes possible. . . . But the baby with no advocate, and threatening no particular persons, cannot possibly be construed to be a legitimate victim of *protective* killing.

12Cf. the works of Ramsey previously cited and Baruch Brody, "Thomson on Abortion," *Philosophy and Public Affairs* 1 (Spring, 1972), pp. 335-40.

the question of what forms of care are appropriate for such a child. The absence of a family community means that society must be at special pains to act in the patient's interest. Interest and longevity are not identical, as we have suggested before. Thus it may be inappropriate to subject a deserted child to all *possible* treatment and he may, in consequence, live a shorter time than technology now makes possible. This sort of procedural consideration does not suggest the illegitimacy of such a course of events. But the baby with no advocate, and threatening no particular persons, cannot possibly be construed to be a legitimate victim of *protective* killing.

IV

Let us now shift to the second substantive argument under review. This is the notion that the death of the newborn is justified in his own interest. One decides for his death because, in his case, such a decision is better for him.

One interesting proposal for a way of arguing this case has been made by Professor Paul Ramsey. Ramsey claims that we are always obliged to care for sick persons, but that the requirements of care alter with the condition of the patient. Normally, caring for the patient requires attempts to cure his disease, but it sometimes happens that a patient begins to die. Once the dying process has begun the obligations of family and physicians shift. Specifically, the obligation to cure is gradually displaced by the obligation to provide "company," companionship, and human comfort to the dying person. Thus one should allow a dying patient to die.

In Ramsey's view allowing to die is appropriate; positive euthanasia is forbidden. This may appear to be a moralistic quibble; the impression is deepened by Ramsey's argument for his thesis which seems to make heavy use of a distinction between omission and commission. He seems to say that a person is more responsible for deaths following his commissions than for those following his omissions. In fact, however, Ramsey thinks that a decision to withhold or withdraw therapy should be described as "ceasing to do something that was begun in order to *do* something that is better be-

cause now more fitting."[13] A decision to cease curing is not an omission at all, but a decision about *which* kind of acts of care to *commit*. The trouble with positive euthanasia for Ramsey is that it represents an attempt to push the dying beyond reach of our care.

Ramsey concedes, however, that some individuals may slip beyond care either because they are permanently unconscious or because they are experiencing nonrelievable pain of a very intense sort. If such cases ever arise, Ramsey argues, the patient cannot receive our care and for that reason other norms become operative. He will allow positive euthanasia in such cases.

All this is tied into the newborn case by Ramsey's claim that the process of dying may begin at any age, indeed that one may be afflicted in utero by the malady from which he will die.[14]

In order to assess this theory about the morality of euthanasia on the newborn, let us consider a real world case which seems to embody similar ideas. John Lorber, in Sheffield, England, is a physician with extensive responsibilities for a clinic specializing in the care of babies afflicted with spina bifida. Spina bifida is a birth defect of uncertain origin. The afflicted children have a split in the vertebrae and a portion of the spinal cord may be extruded, sometimes within a thick blister-like sack and sometimes outside such a sack which has been ruptured. The frequent consequences are paralysis, to some degree, of the lower extremities; bladder and bowel incontinence or malfunction, and, frequently, mental retardation. Death for such children used to be a virtual certainty because the exposed portion of the spinal cord would be very vulnerable to infection and the child would succumb to meningitis. Modern medical technology has made it possible to close the lesion, surgically attempt to straighten the

---

[13]Paul Ramsey, *The Patient as Person* (New Haven: Yale University Press, 1970), p. 151; cf. pp. 144-53, 132-36. Emphasis added.

[14]Paul Ramsey, "Reference Points in Deciding About Abortion" in *The Morality of Abortion*, ed. by John T. Noonan, Jr. (Cambridge: Harvard University Press, 1970), pp. 91-100; Ramsey, *The Patient as Person*, pp. 161-64.

back, drain the hydrocephalus which often develops, and treat, in various ways, both the infections and the frequently recurring renal problems. The result, of course, is to salvage many children who would formerly have died; yet a large percentage of these children are seriously handicapped; many are severely mentally retarded.

For the first twelve years of the Sheffield clinic's operation, a policy of maximal treatment was followed. Everything possible was done for all infants afflicted with spina bifida. The battle against death and deformity was never given up. But accurate records were kept and in 1971 Lorber published an article in which he argued against the past policy of his own clinic and claimed that *selective* treatment should be the rule. As early as possible one should decide which patients to treat and which to allow to die. Lorber writes that it is "easier not to draw a line" but that this would represent a failure to learn the lesson of the "massive therapeutic experiment" which happened at Sheffield. The good specialist can, he argues, accurately assess "the minimum degree of future handicap" even if it is impossible to "forecast the maximum degree of disability."[15] Essentially, the criteria Lorber proposed involve the degree of paralysis of the infant, head circumference (showing likelihood of hydrocephalus), presence or degree of curvature of the spine and "associated gross and congenital anomalies or major birth injuries."[16]

While it is clear that Lorber bases part of his argument for this selection practice on social utility grounds, it is also obvious that he feels this kind of selection for treatment is in the interest of the patients from whom therapy is withheld. This might be because of anticipated serious physical or mental defect. An example of physical problems might be the following:

> One normally intelligent girl of 9 years of age has had 18 major operations so far, including 7 revisions of her shunt and two extensive spinal osteotomies in an attempt to correct her extreme kyphoscoliosis. She still has as gross scoliosis as ever. A long

metal rod was passed through the bodies of her vertebrae along the length of her vertebral column: unfortunately she had such a compensatory lordosis that this rod emerges from the thoracic vertebrae and through the skin to bridge the lumbar lordosis and enter the lowest lumbar vertebrae and sacrum.[17]

Lorber does not explicitly tell the reader what the fate of this patient would have been if his proposed selection criteria had been in operation. On the other hand, most of those treated patients whom Lorber would now refuse treatment are, in fact, mentally retarded.

Now one way of interpreting Lorber's proposal is as an adaptation of Ramsey's criteria. We would then understand Lorber to be suggesting that some children are born so seriously defective that, although not dying, they should be allowed to die. Not all spina bifida children fall into this group, only those most seriously affected. Rather than leave the judgment of *which* children to allow to die to the more or less amateur guesses of local physicians and family, Lorber has gone on to propose some well-tested rules of thumb to guide decision making. Lorber's rules apply only to the decision not to give treatment; he does not favor active euthanasia on the children from whom massive therapy is withheld, any more than Ramsey favors active euthanasia on the adult patient being allowed to die.[18]

I believe, however, that we can see some serious problems with this synthesis. One of these, concerns the adequacy of the criteria for selection which Lorber formulates. These have been called into question by other professionals in the field,[19] who argue both that Lorber's prognosis for those babies whom he would allow to die is unjustifiably bleak and that some of those babies are worse off than they would have been if treated very early in life. They further point to the relative advantages of supportive services such as clinical and per-

---

[15]John Lorber, M.D., "Results of Treatment of Myelomeningocele," *Developmental Medicine and Child Neurology* 13 (1971), p. 300.

[16]*Ibid.*, pp. 290-91.

[17]*Ibid.*, pp. 284-85.

[18]For Lorber, see his "Early Results of Selective Treatment of Spina Bifida Cystica," *British Medical Journal* (October 27, 1973), p. 204.

[19]See Freeman, and Ames and Shut cited in notes 8 and 10.

sonal care over against orthopedic corrective surgery on the spine. In other words, there are possibilities of erroneous diagnosis and less than optimal therapy which make a decision to allow to die problematical. These objections are often raised against positive euthanasia, but they would seem to hold with equal force against Lorber's practice.[20]

The problem of error is in no way unique to these medical decisions, however. If that were the only difficulty, allowing babies to die might be fitting. But there is a more serious problem. Let us assume that there are circumstances in which we might approve of allowing an adult to die. Our approval need not require the patient's consent, if such consent could not have been obtained. Yet our approval would involve a judgment that the patient had begun to die. How such a judgment might be made is a complicated problem. But one plausible ingredient will be a kind of comparison between the adult's past health and future prospects. We would consider past physical health and, to a limited point, his person, character and life-style. On the basis of some amalgam of these factors, we might infer that a particular patient had begun to die.

The striking thing about newborn persons, however, is precisely that they have no visible personal past. They have had no opportunity to develop a normality of their own functioning. No physical plateau, personality, character or style of life has had a chance to surface. The newborn presents himself as totally unexploited potential—if we were cynical we could say, as a field for potential exploitation. Thus, in the absence of a benchmark in past life for saying *this particular person* has started to die, I do not see how one committed to care (as Lorber surely is) could ever switch from cure to companionship. The yardsticks which would give such a division provisional legitimacy in the case of an adult (that is, consent and/or establishment of a norm of life) are absent in the case of the newborn. In their absence we should not disjoin care and cure.

Of course, the question of what is the fitting form of care-cure remains open. I have already claimed that maximal treatment and optimal treatment are not the same. Many religious moralists (including Professor Ramsey) express this point in very sophisticated form using a distinction between ordinary and extraordinary means. Patients are not required to use extraordinary (maximal) means, only the ordinary ones. Which means are extraordinary? One formulation is that those which harm the patient more than he will benefit from them.[21]

I do not want to argue for an obligation on physicians and families to use extraordinary means on all newborns. In the course of the care-cure of some babies it *may* become clear that additional therapy will cost that baby more than he can gain. But it is very unclear that most of the babies Dr. Lorber allows to die fall into this group; it is even less clear that baby B (Down's syndrome and duodenal obstruction), with whom we began, does. It is difficult to see how these decisions to withhold treatment could claim to be judgments made about optimal treatment for the particular babies at hand. Instead they are judgments comparing these babies and their limited prospects to "normal" babies and their different prospects. A judgment about these particular babies' interests would have a better basis later.

On the other hand, it may be that there are newborn human persons who are beyond the reach of our care.[22] As Ramsey suggests, this might be because of their (inferred) unconsciousness or because they experience pain which cannot be relieved. No one, of course, really suggests that a Down's syndrome, or spina bifida, baby cannot receive love. They would not fall in this group. But if infants ever are in cir-

[20]The problems for exponents of positive euthanasia are clearly presented by Yale Kamisar, "Euthanasia Legislation: Some Non-Religious Objections" in *Euthanasia and the Right to Die,* ed. by A. B. Downing (Los Angeles: Nash, 1969), pp. 85-86.

[21]A full discussion of the complex distinction between ordinary and extraordinary means lies outside our scope. These terms have not always and to everyone meant the same thing. My formulation is very freely adapted from Thomas J. O'Donnell, S. J., *Morals in Medicine* (Westminster, Md.: Newman Press, 1960), p. 72.

[22]The serious difficulties with this claim have been pointed out by Richard McCormick, S.J., in "Notes on Moral Theology," *Theological Studies* 34 (March, 1973), pp. 67-69.

cumstances such that care-cure in the conventional sense cannot be received—or where it is received as torture, then the requirements of care would have to be rethought or obligations of other sorts might become more relevant.

V

In summary, I regard withholding treatment from defective newborns as wrong unless (1) it can be argued that the action is necessary to protect the personal life of at least one specifiable other person or (2) the infant cannot receive care in any other form. This amounts to a prohibition of active or passive infanticide on most newborns. I am uneasy with this conclusion, although I cannot see my way clear to any other. As a postscript I should like to make one additional point.

One of the aspects of this conclusion that troubles us is that it leads to the salvaging of a very large number of seriously defective children. Thus Lorber and others who practice selection point with pride to the "high quality" of the children now under their care. Of course, we should be doubly shocked if selection did not have this result,[23] but the problems of the hardships and sufferings of others cannot be denied. This is especially troubling for someone who argues against quality control, for life with defect means sacrifice and hardship for the child, siblings, and parents. It seems the moralistic conclusion of the abstract theorist.

Against this I would note that neither family disaster nor a great increase in the number of living defective children is *inevitable* given my conclusions. The reason these consequences do not *necessarily* follow is that we can allocate resources so as, at least, to minimize them. In other words, we can see this as a problem of resource allocation. As such it would have two distinct levels.

The first of these is the level of deciding which babies to treat and how to treat them. Given finite resources to spend on new-

borns, the issue is unavoidable. I have already argued that the only fair criterion for deciding appropriate treatment for a given baby is that baby's own welfare and ability to receive love. This precludes selection on some qualitative basis and, in effect, forces

But if mistakes are made, we may be able to say that responsibility ultimately lies not with the parents but with a medical system which offered them only unacceptable ways of handling the problem: too much massive intervention, on the one hand, and insufficient help in caring for the afflicted baby, on the other.

a surgical team to a random or, its nearest social equivalent, a first-come, first-served "system" of selection.[24]

What then of the related question of *how* to treat? This cannot be separated from the question of selection since, presumably, some kinds of care are more likely to exhaust our financial and personal resources than others. And, at least to the amateur eye, there seem to be real differences among, e.g., spina bifida centers, over such questions as the relative emphasis on shunting and counseling, orthopedic surgery and physical therapy.[25] It is not obvious that maximal use of technology leads to optimal care.

In fact, a method of treatment in which

[23]It is, of course, possible that patients from whom treatment would be withheld at one clinic are intentionally referred to another with a less selective policy. Cf. James Lister's letter in the *British Medical Journal* 4 (November 10, 1973), p. 355.

[24]An excellent statement of the arguments for randomization is James F. Childress, "Who Shall Live When Not All Can Live?" *Soundings* 43 (Winter, 1970), pp. 339-55. I do not assume that "first-come, first-served" is identical with random selection.

[25]I have in mind the differences in emphasis that emerge from reading the account of the practice at Sheffield as compared with that of Ames and Shut in Philadelphia.

family support is not central seems to border on blackmail. As things stand, the family can often only make the "right" decision at incredible cost. No parents can be sure how they would face such a crisis. But if mistakes are made, we may be able to say that responsibility ultimately lies not with the parents but with a medical system which offered them only unacceptable ways of handling the problem: too much massive intervention, on the one hand, and insufficient help in caring for the afflicted baby, on the other. There seems to be a rough analogy with a weapons technology which produces only megaton weapons, leaving nothing appropriate for fighting conventional skirmishes. Why do we have refined surgical techniques but inadequate institutional supports for handicapped persons and their families?

In any case, given their finite resources, health-care professionals will have to find a workable balance between offering maximal treatment to a very few infants and offering minimal care to all. Limitations of resources will mean that we can offer less than ideal treatment for those afflicted babies who are treated. This will lead to some infant deaths and misery as will the more or less random selection process. While these are sad facts, they are inevitable.

The error we want to avoid is the notion that we should solve our limited resource problem simply by assessing the "quality" of the output. Such an approach leads one to think that the ideal result is either a "perfect" baby or a dead baby.[26] And the

---

[26]While he can in no way be held responsible for the use to which I have put it, I owe this phrase to LeRoy Walters.

root problems of this way of looking at the issue are that both the human rights of defectives and the imperfections of all babies are glossed over. We would be horrified to learn that an obese, myopic professor was refused treatment on the grounds that he would always be a decrepit physical specimen. Why do we tolerate the same *kind* of reasoning when applied to newborns?

Beyond this, of course, lies the problem of the second level of resource allocation. How much of our medical budget should be spent on newborn care, and how much of our GNP should be allocated to medicine? In my view, such decisions should be based on fairness considerations and should in some way reflect the deepest value commitments of our culture. Full discussion is obviously impossible here. But it is not obvious that, within health care, the salvaging of defective newborns should be our highest priority. Extending basic services to more people may be much more important. Further, it may be that we spend too much on health and too little on education and the arts.

Briefly put, we can attack the problem of defective newborns by putting much greater stress on support for the family and by realizing that other obligations force us to restrict the numbers of such children whom we reach. Whether we should develop resources is an open question, as is the question of their ideal form. But once we have decided to develop resources there are moral constraints on the way we may use them. One of those constraints, in a just society, is that we will not refuse treatment to babies whom it is in our power to help.

12

Attitudes toward the newly dead

WILLIAM MAY

Maigret suddenly realized that there was one character in the drama about whom almost nothing was known, the dead man himself. From the outset, he had been to all of them merely a dismembered corpse. It was an odd fact that the Chief Superintendent had often noticed before, that people did not respond in the same way to parts of a body found scattered about as to a whole corpse. They did not feel pity in the same degree, or even revulsion. It was as though the dead person were somehow dehumanized, almost an object of ridicule.

Georges Simenon,
Maigret and the Headless Corpse

JUST one aspect of the problem of organ transplants surfaces in this passage from Simenon's novel. To extract organs from a corpse is, in a sense, to dismember it. And, if Simenon is to be believed, dismemberment is an act of violence; it dehumanizes; it reduces the body to an object of ridicule.

While living, a person is identified with his body in such a way as to render the dignity of the two inseparable. A man not only *has* a body, he *is* his body; it is the medium of his self-revelation. His behavior betrays the bond between the two: pride expresses itself in his carriage; humiliation leaves his body stricken with shame. Thus, when a man is subject to embarrassment, he wishes that the earth would swallow him up; he averts his face, turns on his heels, or blushes and perspires as though he wished to fabricate for himself a veil.

Apparently this association of self and body does not terminate abruptly with death. Admittedly the corpse is no longer a man. The cadaver is a kind of shroud that now masks rather than expresses the soul that once animated it. And yet—while the body retains its recognizable form, even in death, it commands a certain respect. No longer a human presence, it still reminds us of that presence which once was utterly inseparable from it.

Such is not the case, however, argues Simenon, when the body loses its integrity. The detached organ or member becomes, in a sense, a fit object for ridicule. It has lost its *raison d'etre* and therefore its centeredness. It has become an eccentricity, an embarrassment, an obscenity. It seems to have committed the indecency of refusing to vanish along with the self, while simultaneously failing effectively to remind us of what has vanished. The severence of death has been crazily compounded by a different order of severance that leaves the community charged with picking up leftovers rather than laying to rest remains.

Proposals, then, for the dismemberment

of the body, even if that dismemberment is justified as serving important social purposes, such as organ transplants, awaken certain deep-going reservations that ought not to be ignored. If even in a very preliminary way, we ought to bring them into view and interpret them.

These reservations, of course, may vary considerably according to the specific proposal for salvaging organs; therefore we should keep in mind the several options in their variety:

1. A system of routine salvaging of organs from which exemption may be granted only at the special initiative of the pre-deceased or his family;

2. A program of organized giving of organs which is dependent upon the consent of the donor or his family;

3. Provision for the sale of organs by the pre-deceased or his family; and

4. Provision for the crediting of a family account against the day that some member (of the family) may require an organ.

Advocates of routine salvaging argue that it maximizes the number of organs made available for social purposes and spares citizens the awkwardness of wearing donor cards, or physicians the necessity of making ghoulish overtures to the bereaved at the time of death.[1] Proponents of organized giving argue that the system will provide some (maybe not so many) organs, while protecting the perceived rights of citizens and their families concerning burial and encouraging a pattern of *giving* that will have positive moral consequences for the society at large.[2] In matters so fundamental as the exchange of human organs, it is argued, "giving and receiving" is better than "taking and getting" and certainly to be preferred to "selling and buying." If any bartering is admitted into the process of transplanting organs, a system of family credits for donated organs is to be preferred to the debasing effects of their public sale.

Whether a system of automatic salvaging *alone* will provide a sufficient supply of organs to meet social needs, I would not attempt to resolve. The question of adequate supply cannot be answered until a program of organized giving has been given a fair trial. As advocates of the latter point out, such a trial has not been possible until the recent passage of the Uniform Anatomical Gifts Act in over forty-four states, which, for the first time, removes the legal obstacles in the way of organ donations.[3] More restrictedly, I would argue that human attitudes toward death (and the newly dead) are such that a system of organized giving must be granted a serious test before entertaining the alternative of routine salvaging. In the course of this argument, it will be necessary to examine certain primordial attitudes and basic symbols for death, some further specific convictions about the newly dead as reflected in the funeral practices of both traditional and Christian societies, and, finally, certain resources in belief and practice that give moral warrant for sustaining a program of organized giving.

1. Attitudes and Symbols

Drawing his evidence from both traditional societies and dreams, Edgar Herzog argues in *Death and Psyche*[4] that the most primitive response to a corpse is flight. This phenomenon is more than a matter of the aversion of an individual to a cadaver. Entire villages have been known to move to another location to avoid any further traffic with a corpse. If flight is a primary human response to death, then the development of funeral rites must be interpreted as a sec-

[1] Jesse Dukeminier and David Sanders, "Organ Transplantation: A Proposal for Routine Salvaging of Cadaver Organs," *New England Journal of Medicine,* 279:413-419, 1968.

[2] Alfred M. Sadler and Blair L. Sadler, "Transplantation and the Law: the Need for Organized Sensitivity," *The Georgetown Law Journal,* 57:5; Alfred M. Sadler *et al.,* "Transplantation—A Case for Consent," *The New England Journal of Medicine,* 280:862-867, 1969; Alfred M. Sadler, Blair L. Sadler, and E. Blythe Stason, "Transplantation and the Law: Progress Toward Uniformity," *New England Journal of Medicine,* 282:717-723, 1970; and Paul Ramsey, *The Patient as Person* (London and New Haven: Yale University Press, 1970), Ch. 5.

[3] There are additional, non-legal obstacles to organ transplants (such as organ rejection, high costs, logistics, and limits on available medical manpower) that legislation for automatic salvaging alone would not solve. Alfred M. Sadler and Blair L. Sadler deal with these in "Providing Cadaver Organs for Transplantation: Three Legal Alternatives," an unpublished paper written for the Freedom and Coercion project of the Institute of Society, Ethics and the Life Sciences.

[4] Edgar Herzog, *Psyche and Death, Archaic Myths and Modern Dreams in Analytical Psychology* (London: Hodder and Stroughton, 1966).

ondary response on the part of the community to force itself to be present to death. This presence, of course, does not wholly eliminate the original aversion. The community becomes present, after all, for the purpose of removal. It burns or buries the corpse. The community no longer journeys away from the dead, but it sends the dead on a journey, as it were, away from its presence. Thus, the element of aversion and horror persists even within the form of funeral practice.

The modern humanitarian, of course, will grow impatient with this kind of analysis. What does a rather primitive, almost subhuman emotion, like horror, have to do with the resolution of modern policy issues? Surely civilized men should not be distracted by such matters. A discussion of organ transplants should focus on the question of the most efficient way of supplying the needs of those dying for the want of vital organs. Let atavistic emotions give way to the central human issue.

Yet the fact of horror may be more germane to the subject of humane procedures for transplants than first appears. It is not advisable in the pursuit of worthy social goals to sidestep or repress the element of aversion with respect to means.

The Grimm Brothers included in their collection of folk tales the intriguing story of a young man who is incapable of horror. He does not shrink back from the dead—neither a hanged man he encounters nor a corpse with which he attempts to play. From one point of view, his behavior seems pleasantly childish, but, from another angle, inhuman. His father is ashamed of him, and so the young man is sent away "to learn how to shudder." Not until he has learned to shudder will he be brought out of his nameless, undifferentiated state and become human. Ingmar Bergman plays with (and complicates) the same theme in his movie *The Magician,* in which the hero—sometime artist, actor, charlatan, magician—contrives to make an apparently detached scientist acknowledge his human capacity for horror. When the magician succeeds in lifting the hair off the head of the scientist, the latter, with an irrecoverable loss of dignity, denies that he has had the experience. At a somewhat more comic level, the modern undertaker has trouble in securing respect for his

person and work—because of his over-familiar association with death. Our laughter and contempt testify to our deep-going sense of the connection between human dignity and a capacity for horror.

A policy that institutes the routine cutting up of corpses, even for high-minded social purposes, may fail precisely at this point; its refusal to acknowledge the fact of human horror. There is a tinge of the inhuman in the humanitarianism of those who believe that the perception of social need easily overrides all other considerations and reduces the acts of implementation to the everyday, routine, and casual. Even the proponents of routine salvaging have to concede indirectly the awkward fact of human revulsion. A system requiring consent, they argue, has two defects. It will fail to produce as many organs as categorical salvaging and it forces upon staff the necessity of making "ghoulish" overtures to the pre-deceased or his relatives. The question remains whether a system that overrides rather than faces up to profound reservations is not, in the long run, more ghoulish in its consequences for the social order.

Human horror before death does not remain a formless, unspecified emotion. The object of horror is associated with certain images and symbols. Specifically, death is identified in language and imagery with the acts of hiding and devouring. An analysis of these two images is required for further appraisal of a system of routine salvaging.

The name of the nymph "Calypso," who encounters Odysseus as the embodiment of death, means literally the one who hides. The death-demon in Indo-Germanic and even pre-Indo-Germanic times, according to Herman Güntert, is a Hider-Goddess. A "mysterious hiding and shrouding has been experienced as the first essential character-trait of the numinous, hidden power of death from early times."[5]

Eric Neumann has discerned this association of death with devouring, both in archaic myth and contemporary dream life. "Eating, devouring, hunger, death, and maw go together; and we still speak, just like the primitive, of 'death's maw,' a 'devouring war,' a

[5] *Ibid.,* p. 39.
[6] Eric Neumann, *The Origins and History of Consciousness* (Princeton: Princeton University Press, 1970), p. 28.

'consuming disease.' "[6] The association appears in the symbol of the *Uroboros,* the dragon that consumes its own tail, and in the mythic representation of the devouring mother. Being swallowed and eaten up is also a pattern that occurs in medieval paintings of hell and the devil. Cannibalism prevails amongst those who are lost in the land of the dead. In the innermost circles of hell, Dante places Judas, Brutus, and Cassius whom Satan devours; and in his modern representations of hell, the American dramatist Tennessee Williams resorts to images of cannibalism—with special emphasis, once again, on the theme of the devouring mother.

Finally, the two activities of hiding and devouring coincide. The corpse, which is hidden in the earth, is thereby swallowed up and absorbed; the flesh, which is devoured by the scavenger, at the same time disappears.

2. Hider-Goddess and Devourer

Basic images for death have a way of associating with the institution which deals most with the dying. Traditionally, the hos-

W hat is wrong, indecorous, and enraging about placing the burden of proof on the family is that it forces the family to claim the body as its possession, only to proceed with rites which acknowledge the process of surrender and separation.

pital was a place of healing and recuperation for the sick and wounded. More recently the hospital, along with homes for the chronically ill and the aged, penal institutions, and mental hospitals, has acquired certain subliminal associations with the Hider-Goddess.

Prisoners call themselves the forgotten men. The mentally disturbed and the chronically ill are hidden away from the society at large in preparation for their final disappearance. This process of hiding goes on for all the understandable reasons that pertain in a highly differentiated society and its specialization of functions and services. One would hate to do without these technical services, but they have exacted a high price by imposing upon inmates a kind of premature burial. The institutionalized have forced upon them a loss of name, identity, companionship, and acclaim—an extremity of deprivation of which the ordinary citizen has a foretaste in his complaints about the anonymous and impersonal conditions of modern life. The society at large, of which the hospital is destination and symbol, functions as a kind of Hider-goddess, depriving its citizens of significance.

The development of a system of routine salvaging of organs would tend to fix on the hospital a second association with death—as devourer. In the course of life, a breakdown in health is often accompanied by a sense that one has been exhausted and burned out by a world that has consumed all one's resources. The hospital traditionally offered a respite from a devouring world and the possibility of restoration. The healing mission of the hospital is obscured, however, if the hospital itself becomes the arch-symbol of a world that devours. Categorical salvaging of organs suggests that eventually and ultimately the process of consumption that dominates the outer world must now be consummated in the hospital. One's very vitals must be inventoried, extracted and distributed by the state on behalf of the social order. What is left over is utterly unusable husk.

While the procedure of routine salvaging may, in the short run, furnish more organs for transplants, in the long run, its systemic effect on the institutions of medical care would seem to be depressing and corrosive of that trust upon which the arts of healing depend.

3. Antigone, Funerals, and Donor-Consent

A system of salvaging that requires the consent of the donor and/or his family, respects, for want of a better phrase, the "principle of extra-territoriality" in the relations of the person to the social order. This principle of extra-territoriality is already embedded in traditional legal rights concerning burial.

Society traditionally located "quasi-property rights" to the corpse in the family of the deceased. The rights were quasi—in the sense that the cadaver could not be put up for commercial use or sale. But rights they were in the sense that no other party could normally interpose claims upon the corpse that would interfere with the family's right and obligation to provide for a fitting disposition of the remains. In other words, whatever use and abuse, conflicts and tragedies, a person has been subjected to in the course of his public life, at the deepest level he cannot be reduced to them without remainder. He was a human presence that transcended the world into which he was apparently absorbed.

The principle of extra-territoriality is at issue in Antigone's contest with Creon over the burial of her brother. The king claims the rebel for his own; Polynices, and therefore his body, is wholly at the disposition of the state. In defying the king and insisting on a proper burial, Antigone claims that her brother transcends the social order. His person is not fully exhausted by the claims of the tyrant upon him. In covering him over with the "thirsty dust," she signifies that he is not, and cannot be, devoured by the state.

(A mute recognition of this limit on the power of the state is contained in the symbolism of the modern military funeral. The casket of the fallen soldier is covered with a flag, but when the coffin is lowered into the grave, the flag is neatly folded and withdrawn. The symbolism at once attests to the majesty of the state: A man dies for his country, but a country does not die with the man—long live the country. At the same time the symbolism attests to the limits on the power of the state. The state cannot follow the soldier into the grave. There is a remainder that cannot be remaindered. A human presence that cannot be fully enclosed and devoured.)

The question arises as to whether burial rights and duties pertain to Polynices because he is a *man,* or because he is Antigone's *brother*. Put more generally, does the principle of extra-territoriality adhere to the person or to his family? The issue here is partly exegetical insofar as the proper interpretation of *Antigone* is at stake (a question which I will not attempt to resolve) but also partly symbolic insofar as the significance of a funeral service is at issue. In pursuing the latter question, we will have to cope with further ramifications for the subject of organ transplants.

From one perspective, the funeral service (which includes fitting disposition of the corpse) presupposes and reinforces a certain continuity between the person, his mortal remains, and the family unit. This continuity is particularly prominent while the newly dead body has its recognizable form: it attenuates when the body returns to particles. Thus funeral rites are an expression of the continuity of the soul with its body and with the gathered community of friends, colleagues, and family. From this perspective, the principle of extra-territoriality applies to the family group. The corpse, the deceased, and the family belong, as it were, to a continuum which should enjoy a certain sanctuary against the larger society and the state. Within this context, if one wants to proceed beyond traditional funeral rites to a justification for donating organs, then one will have to interpret the donation as a further and different expression of continuity between the generations. Something like Robert Jay Lifton's—or preceding him, Unamuno's, Soloviev's, or Bulgakov's—concept of symbolic or surrogate immortality is at work in this interpretation of the funeral service and the donation of organs.

From another perspective, the function of the funeral service is not so much to maintain continuity with the deceased as to provide public occasion for the acknowledgment that continuity has been broken by death. The acknowledgment of this separation is a particularly acute problem for those intimates whose lives have been so inextricably intertwined with the deceased. The family therefore has a special need for rites through which it acknowledges and participates in the process of surrender. "Dust thou art and unto dust thou shall return." There is nothing like the rigidity of death and the finality of cremation or burial to force the community to acknowledge that the process of separation has begun. Viewed from this second perspective, if one wants to proceed beyond traditional funeral practice and donate organs to the living, this action will be construed not as a way of achieving symbolic immortality but rather as a finite act in

The principle of extra-territoriality is at issue in Antigone's contest with Creon over the burial of her brother. . . . His person is not fully exhausted by the claims of the state.

which one mortal human being assists another.

In any event, this second perspective also argues intensively against a system of routine salvaging of organs because the system places the burden of proof on the family if it seeks exemption from the state's right of eminent domain. What is wrong, indecorous, and enraging about placing the burden of proof on the family is that it forces the family to *claim the body as its possession,* only in order to proceed with rites in the course of which it must acknowledge the process of surrender and separation. Antigone has a right to bitterness in her contest with Creon. She is compelled to claim her brother's body as *her* possession, her territory—not Creon's—precisely at the time that death forces all concerned to recognize a human being who is beyond their grasp.

"Quasi-property rights," directed to decent burial, were wisely vested in the family because the family, most of all, has used up and consumed the person in the course of his life, and the family, most of all, must acknowledge that he has moved beyond its effective control. By way of redaction, the rites tacitly acknowledge that the deceased is now, what he has always been, a human presence whose extra-territoriality must be honored.

In summary, the provision of organs for

transplants should preferably be based on a system of consent. If the state is granted the categorical authority to dispose of the corpse, package it as it pleases, then it goes a long way toward establishing its total and unlimited claim over the person living or dead. Funeral rites, at the center of which are the "remains" attended to by the family and intimates, help establish the principle of a remainder above and beyond the claims of the family and the state. It establishes the principle of extra-territoriality. The person does not belong without limit to his society.

This needs to be acknowledged precisely by those who have most consumed the person in the course of his living—his family, colleagues, and friends—those who have most eaten him alive, who are most torn by guilt and remorse.

4. The Newly Dead in Traditional Societies

The crisis of death in primitive culture cannot be adequately interpreted apart from the structure of other crises in the course of life. As Van Gennep and Van der Leeuw have observed, life for the primitive is not a straight, unbroken line that terminates in death. Rather, the life-line itself is punctuated by a series of turning points which are themselves an experience of death. Conversely, the event of death is followed by a form of continued life for the deceased that structurally corresponds to the earlier turning points.

Examples of such earlier crises are, of course, puberty rites, marriage, birth, episodes of sickness, coronations, war, departures, and reunions. The puberty rite conveniently illustrates for our purposes the three basic elements of which each turning point consists; that is, the three distinct moments of detachment, transition, and incorporation.

The detachment of an initiate from his past was effected in varying ways, perhaps by a mutilation, a whipping, a disrobing, a tattooing, or the pulling of a tooth. These severities were imposed upon the young as the condition of entrance into adult life. They were all symbolic expressions of dying. The second moment of transition that followed often required the special segregation of young men and women from the society at large. This was a period of great vulnerability for them; hence, their life during this interim was carefully hedged and protected by *tabus*. Finally, the young were assimilated and incorporated into the adult life of the tribe, accepting the sacred duties and powers that characterized adult existence. Clearly these new duties and powers could not be interpreted as casual additions to previous life and identity, the way a modern young person (e.g.) might join a club and add it to a long list of his previously defined commitments. The sacred was not in an additive relationship to other matters. That is why this final stage of incorporation had to be preceded by clear rites of detachment. The young, in effect, passed irreversably from one country into another, from childhood into adult life. Childhood had come to an end; the inauguration of adult life must be preceded by the experience of dying.

Correspondingly, the anthropologists have observed, death is not simply an exclamation point with which an individual life comes to an end. The newly dead have a very special status. Structurally, the event of death includes the three aforementioned moments of detachment, transition, and incorporation. The rituals of detachment and separation associated with the funeral were required not only to break the previously defined ties of the community to the man but also the man to the community. There followed a period of transition (emphasized especially in the work of Robert Hertz, *Death and the Right Hand*). This is a period of great vulnerability and weakness for the deceased (and perhaps for the community formerly associated with him). Assistance may be offered in the form of closing up the orifices of the body (so the devil cannot break in) or in the provision of food. This period may last for greatly varying lengths of time—four months, six months, one, three, or four years—but, Hertz argues, even when the transition is abbreviated, it symbolically corresponds to the length of time it takes the flesh to decompose, leaving a bare skeleton. Finally, the deceased reaches his destination, as it were, the dwelling place of the ancestors, the blessed isle of the dead. In some tribes, this final rite of incorporation constitutes a distinct funeral service, more joyous than the first.

This mythic and ritual structure for the primitive has its subjective correlate in the experience of the bereaved. The family of the deceased goes through its own social and psychological process of detachment, transition, and final incorporation and return into the society at large. These rites for the bereaved in varying forms persisted in Western society until World War I (argues Geoffrey Gorer in *Death, Grief and Mourning*) but rapidly thereafter began to disappear. Wearing widows' weeds did not appeal to the large number of women who lost their husbands in the great war; conventional mourning customs disappeared. Funeral rites meanwhile were removed from the church to the funeral home where the services, detached from the sanctuary and religious tradition, became more vulgar, ostentatious, and meaningless. The way was prepared for the kind of reaction epitomized in Jessica Mitford's book on vaulting prices, *The American Way of Death*. In the place of meaningless rites, Mitford recommended, in effect, no rites. In the place of a vulgar event, there is substituted a non-event.

The social and psychological price exacted by this partial or total elimination of mourning rites may be high. In the absence of

Death is not simply an exclamation point with which an individual life comes to an end.

specific modes and times for expressing grief, the bereaved run the risk of plunging into what Geoffrey Gorer has called "limitless grief." "I will never get over his passing," says the widow, in a society without consoling forms. The bereaved (and those who have contact with the bereaved) are in need of clearly defined social occasions and forms in the context of which the work of mourning can go on and reach its completion. If this is true, then the solution to meaningless rites is not the total elimination of ceremonies but the development of meaningful rites for our time.

5. Meaningful Rites; a Jungian Analysis

It helps little to make a general plea for meaningful rites if the absence of meaning is precisely at issue. The bereaved will be little consoled if the sole purpose of an artificially contrived rite is their consolation. Instrumentalist therapy of this kind only produces the smooth efficiency and inanity of current funeral practice.

The Jungian analytic tradition offers a promising basis for investing funeral rites with a meaning. It does so in a form which permits one, additionally, to integrate into traditional practice, provision for the salvaging of organs on a consensual basis.

Funeral rites, the Jungian Edgar Herzog argues, ultimately permit the family to consent to, even assist in, the death of the deceased. Death, as indicated earlier, is associated with concealing and devouring. The burial service engages the community in both acts. To bury is to conceal. To bury is to *let* the earth devour. The imagery of *Antigone* underscores both elements. Sophocles avers that it is terrible to let a corpse lie exposed to sight, for only living things are to be *seen;* or again, it is mandatory that a body be surrendered up to the "thirsty dust."

Thus human aversion to death is not the last word. Funeral services require the community to appropriate the horror. The living can pass on to mature life only *through* death and through consent to death. Herzog works this out in the context of dream analysis. He concludes, somewhat dramatically, that the *arrested* adult is the one who is unable to participate in the final killing of his parents, an act which carries with it the life responsibility of assuming the parents' role and place. This reluctance on the part of the immature adult is more than a question of general guilt feelings between the generation. In taking his parents' place, he must admit to being an adult who, in his own time and place, will also die. In refusing to "kill," he betrays that he is afraid to die, and, because he is afraid to die, he is unready to live in his own right. The arrested adult must pass through death to life.

This analysis, of course, places weight on the importance of funeral services, the occasion for the appropriation of the death of others and the acknowledgment of one's own dying. At the same time, it also permits, where fitting, a restructuring of those services to give a significant place to the donation of organs destined to be concealed and accepted into the bodies of others. Because, however, the relationship to one's own death and the death of others is not a casual matter, because, indeed, it is a touchstone of the mature life, a system of organ salvage should depend not upon automatic procedures but upon active participation and consent.

Admittedly this kind of justification of funeral rites in its own way is therapeutic, but at least it is therapeutic in a form that requires men and women to face the reality of death instead of disguising the event with pink gels and flesh-colored veils.

6. Christian Tradition and Donation of Organs

No essay on the possibility of organ salvage within the context of Western culture would be complete without inquiry into that religious tradition under whose auspices most funerals in the West occur. Not that the Christian tradition could or should be legislatively decisive on the subject. Even if it could be demonstrated that Christian ethics justified a system of routine salvaging of organs, it would be unwise to legislate such a system on that basis alone. The Christian tradition no longer occupies an official regulative position in Western life and culture. Law based on Christian ethic alone would be divisive (and therefore objectionable even on Christian grounds). On the other hand, the Christian Church remains a major institution in the West, with significance for millions; its attitude on the subject could have considerable impact on the acceptance of a system of giving and receiving organs. This paper closes then with a discussion of potential obstacles and warrants for a system of organized giving in the light of Christian thought and practice.

There is an important feature of traditional Christian teaching that would seem to stand in the way of organ transplants, the doctrine of the resurrection of the body. Christian expectations for future life were not dreamy and spiritual. Christians looked forward to a future life which was bodily life together in the presence of God. On this point Catholics and Protestants have recently differed in one important respect. Catholics have carried forward the Greek concept of the immortality of the soul. They have postulated an interim period of future life for the soul without the body. But, even so, the soul would not persist forever in this bodiless state. Final bliss required the graded purgation of the soul and its final unification with the body—in the Apostle Paul's words, a glorified body. Protestants, on the basis of

---

Both Catholics and Protestants have held to what Archbishop Temple called a "holy materialism," the full participation of human existence in eternal life; that is, a future human existence which in some sense is embodied.

---

recent biblical scholarship, rejected even this minimal concession to Greek spiritualism. The biblical doctrine of the resurrection of the body had to be radically distinguished from Greek teaching about the immortal soul. The soul, no less than the body, is in need of reconstitution and healing; the soul no less than the body is mortal. Future life therefore depends exclusively on God's final act of resurrection and recreation and not on the soul's own natural immortality or virtue. Despite these differences, however, both Catholics and Protestants have held to what Archbishop Temple called a "holy materialism," the full participation of human existence in eternal life; that is, a future human existence which in some sense is embodied.

Given these views of future life, it is no wonder that early Christians in the funeral customs settled on the convention of burial, rather than the total obliteration of the

corpse through cremation. Historical inquiry into funeral practice in the Roman empire makes it clear that for centuries preceding Christianity cremation had been the prevailing, though not the sole, practice. In the Christian era, burial became the accepted custom. Jocelyn Toynbee warns us, to be sure,[7] against assuming a cause and effect relationship here. For the centuries immediately preceding the emergence of Christianity, there is evidence of a shift in Roman practice in the direction of burial. But, in any event, the Christians did not reverse this tendency. Quite the contrary, they seemed to set the seal on burial as standard practice in the disposition of the remains.

Our question, then, is whether Christian belief in the resurrection of the body would operate today to place obstacles in the way of a new kind of destruction of the body—not through cremation but through the extraction of organs from the corpse. (The body contains some seventeen salvageable organs, to say nothing of usable tissue and nerves.) I leave aside the sociological question as to how many Christians today would prefer to by-pass the question—allowing the traditional doctrine of the resurrection to be demythologized or permitting this once cardinal tenet of the faith to drift from a central to a marginal position in Christian teaching. The question is whether Christian orthodoxy (whose strength ebbs and flows, and may flow again)[8] would find insuperable obstacles to a medical procedure that entailed the human destruction of the integrity of the corpse.

In searching the tradition on this question, I have found most helpful St. Augustine's essay "De Cura Pro Mortuis."[9] At no point in this defence of burial does Augustine make the practice of burial a *condition* of the resurrection, as though God were somehow prevented from accomplishing his purposes with those who were smashed to pieces

---

[7] Jocelyn M.C. Toynbee, *Death and Burial in the Roman World* (London: Thames and Hudson, 1971).

[8] Who could have predicted at the time of the American Revolution, when Christians dwindled to ten percent of the population, that Christianity would have a significant future?

[9] St. Augustine, *Nicene and Post-Nicene Fathers*, 1st Series, Vol. III, ed. by Philip Schaff, tr. by H. Browne (Grand Rapids: William B. Eerdmans Publishing Company, 1956).

or incinerated. Burial is "no aid to salvation" but "an office of humanity." Burial is
simply a *fitting* testimony to the resurrection,
declaring that the faith does not condemn
the body or devaluate it to the position of a
disposable cartridge. The full text from St.
Augustine reads:

> But as for the burying of the body, whatever
> is bestowed on that is no aid to salvation, but
> an office of humanity, according to that affec-
> tion by which "No man hateth his own flesh".
> (Eph. 5:29) Whence it is fitting that he take
> what care he is able for the flesh of his neigh-
> bor, when he is gone that bare it. If un-
> believers in the resurrection of the flesh do
> it, how much more beholden to do the same
> who do believe; that so, an office of this kind
> bestowed upon a body, dead, but yet to rise
> again and to remain to eternity may also be
> in some sort a testimony of the same faith?[10]

Clearly Christian faith in the resurrection
does not present an insuperable obstacle to
the extraction of organs from the corpse.
Must the church, however, merely acquiesce
to such procedures reluctantly or does the
faith provide positive warrant for the donation of organs and for the institutional
mobilization of resources to that end?

My own response to this question is colored by a personal memory which at first
glance does not seem too germane to the
subject. I recall seeing many years ago in a
series of photographs of Northern Renaissance sculpture a sarcophagus, with a statue
of the deceased located nearby, a half-erect
skeleton. Decomposing flesh hung from the
skeletal frame, but the right arm was extended with the hand open, and, in the hand,
the figure offered his heart to God. The
heart, of course, is the site of the soul in the
body; thus the figure offered, in effect, himself under this form. When I saw this figure
over twenty years ago, it expressed my understanding of the status of the soul before
God. A person could not claim salvation for
his own possession or desert, but neither
could he face life—or death—as though he
were denied communion with God. He could
only make his offering. He need not make it
anxiously or tentatively, but rather, with
some measure of gratitude, confidence, and
hope for its acceptance.

The development of a technology for organ transplants, and most dramatically the
heart transplant, has opened up now the possibility of another kind of offering of the
heart—somatic rather than symbolic—the
offering of almost all that remains bodily of
the self to the neighbor, in the hope of, and
even gratitude for, acceptance and use. This
kind of donation, moreover, may actually be
closer to the heart of the Christian message
than the too-pious Renaissance figure. The
statue, even though it denies to itself salvation as a possession, relies still on a certain
image of acceptable piety—a sacrificial offering from the human to the divine. It over-
looks the self-donative activity of the savior
who reportedly freed men from the need to
make some kind of saving sacrifice to God
and freed them for a donative life toward
the neighbor.

There is positive warrant in Christian
liturgy and Christian ethics for a system of
organ donation. Christ shares, under the
form of bread and wine, his body and blood
with his disciples. The disciple is invited to
share in this life of self-donative service by
expending himself for the neighbor. Not
many people within Western societies today
share these special motivations that would
obtain for Christians but the society at large
could benefit from institutional support on
this issue from the church. A system of organ
donations would shore up and encourage the
development of "consensual community in
general." For the theologian Paul Ramsey,
this is an important reason why organized
giving is to be preferred to routine salvaging.
"A society will be a better human community in which giving and receiving is the
rule, not taking for the sake of good to
come. . . . The positive consent called for by
Gift Acts, answering the need for gifts by
encouraging real givers, meets the measure
of authentic community among men."[11]

While justifying and encouraging organ
transplants, the Christian, I would suspect,
would have to shy back from the inflationary
language of those who would want to interpret such deeds as acts of "symbolic immortality." Such deeds in themselves, for the
Christian cannot be called divine; they are
simply signs of a self-donative love which
they themselves are not and cannot produce.
The language of symbolic immortality is too
exaggerated for a monotheist. It would be
better to talk simply about the assistance
that one mortal renders another.

---

[10] *Ibid.*, p. 550.
[11] Paul Ramsey, *Patient as Person*, p. 210.

Coincidentally enough, Augustine had to face this issue of inflation in a different form in the aforementioned essay on the care to be given to the dead. One justification for respectful (and elaborate) funeral services in Augustine's time was the notion that the

Augustine wanted to eliminate from funerals all suggestion of an immortalizing continuity between generations. The funeral was an occasion in which the full reality of death had to be acknowledged.

dead have the power to return to and care for the living. Partial proof of this was offered in the appearance of the dead to the living in dreams. Since the dead are, in effect, both immortal and providential, it behooves the living to treat them right. Augustine undercuts rather matter of factly this proof by pointing out that the living appear to the living in dreams without knowing or caring one whit about them! Why assume that the dead watch over and provide for us as guardians?

Augustine's radical monotheism forced him to be wary of a religious sentimentality that substituted the providence of one's fathers for the providence of God. Consistent with this rejection of ancestor worship, Augustine wanted to eliminate from funerals all suggestion of an immortalizing continuity between the generations. The funeral was an occasion in which the full reality of death

had to be acknowledged. Far from continuing to watch over men, the dead have forsaken the living! The funeral is a two-way farewell. The dying man is removed from the care of the community, but also the community, from the care of the dying man.

The fundamental situation is structurally unchanged by procedures for the post-mortem extraction and redeployment of organs. The receiving of an organ does not rescue the living from the need to die. It only defers the day when they will have to do their own dying. Nor does the receiving of an organ, in and of itself, teach the living how to live—unless—the recipient, in receiving the organ discerns a self-donative love of which the giving of the organ may be a modest sign.

This is not the place to take up the further and final question of the Christian warrant for a funeral, but one restricted issue remains.

If there is warrant for the giving of one's organs, nerve, and tissue to unknown recipients, is there also still warrant in such cases for funeral services? Has the liturgy already been held in the hospital? What about the gutted remains? I would suggest that Christians on this point might consider an analogy taken from their chief sacrament—the eucharist. This central liturgical action of the faith is particularly pertinent to the question since it is, after all, an act of devouring— a sacred meal—in which Christians eat bread and wine, as the body and blood, as the symbolic presence of the self-donative activity of their Lord.

In current practice—the Catholic and Episcopal churches and others—have developed customs for the respectful disposition of the remaining elements—the so-called reserved sacrament. The remaining host will either be taken to the sick, consumed, or poured into the ground. It is held inappropriate to flush it down the toilet. This respect toward leftover bread and wine has some bearing on funeral practices in the cases of bodies from which organs have been extracted. Ritual provision should be made for the respectful disposition of the remains of remains which have been the "matter" of a fraternal action within the human community. Such ritual provision is hardly a condition of salvation, but it is a testimony to the privileged place of the body in acts of love.